HARDPRESS.NET
HOME OF HARD-TO-FIND BOOKS

An Autobiography, and Letters, of the Author of "The Listener," "Christ Our Law," &C
by Caroline Fry

Copyright © 2019 by HardPress

Address:
HardPress
8345 NW 66TH ST #2561
MIAMI FL 33166-2626
USA
Email: info@hardpress.net

E - sl
Bie

DATE	ISSUED TO

AN AUTOBIOGRAPHY,

AND

LETTERS,

OF

THE AUTHOR OF "THE LISTENER," "CHRIST OUR LAW," &c.

Mrs. Caroline (Fry) Wilson

PHILADELPHIA:
J. W. MOORE,
193 CHESTNUT STREET.
1849.

Isaac Ashmead, Printer.

PREFACE.

THE Editor considers it due to the memory of the subject of the memoir, which is placed at the commencement of the present volume, to state, that it was written by his beloved wife at different periods, as memoranda of the most important part of her life; intended to be continued from time to time, until they should be ultimately remodelled into a connected narrative.

She did not live to fulfil this intention; and it must therefore be remembered, that these imperfect records were never designed to be published in their present form; but well knowing her anxious wish to proclaim the Saviour's love to one who had despised and rejected him, and her conviction that by such an avowal, his grace would be magnified, the editor deems himself entrusted with a sacred duty, which he cannot better perform, than by giving the narrative, scanty and imperfect as it is, in her own words. He presents it, therefore, without comment, and unaccompanied with any particulars of her history subsequent to the period at which her own memoir closes.

After the change which had taken place in her religious sentiments, the subject of this memoir was severely disciplined in the school of adversity, and no doubt her sorrows were instrumental in establishing her faith, exalting her Christian profession, and fitting her for the special service of that Master, whose love was the constraining principle of her life. Of this devotedness her published works furnish abundant testimony; and those letters of the present collection, which were written within a few days of her death, will give evidence of the power and permanence of that faith which sustained her through a long period of trial, made the approach of death joyous, and prepared her for the heaven which she so ardently anticipated. No one who witnessed the closing hours of her life could refrain from adopting the prophet's exclamation, "Let me die the death of the righteous, and let my last end be like his!"

Many of the letters now published are interesting, as containing valuable reflections on topics of the deepest interest to the Church of Christ at the present period; and the others are replete with the sentiments and opinions of one "who walked with God."

The Editor dismisses these collections, ardently hoping that the perusal of them may be accompanied with the Divine blessing, and that while they conduce to the edification, comfort and encouragement of many, they may be subservient to the praise of Him, who, in accomplishing the mysterious designs of His grace and providence, not unfrequently condescends to employ the humblest instrumentality of human agency.

CONTENTS.

AUTOBIOGRAPHY.

    CHAPTER I.—Birth and Childhood, - - 13

        II.—Early Youth, - - - - 39

        III.—Early Womanhood, - - - 46

        IV.—Conversion, - - - - - 60

LETTERS, - - - - - - - - 82

AUTOBIOGRAPHY.

SINCE it has pleased God to give publicity to a name obscure, to an extent that may hereafter excite the public curiosity respecting her that bore it; and since it may please Him also to get himself honour by the manifestation of His goodness and mercy, in the record of her life—feeling that it will be impossible for any one else, to state truly that which alone is worth recording,—the history of her mental and spiritual existence,—she is induced to put down at her leisure these notices of herself; rendered the more necessary by the fact, that she has never kept a diary, or any kind of memoranda, of even the most important occurrences of her life. Should that time ever come, which in the plenitude of her happiness it becomes her to anticipate, when with powers and faculties remaining, the interests and affections of this world will have terminated, it is her present thought to collate these materials, and such of her letters as can be collected, into a regular memoir. Of this, God knoweth. 1839.

MEMOIRS, &c.

CHAPTER I.

BIRTH AND CHILDHOOD.

CAROLINE FRY was born at Tunbridge Wells on the 31st of December, 1787, being one of ten children, and seven daughters.

Of her who makes these records, the remotest recollections are of a most happy and too indulgent home, where, without the elegances or the restraints of polite, or even social life, every comfort was in profuse abundance, and all pleased themselves after their own manner.

Being the youngest but one of a family whose births extended through more than twenty years, she remembers but few of her brothers and sisters as children, and the prescriptive right by which the youngest child of a large family is spoiled, was extended in her favour to the two youngest, the humoured pets of a most loving father. He never walked out but they were one at each side of him—they accompanied him during great part of the day to his farm, or his houses, the building of which was his great pursuit and pleasure. He called them his ladies, chose their dress, taught them to read the newspapers, talk of politics, and play at whist with him every evening, and above all, under surety of his protection, to set at defiance all other authority and control. I have been told that on his death-bed he spoke painfully of having spoiled his two youngest children, then about twelve and fourteen years of age. He did not foresee what adversity and the interposition of divine grace would do to mend his work; so that, however their difficulties were increased, and their sins accumulated by this early indulgence, they grew up to be neither the least beloved, the least useful, nor the least prosperous of his children.

And yet the fear of this indulgent father's disapprobation, was the only restraint Caroline remembers to have felt. His absence from home for a whole day, which never occurred but at a general election, a special jury case, or some other such event, was a signal for the outbreaks of insurbordination, and the doing of all sorts of prohibited things:—her other parent being a quiet, careful, domestic woman, an object more of affection than deference, at least to these little people, who held themselves out of her jurisdiction.

More influential even than this partial fondness, was the father's abiding impression, whencesoever derived, that his children were, or were to be, or ought to be, above the position of life in which they were born—his sons were not to be brought up to trade—his daughters might not marry men in trade—his little girls might not associate or play with any children of equal condition with themselves. To this inborn, inbred opinion of their own importance, productive of some good results no doubt, must be attributed no small part of the difficulties and misfortunes of their family after their father's death, and the little success that attended most of them notwithstanding the more than ordinary talents distributed to them by Providence, and in a moral and human sense, their actual deserving. The grace of God, and the calling of his Holy Spirit, determined, we cannot doubt, the destiny of the eldest son, the Rev. John Fry, Rector of Desford, sufficiently well known as the author of many works of talent, piety, and learning.

On Caroline the only effect of this parental ambition, was probably that which it had upon her education, and early associations, rather than upon her ultimate destination. She inclines to think that even education rather left her what she was, than made her anything. Her recollection of her own character, temper, feeling, is from the first so very like to what it was at last, it would appear to her that nature has been too strong for any influences acting from without—at least till a divine power interposed to alter its own workmanship, and that but slowly and partially to the last, rather to modify than to change. Back to eight or ten years of age, she can well remember that intense, unreasonable, almost maddening anguish, which through all the changes of her changeful life has known no suspension, and up to this day no diminution, produced upon her by a sense of unkindness, or injustice, or discouragement, often imaginary, always exaggerated. Nobody knew then, or ever has known, or ever can know, the mental agony of these moments, followed by fits of depression, self-reproach, and despondency heretofore scarcely endurable, but now, blessed be God, commixed with that prostration of spirit, and utter self-abandonment, which is not all misery, since in it is realized the full value of redeeming love, and the sweet sympathy of a once-suffering Redeemer. He knows, what she never herself has known, how much of this passion is sin, and how much is only misery. The bitter and resentful words to which, if the occasion serves, it will give vent, are sin of course, and the pain thus given to others, is often the bitterest and most abiding woe; but this is rather the casualty, than the character of these passionate fits: —unless something from without unhappily strikes upon the wound in the moment of irritation, the originating cause of which may be no party to the suffering, it is endured in secrecy and silence.

Reverting to her childhood, she remembers to have often passed whole days and nights in tears;* and when pressed by her parents for the cause, unable or ashamed to give the true one, has complained of pain

* At all times of her life these violent and prolonged fits of crying have occasionally occurred. Were they not the safety-valves of an over-actuated brain?

and sickness which she did not feel, and suffered them to administer remedies as for a bodily ailment. She has often questioned since, whether those tender parents did not judge more accurately than appeared, of these fits of aggravated feeling; for she well remembers that the remedial measures taken to restore her, were a piece of cold meat at breakfast, a glass of strong ale at dinner, or a cup of coffee in the evening. Whatever there may have been since, when knowledge of the extravagance, and experience of the mischiefs of these morbid sensibilities might have afforded some defence against them, there was no sin in them at that early age, and the memory of what she suffered has throughout life produced in her the greatest tenderness and forbearance towards the tempers and feelings of children, and a disposition to treat them more as maladies than faults.* To the truth of this, though ignorant of the cause, many can

* It is distinctly in her recollection that on one occasion, wanting to make known to her mother the depression of her mind, and not having courage to speak of it, being then a professed rhymer, she wrote to her in the following terms,—of the last word she did not know the meaning, and remembers being told it afterwards. She was probably about nine years old:—
>I am not very well,
>And no mortal can tell
>What is my pain,
>When I am profane.

—no specimen of early genius, but certainly one of premature mental suffering, without external cause—for to misfortune or bodily pain she was a stranger, and almost so to the slightest contradiction.

testify who may hereafter read these pages, some perhaps who have either suffered or benefited by indulgence, according as it was good or evil in its effects upon those committed to her care. For herself, through those long and many years in which she lived a stranger in the stranger's home, her thoughts untold, her feelings all unshared, it may be, there were some who understood her better than she understood herself; and can tell in what manner this feeling manifested itself, and will call it by its right name. They need not spare to do so, for she would if she knew. All she can recal with certainty, is the intensity of her sufferings, and the strangeness and unfitness, to say the least, of the conduct it occasionally produced, of which more will be told hereafter.* In these her last, best days, when all is viewed by the clear light of heaven, all transacted under the eye of the Omniscient, all shared, all treated of, all prayed over in close communion with the blessed Saviour, the only amelioration of the pain is found in that sweet sympathy.

But that which through all her life she longed for, as an impossible solace, that some one could dwell within her, and see what she herself could never understand,—that solace, that impossibility, has been attained. Jesus, before whom these irrational tears

---

* Sleep—even the peaceful slumbers of her most happy days, is often no defence against this suffering—under the influence of a dream of some act of unkindness or injustice done her, she often wakes in an agony of tears.

are shed, Jesus, with whom these morbid sensibilities are shared—He does know—He knows how much is sin, how much is misery—how much to be repented of, and how much only to be borne; and He can sympathize alike with all, for He and He only pities sin, as much as He pities sorrow, and speaks peace to the contrite, as well as to the afflicted. Under the deep sense of sin, and helplessness, and self-abhorrence, that now accompanies every return of this mental anguish, and adds to its poignancy, she need not tell him, and He need not tell her, the source and nature and culpability of her feelings. She can say to him—and O thou blessed one! how often hast thou heard it!—"Lord! thou knowest," and he can answer " My grace is sufficient for thee." It is sufficient; sufficient for Jonah in the great deep, whither his own wilfulness had brought him; and for Daniel in the den to which his enemies consigned him, and for her who in hours of such deep and untold anguish, as made her cry aloud to God for release from the body of this death, knows and feels and proves He is sufficient—and puts it here, where properly it does not belong, lest she should never reach that part of her soul's history, in which it should be found:—1839.

To return to her childhood; the same restless impatience of what she did not like, even when personally unaffected by it; the same eagerness in the pursuits of the moment, and speedy indifference to the objects so eagerly pursued; the same extreme enjoyment of simple and trifling things, even existence itself without adventitious pleasures, when there was no actual cloud upon it, the same disproportioned pain from trifles, also, brief as it was excessive—the same very peculiar contrariety of character, that kept perpetual dissonance between the intellect and feelings,—in common language, between the head and heart, the judgment that seldom erred, and the feelings by which it was always overpowered—the same excessive desire to please, and aptness to displease by precipitancy and want of tact—the same innate consciousness of talent, and painful timidity in the exercise and exhibition of it—all this, through all her life, she can trace back to her remotest memory of herself; much indeed that education might have corrected and did not, but left to grow like the wild rose of the wilderness, in strange and rude luxuriance, all redolent alike of thorns and flowers, to feel and know, and painfully regret through all her days, she was not, and could not be, what her natural endowments seemed designed to make her. Now she knows that herein God was right, though man was wrong; for it resulted that the consciousness of talent was at all times more a source of humiliation than of pride. When she might have felt elevated above her fellows, she felt only degraded below herself; and where is the sinner so safe as in the dust? True these are late conclusions, that did not cast their consolatory influence through the years gone by, but they are conclusions, and she has come to say with Paul, " I glory in my infirmities, since when I am weak, then am I strong;"—it is best to be nothing, that Christ may be all in all. How little is it known to the aspirants of mankind, that such a feeling, when it can be realized, is bliss, with which the triumphant successes of the creature have nothing to compare.

Caroline had not to complain of a neglected education, as far as education is comprehended in mere instruction. School was not to be thought of; she never slept from under the same roof with her father during his life-time, nor as she believes ever was ten miles from home but once, when he took her and her younger sister, on a visit to their brother, then recently married and settled in London. The instruction of the younger girls was therefore committed to the elder, who had been educated at what were then thought good schools; the aspirings of the family extended both to knowledge and accomplishments, and though the opportunities were small, the most was made of them; and at a time when girls in that station of life learned very little, and were thought best employed in domestic duties, and the operation of the needle, in this family every thing was at least attempted, and books, drawing, and music were the occupations of the younger people—the return of the eldest brother from Oxford at each vacation affording a great stimulus to this literary taste, by accession of books and other information which could scarcely otherwise have reached them, in their exclusion from the reading world. Many studies were thus introduced, which common as they are now, were not so then—such as Botany, Chemistry, Astronomy, &c., and the young people being all considerably gifted by nature, were prodigies of learning in the estimation of their equals. Often as the recollections of this irregular school-room and its high pretensions, have since provoked a smile, Caroline knows she was indebted to it for a great deal of solid, early acquired knowledge, which the most expensive school at that period would not have afforded; while some of its deficiencies have never ceased to be inconveniently felt.

She has no recollection of pain or difficulty, or unwillingness in learning—but a distinct one of pleasure in buying a sixpenny book, (the History of a Mouse) the first she remembers to have possessed, when she could have been but a very few years old. It is not to be supposed, that her partial and loving parents should underrate or disregard the first development of talent, little as they did to cultivate and direct it. At eight years old, little Caroline was an established poet laureate in the family, who was to write a copy of verses on every birth-day, saints-day, fast-day or thanksgiving-day, and every victory by sea, or land, sufficiently numerous in those warlike days; in the inspiring hope of receiving presents of money or pretty things, from whoever had the good fortune to receive the dedications of her muse. It is doubtful whether any of those, at least profitable productions, extending as they did from eight to fourteen years of age, are still in existence;—if they are, it must be in the hands of her sisters. She has the impression that they were not so good as a great many children write at that age.

However, they were not thought slightly of then, and that destiny so vainly afterwards resisted, was the first ambition of her life—to be an author, especially to be a poet; for general as was her taste for reading, and eager as her interest in all kinds of knowledge, poetry was undoubtedly the predominant taste. Some trifling circumstances, distinct, as if of yesterday, upon her memory, may evince how strong and inborn this literary ambition was. Well is the feeling remembered, with which, sitting upon her father's knee, she heard a conversation between him and her mother, originated by his declaration, that he would have his two youngest girls taught Latin. It was an extravagant proposition certainly, considering the actual station of the parties, and the rarity of the accomplishment at that period, but proportioned to her intense desire for learning was her silent resentment against her mother for the opposition that defeated this intent. Her childish impression of the necessity of knowing other languages, in order to become an author in her own, was a source of continual discouragement and depression to her, for she guessed not how easy it would be to attain them for herself. She remembers saying to some one of her family, on it being suggested that she might be a Milton, her then favourite author;—that she could never expect poetical fame, because she would never have the means of knowing any language but her own; a saying that often recurred to her in after-life, when the study of languages became her favourite pursuit, after poetry had been pretty nearly relinquished. Illustrative of this learned ambition, the only ambition perhaps that she was ever susceptible of, she recals another of her childish feelings. Her father's house was opposite the Parade, or Pantiles, as they were called at Tunbridge Wells, the resort at that time of the greatest and noblest of the land, whom, as children do, the little girls were in the habit of looking at, and watching from the windows most particularly those who happened to have children of their own age,—indeed, as their father's objection to his children associating with others, did not extend to those above them, the two little girls, being pretty well dressed, and well-mannered children, often went to play or walk with the young ladies whom they contrived to become acquainted with as children do. Among the great things and gay things thus constantly before their eyes, was the handsome equipage of the Duke of Northumberland, whose carriage and four brought every day under the windows two little girls, some few years older than Caroline, then about ten or eleven; who became, as was so natural, the objects of her curiosity and envy; but the envy took a single direction, it never occurred to her to want the titles, or the equipage, or the dress of these little girls, but she remembers now the painful moody sadness, with which she sat and looked at them, and thought how many things they could learn, how many masters they could have; —it may seem an overdrawn statement, but it is distinct to her as if of yesterday; a bitter repining at her lot, which no one can remember but herself, because no one ever knew it—had the feeling been less strong, the impression would not have remained. From this and other recollections, it has always appeared to her a great disadvantage to young people of the middle ranks, to be brought up in a public watering-place, where they are in juxtaposition and more near comparison with their superiors in wealth and station, than is likely to occur elsewhere—the stirrings of rivalry and ambition so excited, are not always of so harmless a nature in the issue, as little Caroline Fry's longings towards the house of Percy.

Among the means of instruction within her reach indiscriminate reading was the most important. The house, for the period, was not very ill supplied with school-books, and childish literature—such as it was when Mrs. Trimmer was a high authority, and Mrs. H. More, and Mrs. Hamilton, &c., were beginning to write. But the great supply was in the two circulating libraries, usually pertaining to a watering-place, to both of which her father was a subscriber; and, whence she was allowed to fetch what she pleased, without the smallest guidance or restraint, or so much as advice upon what she had better read or not read. As no other person read much in the house, the library catalogues were little C's peculiar treasure and sole counsellor; and, since she had nothing else to choose them by, the books had to be chosen by their names only. And now let not the incautious mother, or the adventurous daughter, take courage, and assume that the result of unrestricted reading may not be so bad as people think, and the trash of a circulating library not so certainly destructive of moral and intellectual taste. What parental prudence did not, a beneficent Providence did—partly by the effect of their example, and partly by the natural character of her own mind. Little Caroline never saw any body read pernicious books—she never heard of pernicious books—or heard anything about what they contained. She never saw a novel in her father's house, and never spoke with any one who had read them. The exact morality of her father's house was such, that she does not remember to have ever heard a free expression, or an indelicate allusion, or a profane or immoral word in jest or earnest. The very name of vices and follies, was strange to her ear—and all the knowledge of the living world, its passions and pursuits, was no more than she learned from those parts of the newspapers which her father desired to hear, and which were generally read aloud—consisting chiefly of the parliamentary debates, the court circular, robberies, accidents, and most especially theatrical reports, which in a newspaper are innocent enough. If the common talk of young ladies about love and marriage, &c., went on, as it must be supposed it did, among her grown-up or growing up sisters: it never transpired in the family circle, or within hearing of the little ones.

How much, in the absence of all other moral instruction and restraint, Caroline owed to this ignorance and simplicity concerning evil, will appear as her tale progresses; but the first effect was that she had neither curiosity nor understanding for any sort of reading that might have been injurious. With all her passion for poetry, she never read any but Milton, Cowper, Virgil, Pope, Young, Dryden, and Thompson—she does not think even she had any taste for Shakspeare before she was fourteen—and of those authors, it was the graver, not the lighter pieces she enjoyed;—Milton's Paradise Lost, and Pope's Homer's Iliad, being certainly the earliest, and most habitual diet of her poetical appetite—as Young's Night Thoughts and Cowper's Task, were a little later, and she recollects what she cannot well account for, and what is certainly not the case now, and very unusual to a child, she had a decided preference for epic poetry, and for blank verse. As far as she remembers, her prose reading was quite as good. The heroes of Lacedemon, were the idols of her imagination, second only to Achilles and Agamemnon—Plutarch's Lives were her exhaustless feast —the pious heroism of Gustavus Adolphus—the adventurous spirit of Charles of Sweden—the courtly Francis, and the sagacious Charles—whatever was great, or noble, or bold, or proud, was the food of her reflective, as well as inquisitive, faculties—divided only with her love of whatever was philosophical;—she believes, that before she was fourteen, she had read, and enjoyed, and reflected upon all the standard classical works, in translations of course, and a great many books upon natural philosophy and science, such as were then most in circulation. We say reflected upon, because all reading was to her, through all her life, only so much material for thinking and feeling. She never took delight in mere facts, nor turned over pages for mere information—nor could well retain these when she had got them; whence it probably resulted, that with all her knowledge, she never was an accurate scholar, her memory had no verbal stores, she had nobody's thoughts in her head but her own, could never quote from any other writer, or bring what she had read to bear upon her arguments. It is commonly said in youth that it is of no use to read more than you can remember. This is not true. The use of reading is to form the mind, to enlighten the understanding, to direct the opinions, and provide the materials for thinking and for judging. It is the mental aliment, which it is no more indispensable to remember in detail, than the things we eat and drink, and grow up upon bodily. No doubt, the addition of a strong, verbal, and eventual memory, with the higher intellectual powers, is a very great advantage in writing and conversation, of which Caroline has always felt the want.

In nothing has C.'s ultimate character been so true to the first impulses of nature, as in her pleasures. There is every appearance that the first-born will be the survivor. Little C. never liked the dull, the artificial play-thing, nor the game of play, unless it were one of skill and exercise, such as throwing the ball, and skipping the rope, &c. Her earliest remembered pleasure, was the first-blown flower of the spring, or the new-born lamb in her father's meadow; she knows distinctly,—and never returns to her native place without a vivid recurrence of the impression,—where she used to go with her nurse, to see if the wild snow-drop was budding, to gather the first primroses, to hunt the sweet violets from among the nettles where they were yearly to be found. The long romantic walk, the nutting, and the blackberrying, were the great occurrences; the hay-field, the barn-floor, the sheepcote, the many hours of the day she spent with her father upon the farm, listening to the detail of the bailiff, watching the plough, and the various operations of the field, are recollections of such exquisite pleasure, as never fail to return upon her memory and her feelings, whenever she sees anything of farming operations; she doubts if she ever sees a cart, or so much as hears a wagoner's whip, without the stirring of some vague reminiscences of bygone pleasure—pleasure as regards the farm, which never happened, in all the varieties of her subsequent life, to be renewed; yet she longs for it, even now that the garden feeds the still prevailing passion, but never bears a snow-drop so white, nor a violet so sweet, nor a primrose so smooth, and round, and pure, as those that grew for her without her care. If any one who loves her should like a proof of this, perhaps they will find them growing still in the same place, upon the farm of Hangershall, hard by the clear rivulet that divides Kent from Sussex, under shelter of the high rocks. This, amid the beautiful scenery of Tunbridge Wells, it will be judged, was no bad training for a poet; and whatever she may, or may not owe to it, in the culture of the imagination, she no doubt owes to it her escape from one of the dire penalties of authorship and reading—the miseries of dyspepsia, and hypochondriasis. Born of very handsome and healthful parents, and leading through all her first years the most healthful life possible, her constitution outbore the long intermediate pressure; and she is, when this is written, a remarkable instance of bodily activity and animal spirits, not worn and injured by mental toil and suffering—long and weary as they were.

It has been remarked that example and ignorance of evil were the principal moral restraints. Intellect itself, if not perverted, is so; and the habit of reflection is so. But all that comes of these is the morality of this world—the morality of self-interest and self-respect.

Caroline never learned to fear sin, as sin,—least of all as measured against the law of God. Her first notions of right and wrong were such as she gathered from her reading; a purely heathen code, in which heroism and high-mindedness stood as the first of virtues, weakness and pusillanimity as the worst of vices. To be faultless, to be perfect, was her early and long-continued desire and determination, and much of the suffering of the first part of her life, arose from her conscious ill-success in the government of herself. No one ever told her where she might have help, or why she could not be perfect. The only thing, of which she never thought, for which she never asked, never felt, never cared, was religion. True, it was never brought under her observation; but that was true of many other things about which her curiosity and consideration were insatiable. The religion of her father's house will seem almost a caricature in these bestirring days; but it was common enough in the high church then. Caroline does not remember an individual in the family ever omitting to go to church twice on the Sunday, except from illness; it would have been thought absolutely wicked; neither does she remember any instance of the Sabbath being profaned by week-day occupations and pleasures; certainly she never heard in jest or earnest the Holy Name profaned, or His word and power disputed, or irreverently treated. But except on Sunday, the Bible never left its shelf, and religion was not any body's business in the week. During the Sunday, religious books, if they may be so called, came forth out of their hiding-places, and all others disappeared. The children learned and repeated the collects, and the church catechism, the only lesson which to Caroline appeared a hardship, and with good reason, for no one ever told her what it meant, and how she was interested in it. The catechism is a most beautiful compendium of the Christian faith, such as the most advanced Christian studies with satisfaction, and finds no better mode of expressing his own belief. But I have always been of opinion that it is unfit for children, and not meant for children; it is, generally speaking, not true of children into whose mouth it is put, as a confession of faith, of which they understand and believe not a syllable. On my own judgment I would never teach it to any, till they came of age to answer for themselves; and I would remark on this, that it is our church's direction to the baptismal sponsors, that the child be taught the Lord's Prayer, the Belief, and the Ten Commandments. Is not this because it is all of the catechism that was considered proper for childhood? This I think, of the best instructed child; to one not instructed, it was a mass of unmeaning words that she learned with difficulty and disgust, and cared as little as she knew, what was meant by it. No nurse nor mother ever talked to her of Jesus' love, nor told her stories of his sufferings; nor ever warned her of God's displeasure. Her infant mind was never stored with sacred words—nor her memory exercised with holy writ. When she listens now to the exercises of the Infant or the Sunday-school, deeply can she estimate, while they cannot, the value of the instructions thus received, in preparation for the day of grace. Her reading of the Scripture was confined to a chapter read every Sunday evening by each of the four younger children to their parents and the family assembled; but as they always chose what they would read, it seldom varied beyond the stories of the Old Testament. David and Goliah, Joseph and his brethren, Daniel in the lion's den, &c. &c.—never applied, never remarked upon by any one; this was followed by one of Blair's, or other similar lectures, read aloud by some one of the elders, and then religion was dismissed till the next Sabbath. The only unseen world that occupied little Caroline's attention was that of the classic poets. In this she was interested enough, and had all names and attributes of heathen deities to adorn her childish verse, and delighted in nothing more than a visit to Olympus or to Hades, with her favourite poets. It was a little after her childhood, perhaps at about twelve or fourteen years of age, when her brother, returning from Oxford, tried to introduce rather more serious reading; Bishop Porteus' Lectures, then just delivered, and Mrs. H. More's Works, then become fashionable; but the former was declared by her parents to be methodistical, and for the latter, Caroline at least had an avowed distaste, except the Sacred Dramas, which she got by heart. It is a remarkable circumstance, strongly imprinted on her memory, that the first desire she conceived for the pleasures of fashionable life, was in reading Mrs. H. More's strictures against them. To their alleged sin and danger, she was indifferent; to their zest she was then first awakened.

Living so much excluded from society, at a period when evangelical religion was little stirring in the church, (to have entered a dissenting chapel would have been esteemed by her father a mortal sin,) it is not surprising that vital religion should never have come under Caroline's observation; still it seems remarkable, that to a mind so reflective and inquiring, the things of another world should not have become a subject at least of curiosity. It was during this period, as she thinks, that Young's Night Thoughts became her supreme delight. Having possessed herself of an old copy, she was in the habit of rising very early, and retiring into a little copse-wood not far from the house, where, seated upon a stile, the nightingales singing over her head, and the beautiful grey snake slumbering amid the wild flowers at her feet, she passed delicious hours in committing to memory that romantic and deep-feeling poetry—than which few things could be more unwholesome for such a mind as hers, predisposed to exaggeration in the good and ill of all things, and prepared to take the poetry of life, of time and of eternity, in the stead of its realities. To the continual study of it at that important age, she has been used to attribute mnch influence on her early character; if it did not create, it certainly encouraged a contempt for the usages of the world, and a tone of independent mental existence, a lowered opinion of human nature, and quickened sensibility to its follies, viewed as follies, not as sins; weighed by reason and philosophy, not by the Word of God. A melancholy presage of that life of which she knew nothing, its injuries, its unkindness, and its injustice, amounting to a desire to escape from it by a death, of which she knew far less, is an impression well remembered in her childhood, produced by the influence of poetry in general, but of this poem most particularly, upon the morbid sensibilities of her nature. Fresh with the breezes of the morning, little Caroline was used to return to the family breakfast-table, moody and whimsical and abstracted, but full of the delights of nature and of poetry, in which nobody crossed her humour, or questioned the disposal of her time; this, with the exception of about four hours a day, called school-hours, was left to her entire disposal, at an age when most children do every thing by rule and dictation. From what has been stated, it cannot be said that she was a good-tempered child; violent and wilful she thinks she must have been, or would have been, had she been contradicted and restrained, but this she rarely was by anybody, and when left to herself she was to the greatest degree a good-natured child, and as such, a favourite with her elder sisters. If anybody wanted a thing, Carry would fetch it,—if any little service was to be done, Carry would do it—if any secret to be transacted, Carry could be trusted—anybody might use Carry's books or papers, or thread or pencils, she would never be angry; there was nothing that she would not do to assist or oblige any one, for she was as quick with her fingers as with her brain: "Let Carry try," is a sentence well remembered, when any little difficulty occurred among the sisters. She cannot well remember, that any individual of her large family, living as they did invariably together, ever treated her unkindly, or otherwise than with the greatest indulgence and affection. A happier childhood, perhaps, has seldom been past. Out of hearing, almost, of the world's cares, except the divisions of Whig and Tory, Opposition and Ministerial, Pitt and Fox, about which her father troubled himself by his fireside, and talked among his children, with as much interest as if he had been a placeman, with all the stirring interests of the long war, the taxes, the invasion, &c. &c.—provided abundantly for anything she ever heard or saw, or thought of, with the comforts of life, free in the exercise of her tastes and powers, in the absence of all temptation to misuse them—leading in the simplicity of country hours and habits, the most healthful existence possible—occupied in all natural pleasures and rational pursuits, there seems not the shadow of a cloud upon the first division of her history, but that which she probably brought with her into the world, and must take with her out of it—the morbid sensibilities of her own nature—the capacity to suffer without a proportionate cause—the heart's indwelling and inburied torment.

She closes at fourteen the first division of these

memoranda, because she was about that age when her father died; the first great change in her changeful life; for though many years elapsed before there was any alteration in the external mode of life, it was the source and cause of much within herself, and ultimately of all relating to her. It must not be omitted, that before this period, little Caroline had actually attained the inborn desire of her heart,—to be an author. The fond father, whose pride and pleasure in her talents were very great, had pleased himself with printing and publishing, at the Tunbridge Wells Library, a few hundred copies of a History of England in verse, which little Caroline had composed for the use of her own school-room. They sold immediately, and were much thought of as the production of so young a person; the printers, and no doubt the author, much desired a second edition, but the prudent parent, who perhaps never seriously looked forward to his little girl's literary character, was dissuaded from permitting it, as likely to spoil her with public approbation. If he anticipated, as she surely believes he did not, that his children would depend on their own talents for the means of existence, this was a great mistake. If he thought to leave them in the comfortable obscurity of domestic life, perhaps it was judicious. At all events it was the commencement of the prolonged course of opposition which circumstances seemed to make to the dictates of nature, by which her early propensities and powers were baffled and suppressed;

—in mere human language, we should say, by which her destiny was crossed. Is it not rather good to say, by which a merciful God kept in reserve for his own use, powers which might else have been expended in opposition to his truth. Had Caroline Fry been an author earlier, what would she have written? Blessed be God, and to Him alone the praise, that she never has written anything of which the memory is painful to her best and holiest moments.

If any manuscript record of this period remain, it must be with Caroline's own family; she knew no one else. Most likely there are not any in existence—she believes they were not worth preserving, even as the productions of a child.

In reading the memoirs of other female writers, it has often come into her mind to think what the result would have been to her, had her powers been stimulated, as most others have been, by early opportunities and associations. . . Greater she would perhaps have been, but far less happy, there is little doubt.

CHAPTER II.

EARLY YOUTH.

CAROLINE was about fifteen when her father died. Everything for a time went on the same—the same house, the same habits, the same establishment, but all was materially changed to Caroline. She passed from a child to a woman. The only control or influence she had ever known was withdrawn; nobody any more attempted to guide or to control her; the form of education was relinquished; her young sister and companion being sent from home, Caroline became the companion of the older ones; and was solely committed to her own discretion and responsibility, treated in every respect as a grown-up girl. For the first year or two, as might be expected, the little poet became more moody and whimsical than ever. She passed the greater part of the day alone in her chamber scribbling at an old escrutoire of which she had got possession, or sitting for hours together at a high window-place with her feet upon a table, looking at the moon, and making verses; but her compositions at this time were shown to nobody; her father who liked them was no more, and none else cared to encourage her propensity. She wrote none the less, but kept them to herself. She chose to walk out alone at dusk, or sit on the common with her book. The most dangerous susceptibilities of her nature, its most romantic and exaggerated feeling as well as its selfish and self-indulgent propensities, were in danger of being thus fostered and encouraged to an unlimited degree; but nature came in to its own rescue—the growing feeling of womanhood, and the whimsies of the child, spoiled the poet, and went nigh to defeat the designs of nature and change the destiny entirely. May we not rather say, Almighty power and mercy interposed, to effect its own distant ends. Is it not as if God had said, "Go your way into the world, try its pleasures, exhaust its interests, enjoy its vanities and smiles, spend there your youth and health, and spirits, but this talent is mine, it must not be with you. I take it and keep it, that when hereafter I require it, it may be found unused and undegraded by a baser service?" Blessed be his name, it was so. He took from her senseless and unguided hand the dangerous weapon with which she might have injured and wounded many, and perhaps have slain herself, and kept it bright and unspotted from the world, till the day when he gave it back to be used under the guidance of his Spirit and his word. She left it, and neglected it, and forgot it; from about sixteen years of age or a little sooner, she left her books and her poetry, neglected her talents and forgot the inborn desire of her heart, to occupy herself with the commonest interests of common life. It is a curious chasm and a curious fact, that this pleasure, this pride, this ambition and determination of her childhood, was as much gone as if it never had existed, and returned only by compulsion of her fortunes, to the involuntary resumption and exercise of her mental powers. While she looks back with shame and wonder on those vain and wasted years, let her ever give glory to the Divine purpose therein, for without them, she had never known the secrets of the kingdom of the prince of this world, whose machinations it has since been her business to expose and combat. It was in keeping with the whole current of circumstances, by which she was fitted for God's purposes, and unfitted for her own, rendered more capable of being useful to the world in her writings, and more incapable of succeeding in it to her own temporal advantage and distinction.

The death of the father had in a measure broken up the extreme seclusion of the family. The young ladies made a few more acquaintances: one was to be married; other young men were introduced, and came to the house, or joined in their walks; the merry, chattering, bright-eyed child was very distinguishable at the bottom of the long family supper-table. The kind elder sisters, unlike it must be confessed to many sisters of large families

I have seen, had no disposition to extinguish her, and she who by birthright had been the admitted genius, was now to be by consent, its wit, its life, its plaything, its spoiled child from first to last. Caroline's natural mirth and gaiety, and disposition to raillery, if not to satire, was now given way to, and excited to the utmost possible extent, for the amusement of her mother and sisters, or anybody that happened to come in the way; in the retrospect it seems to her that she was wild with enjoyment and excess of animal spirits, and happy beyond all expression in the love of those around her, and the every-day amusements of domestic country life. The walks, the woods, the garden, they had not lost their zest, whatever became of the books and of the poetry. Her solitary rambles had become inconvenient; subjecting her, as she began to look more a woman, to some annoyance in a public watering-place. They were given up, as were all her solitary amusements; and with that strong, but capricious attachment which characterized her in after life, she attached herself to two of her sisters in particular, the next older than herself, and became their constant companion.

Of the period between fourteen and seventeen, Caroline remembers nothing but happiness, freedom, mirth, hilarity, good humour with every one, and delight in every thing. She loved her sisters, she fell in with their occupations and pursuits, walking, drawing, gardening, work, the latter most particularly filled up her busy days; and she thinks she read very little. In the capacity of woman, the care of her own wardrobe fell into her own hands; and as was the custom of the family, she had to make all her own clothes, even her own dresses, for no such thing as a dressmaker or a sempstress had ever been heard of in the house. The vivacious eagerness that made Caroline outstrip others in their learning, bore equally upon every thing, and whatever was to be done, she must do most and best; even to the platting of a straw bonnet,—she must do two in the year when others were content with one; and she liked all, she liked every thing, but most she liked the long, fatiguing days, when the sisters used to repair to some distant corn-fields to gather straw for their platting, furnished with a dinner of cold meat, and seated all day on the sod or barn-floor; and if she no longer made poetry, she felt it in the deepest recesses of her soul. She had learned to like the ball-room, the half-romping excitement of the English country dance, which was all she knew of dancing, for the same reason and no other, that she liked playing at ball or skipping a rope, and talking and laughing, it was yet no more to her, but nothing gave half the delight in these days, which the corn-fields at harvest time afforded, a delight as vivid in her memory as if she had felt it yesterday. She may not perfectly recal, but she thinks this period was free from those returns of violent affection and depression, of which she has previously said so much. No one crossed her pleasure, no one contradicted or found fault with her, no one was unkind or unjust to her; perhaps her feelings as well as her intellect, had a slumbering time, to gather strength, for harm as well as good, for good as well as harm.* When Caroline was nearly seventeen, this happy family for the first time prepared to separate. With the view of providing for themselves, if it should become necessary, it was advised that those who were young enough should go to a first-rate London school. The year and quarter that Caroline remained at ———, left no impression but what is painful. There were good masters, and Caroline was well taught in music, drawing, &c., but time ends all things; the anxiously-counted days and weeks escaped, and Caroline returned to her happy home, somewhere about eighteen years of age, with some increased knowledge of the world, and a stirring desire to be better acquainted with it.

We have said, that she returned to her own happy home, but much was changed, nothing so changed as she was; things went on as usual, yet all seemed changed and changing, herself the most of all. Perhaps the young blood no longer flowed so healthfully in the veins. She remembers no more exuberance of spirits—no more gaiety of heart. She remembers no more harvest-fields, or

---

* If this is a fact—it might appear physiologically to connect those morbid sensibilities with the actual exercise of the mental powers—suspended by their disuse.

gardens, or country rambles. She had seen London, she had heard of London life. She had mixed with girls of other habits, and of other tastes; the yearnings of vanity and ambition were in her heart; she wanted to see life, to be—to do—though she knew not what. She remembers walking after dark, up and down a paved court in front of her mother's house, whence she could see the carriages set down at the door of the assembly-room; and wishing she might partake of the gaiety, the dress, the splendid equipage, and the expected pleasure. She remembers walking on the high London-road, and as the travelling carriages went by, wishing she too might go—somewhere, anywhere. The house, the country, had gone after the poetry and the books—all had lost their charm. Altered, indeed, is now to be our story—the artless, the healthful, the peaceful youth was ended. She was to have her way—and more than twenty years were to be given her to try that world she longed for, before she found again a happy peaceful home. Most wonderful art thou, O God, in all thy ways; most good, most wise, most merciful!

CHAPTER III.

EARLY WOMANHOOD.

CAROLINE was to have her way. "Ephraim is wedded to idols, let him alone." It is a sad, sad chapter we have now to write. Before we enter upon it, something should be said of the state of her mind, in respect to religion, during the last-named period of her life. From the time of her father's death, during her school-days, and the short time she remained at home afterwards, Caroline used to go frequently, for the sake of going somewhere, and doing something, and at the instigation of an elder sister, already a decided child of God, to various places to hear the gospel preached, far more interesting of course to her intellect and feeling, than the ten minutes' essay to which she had been accustomed. She does not very well remember whom she heard, except an impression that Mr. Foster, of Long Acre, gave her the most satisfaction, of the few she heard in London, when taken out on a Sunday by her sister from school.

At Tunbridge Wells, it was in Lady Huntingdon's chapel she heard the gospel. She liked to hear a good sermon better than a bad one; and the better it was, the better she liked it; for the same reason that she liked a good poem better than a bad one; and she acquired from them a full and correct knowledge of the evangelical doctrines of the gospel, and the variations under which they were exhibited by different preachers; she may be said thenceforward to have understood the gospel as far as it could be learned of man, without the help of the Spirit or the Word. She never read—she cannot remember whether she ever prayed, or whether she ever felt or cared about religion. It is scarcely to be supposed there was not some personal interest excited at the time in the divine truths set before her, but she cannot recul it; they took no effect at the time, and were soon afterwards revolting to her.

Caroline was eighteen years of age, when the yearning desire of her heart to mix with the world, and taste the pleasures of a London life was gratified by a proposal from a near relation then practising as a solicitor in London, and residing with his wife and family in Bloomsbury, that she should live with them. Seldom has the young heart's satisfaction been more full; not one regret for the home she was leaving, or the sisters whom alone she loved in all the world, was mixed with her delight. To be the companion of . . . and assist her household and maternal cares, was the ostensible object of her removal to

Bloomsbury; the real intention could be no other than her advantage,—to introduce her to society, and afford her an opportunity of making such a settlement as he anticipated. The society was of that class in which there is perhaps the greatest degree of enjoyment; the refinements of polite life, without the restraints of rank; gaiety without dissipation; enough to keep up the taste for amusement, but not enough to sate it. The mode of living was the same: a small genteel establishment, everything elegant, but nothing luxurious or extravagant; no sense of or appearance of wealth; economy without stint—hospitality without display. This was what Caroline saw and shared— her simplicity and ignorance veiled the rest. She was grateful and contented. She loved . . . which was natural; most people loved him and he was always kind; she admired him, so did the society in which he lived; his manners were polished, and his wit was brilliant. It would seem as if her mental powers had actually been extinct during these years, in which her intellect was prostrated to folly, ignorance, and misjudgment; was contented with its humiliation, and had no misgiving of the degradation. In her father's house she had never heard a profane or licentious expression; nothing came amiss here to point a jest, provided it was not coarse or low. Caroline does not remember to have been shocked. In her father's house, nobody ever thought of absenting themselves from Church, or profaning the Sabbath-day;

here, though the latter was no otherwise done than by driving in the Park and paying visits, the former seemed scarcely to come into anybody's head; no mention was ever made of going to church; a few times a year it might happen, the master of the house being absent, that Caroline and her friend, wanting something to do, took into their heads the extraordinary fancy of going to some church on the Sunday morning, for no purpose and intent certainly, but to pass the time. It was in one such freak, Caroline heard for the only time, that eminent man of God, Mr. Cecil, then, probably, in his prime, at St. John's; and absolute offence and disgust are all her remembrances of it. Whether this neglect was then fashionable or not, Caroline does not know, but it was so to a much greater extent than it is now. That the habits and influence of a whole life should have left on Caroline's mind no desire for external observances, not the least compunction in the total neglect of them, does seem extraordinary, and is an impressive lesson. She had been taken to church in her childhood, because it was the custom, and because it was right; to her, at least, no other motive had been supplied; she ceased to go, without a thought about the matter, as soon as she found herself where it was not the custom. It was no doubt at this time, although she cannot recal anything about it, that Caroline ceased to perform the ceremony of prayer in her chamber night and morning, (she has no reason to believe that she had ever really prayed;) from that time never more to bend her knee in private, or her heart anywhere before the God of heaven, until of his sovereign grace and mercy she was born anew. Things could not rest there, and they did not; she was no thoughtless, careless being, to remain indifferent:—but of this hereafter. There was one dogma received without disputation in this new abode of the sometime poet, the precocious bookworm—the letter-devoted child; namely, that it was not genteel for ladies to know anything, except to dress and dance, and behave themselves in company; and manage their families, and ply their needles out of it. Never, certainly, was doctrine more practically exhibited, than this; for there was not, during the first year of Caroline's residence there, a single book in the house, except a stray volume of Cowper's Poems, for reading on Sunday, when the needle-work was suspended. Of course the credulous disciple took care never to remember that she had read so much beyond her years at one time: this had been long relinquished; she was a willing, well-convinced believer in this new code of politeness. Whether anything occurred, to shake the decision against books in general, we cannot say; but, all at once, an elegant book-case made its appearance in the back drawing-room, for the reception of a lot of handsomely-bound books, bought at a sale, without the smallest respect to what they might be about. It did not signify, it was Caroline's business to keep them properly arranged, according to their respective heights and sizes; and no further notice was taken of them. In fact, Caroline strongly felt the obligation she considered herself under, for her residence in * * *'s house; she was led to believe that she was totally dependent, and that every thing she received was his. She was very grateful and very happy, even in the enjoyment of much that she had not been used to in her early home; and she must have been deprived of more in the declining circumstances of her family : in short, she was told and thought she was wholly dependent. Her great desire was to be useful, in return to * * *'s family; there were five or six young children, and the mother delicate. Caroline's whole time, therefore, was occupied with the sublime arts of millinery and dress-making, or dress-trimming; for it was mostly the ornamental parts that fell to her share; it may be inferred, that in the suspension of every other exercise of her talents, this was a real pleasure to her—and she thinks it was. The same faculty that draws a flower, makes a cap, and puts a ready-made flower elegantly into it; the same taste that is brought to bear in the composition of a poem, will please itself in the arrangement of a dress, and Caroline's talents were brought to bear; with the pleasure of pleasing, extremely great to her at all times, and pleasure no doubt in the exercise of her skill, she had also the necessity of her own vanity to be supplied—though to do her justice, it was little enough; she never cared for dress, but dressed she must be, as became her position; and the bargain usually was, that if Caroline would make and ornament * * * *'s ball-dress, she should have one like it for herself. This, with making a fac simile of every beautiful and newly finished cap that was caught sight of at a party, or even in a shop window, and cutting out for the sempstress all the children's clothes, and making all her own, where every thing was to be of fashionable and economical admixture, was no sinecure; and from an early hour in the morning, to a late hour at night, when not engaged with company abroad or at home, Caroline laboured unremittingly in her vocation, and would have thought half an hour abstracted for a book, a real dereliction of her duties. There was an exception, however, and most curiously it served to supply what in her previous reading had been totally excluded; and made her widely acquainted with a class of literature of which she might else have remained ignorant; the indiscriminate trash of the circulating library, and which at that time, circumstances gave the opportunity of perusing.

Was Caroline injured by it? I think she was not; perhaps for the destiny for which Almighty love and mercy was preparing her, she was considerably benefited. The only case in which novel-reading can be harmless, is, where the mind has been previously solidified by much reading and reflection, so as to be capable of no impression from them beyond the surface, which may then receive a polish from works of taste and fancy, without the mind being vitiated or enervated by them. That the mind of a young female should receive no injury of another sort, to taint its delicacy and purity of thought and feeling, requires a case of great peculiarity, such as never may be presumed upon at nineteen; a childlike insensibility. Yet so it was, and Caroline gathered in this manner an insight into humanity, into life and manners, such as no previous opportunity had afforded her the means of observing, without any injury to her mind and morals, in its measure counteracting the absolute seclusion in which she had grown up, and amalgamating, very harmlessly and beneficially, with the very grave and solid reading of her early years. Thus out of every evil, Almighty power wrought something towards his purposes of good. For any purposes but those of his great mercy, never was unhappy child more ill-placed or ill-conditioned, or so ill-suited to her position. Her natural capabilities, suppressed and forgotten by herself, her natural defects brought into distressing observation to others, and conscious embarrassment to herself. If any one of her society then, should read these memoirs, (it is not likely, for she was youngest among them,) they may remember the country girl, who blushed whenever she was spoken to, and blundered whenever she spoke; who never opened her lips in presence of ——, for fear of being laughed at or reproved, who snuffed out the candles, and stirred the coals over the bar for the very fear of doing it; who laughed when she was flattered, and was rude when she was courted, whose very modesty made her stupid, and her artlessness ill-mannered; all suppressed in her that was natural, all impossible to her that was artificial, trying to be every thing but what she was, incapable of every thing she was desired to be, she grew daily more timid and consequently more reserved, more abashed and consequently more awkward. What Caroline was at this time, or passed for mentally, we wish there was one left to tell, for it is her mind's history we alone desire to write, yet tell we cannot. If any one who knew her at that time, and lived even familiarly in company with her, took her to have any talent, understanding, or mental power and cultivation of any kind whatever, they knew her better than she knew herself; but we should be surprised to hear of it; she supposes she talked the nonsense she enacted for those three whole years of vanity and waste. The society she moved in was much of the kind which prevailed in that neighbourhood, but the rapid movement of her subsequent life has worn out every impression of the greater number of them, names, persons, characters and all, very few having crossed her later paths, or been anything to her, then or since, but the companions of her hours of amusement; she cared nothing about them, and has known nothing about them since. If they have heard of her, they must have thought it strange material for a blue-stocking and a methodist. But His ways are not as our ways, nor His thoughts as our thoughts. One person there was however, in the society of this period, who claims a particular mention, both for his own reputation, and the influence his society may have had upon the subject of this memoir. His acquaintance proved another ray of literature in the dark ages of this her unliterary life, which, like the novel-reading, served its purpose, for it made her familiar with the transactions of the stage and its purveyors. Mr. C. was at this time above seventy years of age, and for the fineness of his person, the dignity and elegance of his manner, might have been monarch of the realm. It is possible that distance may have exaggerated the early impression, but it seemed to her she has never seen any one, whose whole person and manner were so courtly and high-bred, his tall upright person, his snow-white hair, and fine, benevolent, and yet impatient and irritable countenance, his easy and yet important air, of condescending consequence, his hat on one side of his fine and carefully-dressed head, the one hand in his bosom, and the other in a sort of consequential swing at his side, is an impression still fresh, made permanent no doubt, by the absolute and unmixed pleasure the sight of it produced. Caroline had known him first at Tunbridge Wells, where her childish poetry used to be submitted to his admiration by her father;

but that was at a distance, now he was the familiar of . . . . 's house, where, living great part of the year at an hotel in London, he found it very convenient to dine every day that he happened to have no engagement, where he was courted, humoured, almost idolized, and every thing that could be done to please him, was felt to be repaid by the mirth which his never-failing wit inspired. Wit that spared nothing human or divine, friends, life, morality, religion, nothing barred the jest; and they who laughed most heartily at the last joke, had reason to believe themselves the subject of the next, as soon as their backs were turned; excess of compliment in their presence was sometimes scarcely less a satire, though the high polish of the manner hid the fact. As was most natural, Caroline attached herself entirely to this fascinating old man. The first scholar—the first literary man—the first courtly man she had ever had any intimacy with, and who, to all appearance, loved and admired her. Whether so or not, he loaded her with flattery and caresses, poured ever in her ear the praises of her person, repeated all he heard from others of her beauty, and frequently remonstrated with her upon the *insouciance* with which she received the attentions of persons whom he wished her to attract; and it was finally decided by all about her that she had no heart, since nobody made any impression on it. It was a remarkable providence, in connection with her subsequent life, that she did not marry then, when she would as soon have accepted one as another, if externally agreeable and desirable.* If the insidious flattery of this dangerous old man, whom she admired, revered and loved, failed as it did, to make any impression on her delicacy, artlessness, and purity of thought and feeling, there was that in which the influence of his corrupt companionship did not fail: she was too innocent for his immorality, she was just ready for his irreligion. Never perhaps at the early age of nineteen and twenty, in a heart of such simplicity and incorruptness, and real ignorance of evil, was the enmity of the fallen nature so developed. We wish to call attention to it, and if we have been writing what seems useless detail, we have done so on purpose to give the full value to this particular point. It is written that the natural heart is "enmity" against God. Who believes this as a universal truth? When vice has indurated the heart, when habit has vitiated and the world corrupted it, it may be so, but what virtuous, happy, young and unspoiled nature, ever thought of hatred towards the God that made us? Fearlessness,

---

* There is surely one lesson deducible from this; a virtuous and moral childhood was sufficient to secure the youthful mind from subsequent moral corruption—the formalities of religious propriety were no defence against the insinuations of infidelity and ungodliness—and why? the one was a reality, and the other a fiction—the habits were virtuous—they were not religious. The pure, clear mind of youth is rarely impressed with what is false and fictitious in itself.

indifference, forgetfulness is natural, but not, surely not, "enmity." Perhaps there are very few believers, looking back upon their days of gay and joyous godlessness, that can at all verify the Scripture statement in themselves; how should they have hated the Being they never thought about and cared for, who never crossed their path with present ill, nor marred their pleasures with fear of retribution? But here, in the bosom of a simple girl, brought up in all the virtuous regularity and real religious observance of a secluded country life—a stranger to all that is morally evil, to a degree, that would not be credited if it were fully explained; with a mind solidly instructed, and unused to any manner of evil influence by books or company, hitherto a stranger to sorrows, wrongs, and fears, that tend to harden the ungracious heart—in this unvitiated, unworldly bosom, was manifested at that early age, clear and strong to her memory as if it was of yesterday, a living, active hatred to the very name of God. She persuaded herself there was no God, and thought she believed her own heart's lie; but if she did, why did she hate him?—why did she feel such renovated delight when his name was the subject of the profane old poet's wit? "No God" was probably with her, as it probably is with every other infidel—the determination of the heart, and not of the judgment. Thus while she thought herself above all religious doubts, she seized delightedly on every manifestation of infidelity in those around her, and laughed with the very utmost zest of gratified aversion, at every profanation of the holy name. There was no such thing as religious discussion in society there, nobody talked about the Gospel but those that believed it; and no so-called religious people were met with in ordinary society. All mention of religion therefore was casual and jocular; ridicule and not argument; nobody reasoned against the faith of Christ, every body despised it, the most knew nothing about it. Its professors were too little known or heard of generally, in such society, to be the objects of malignity. No, it was the master, not the servants then, on whom we spent our malice. Caroline recals one instance only,—it was just then that Mrs. H. More published her Cœlebs. It never reached this bookless mansion, but it was talked of every where and almost every body read it. It was a very unlikely book to commend religion to any worldly mind; and the general decision was not altogether unjust, that no such man should be or would be endured in polite society; the existence of a world in which he could be acceptable, was wholly unknown to the circle in which Caroline was then placed.

The three years of vanity and folly and mental degradation had expired—the altered habits of her life had told on the body—habitual sickliness had taken place of the fresh bloom of health—the total want of air and exercise, inseparable from a London life, had unnerved the limbs and paled the cheeks, and damped the spirits—while nervous sensitiveness and irritability had increased in due proportion.

CHAPTER IV.

CONVERSION.

LIFE is very uncertain, and intellect precarious. She who writes the beginning may never write the end. There is an event in every Christian's life more important to ourselves, and more redolent with the glory of God, than all events beside—"the new birth unto righteousness." Extraordinary as the manner of it was to her, and in its minute particulars known only to herself, ought she to postpone such a brief record of the circumstances as will secure to the sovereignty of divine grace, the praise and glory of this undeserved interposition of redeeming love? She will here narrate in brief, what may be amplified hereafter, should the writer live to complete her purpose.

It will be seen, if these pages are ever filled—if not, it might never have been known, that at twenty to twenty-five years of age, Caroline was an atheist in heart—and only not quite one in understanding: she wished that there should be no God; but because she was not quite satisfied that there was none, she hated the very utterance of his name, except when it was made a jest of.

In what company that occurred may appear hereafter. She was no longer ignorant, thoughtless, uninformed upon religion. She had read books, heard preachers, known saints—several of her own family were already under the influence of divine grace—she knew and hated all, and most intensely Him of whom is all. Years had passed since she deigned to bend the knee in prayer. His word she never read except upon compulsion —being required to do so with her pupils—the most disliked of all her daily tasks. She never went to church but for decency or necessity, and made it a rule and a deliberate effort not to listen or to join in the service; a systematic wickedness of which to this day she reaps the fruits, in the insurmountable difficulty she finds in keeping her attention to the service; now that with all her soul she loves it. The natural heart is said to be enmity against God—no doubt it is so always—but there may be few cases in which the fact was so palpable and demonstrable—so known to the heart itself, so actually in conscious operation, within herself; for it is not probable that any one ever heard it from her lips. Though talkative in trifles, she was exceedingly reserved as to her actual thoughts, and still more as to her feelings, and she had no bosom friend or kindred soul to tell them to. She never did tell them. To the few who would speak to her upon religion, she listened with silent amenity, or studied philosophical indifference: they had a right to their opinions—she would not have disturbed them on any account, since they liked to think so, there was no harm in doing it. So well did she understand their feelings and opinions, and so indulgently consider them, that one time sleeping in the same room with a sick sister, whose mind was morbidly, but most spiritually and truly affected with religious melancholy, that sweet sister would sometimes, in her sleepless nights, ask Caroline if she might repeat some hymns to her, and Caroline would kindly answer, " Do, my dear ;" and when in return, Amelia asked Caroline to repeat hymns to her, she answered that she did not know any, but she would make some against another night, and she actually did make some, that not only satisfied her sister, but continue to this time as acceptable to believers as her more recent verses. It is a curious fact, that one of these hymns—beginning " For what shall I praise Thee,"* of which, when she wrote it, she did not believe a word, and had no intention but to suit the feelings of her sister,—was ten or

* For what shall I praise Thee, my God and my king;
  For what blessings the tribute of gratitude bring?
  Shall I praise Thee for plenty, for health and for ease,
  For the spring of delight, and the sunshine of peace?

  Shall I praise Thee for flowers that bloom'd on my breast;
  For joys in perspective, or pleasures possess'd?
  For the spirits that heightened my days of delight,
  And the slumber that sat on my pillow at night!

twelve years afterwards shown her in manuscript as a great treasure, by a pious young lady who did not know whence it came, and hesitated to believe her assertion that she had written it herself. This was an awful state, but it resulted, in the wondrous power of Him who makes even of evil the ministers of his good, that when faith was given, knowledge had not to be waited for; difference of doctrine and modifications of belief, and all scriptural or unscriptural arguments in support of each were perfectly familiar to her—like one acquainted with the localities of a country, its languages and habits—when it was given her to enter by the gate, the way was plain before her. Indeed she had even so far considered the various views of christianity, as to have concluded that, if there was anything in it at all, the Calvinists had the better of the controversy; a conclusion to which she was

> For all this should I praise Thee, and only for this,
> I should leave half unsung, thy donation of bliss:
> I praise Thee for sorrow, for sickness, for care;
> For the thorns I have gather'd, the anguish I bear.
>
> For my nights of anxiety, watching and tears;
> A present of pain; a perspective of fears;
> I praise Thee, I bless Thee, my King and my God,
> For the good and the evil, Thy hand has bestow'd.
>
> The flowers were sweet, but their fragrance is flown,
> They left me no fruit, they are withered and gone;
> The thorn it is poignant, but precious to me,
> As the message of mercy, that led me to Thee.

most decidedly brought by the reading of Dr. Tomline's famous work, "The Refutation of Calvinism," one of the latest theological works she read before her conversion.* How was a mind to be reached thus trenched and fortified? Opinion had no weight with her; authorities had no influence. She had no dislike to hear the truth preached, or to the conversation of those who believed it, or to their persons. She would as soon have thought of disliking the Copernican system or its advocates, or any other scientific controversy. Her eldest brother was at this time a distinguished minister and writer in the Church of Christ—a man of acknowledged talent and learning. Caroline had heard him preach, and read his works, and held him in very high esteem and much affection; but his religious opinions had not the smallest influence. He considered Caroline as the most hopeless of his family, several of whom were beginning to be spiritually affected. He is said to have remarked about this time: " There is the pride of intellect, that will never come down!"—humanly speaking, what was to reach it? It was always the judge, and not the pupil, of whatever authorities might be brought before it. It has been said

---

* Calvinism would have been little proud of its proselyte—for whatever she had studied beside, she had not studied the Scriptures to discover who was right; but as an impartial and disinterested judge, exercised her own intellect and reason upon human statements.

she did not dislike to hear the truth, but there was that which she did dislike, which she hated, the Word that taught it. Neither the poetical beauties, nor the historic interest of the Bible could give it any charm. She could not endure it, she would not read it, and when read before her, she deliberately determined not to listen. O, blessed and immutable Word! now the joy of her heart, the comfort of her life, the exhaustless feast of her intellect and feelings! Why was it that she could amuse herself with the same truths from the lips of man, and take no offence, and feel no hatred; but could not bear it there? Surely because it has a potency which is not any where beside—"a savour of life unto life, or death unto death," which with all her philosophy and scepticism, she dared not meet.

It is always worthy of remark, that the Omniscient God works with, and not against, the natural disposition of the mind. This independent intellect was to be left unassailed, in the strongholds of its pride, and Caroline was to be reached, where only she was vulnerable, through her affections. At this momentous period Caroline was residing in the family of the Rev. T. M.—., where everything was against the probability of her receiving religious impressions, except the restless, unsatisfied, unhappy state of her own mind, displeased with every thing around her and within her; weary and disgusted with the present, and gloomy and hopeless of the future, without a single sorrow but the absence of all joy, kindly entreated, humoured, flattered and indulged by every one; her dependent situation notwithstanding, she was humorsome, rude, discontented and ungrateful. What wonder that she was so to those kind friendly creatures, who to the latest years of her intercourse or knowledge of them, continued to admire and love her, this conduct notwithstanding, —what wonder, when her heart was locked and scared against the love of Him, who at this very moment stood at the door and knocked, and was not asked to enter!

It has been said she never read—she never prayed—she never listened—wishing to be very exact in this particular, she will not omit, however, to mention what might be the first stirring of the Holy Spirit within her. She recollects a few nights when having laid down as usual without any attempt at prayer, in the intense feeling of her depression, as about to close her eyes, she mentally uttered something to this effect;—" God, if thou art a God, I do not love thee, I do not want thee, I do not believe in any happiness in thee; but, I am miserable as I am, give me what I do not seek, do not like, do not want—if thou canst make me happy; I am tired of this world, if there is anything better, give it me!" This, or nearly to this effect, felt between sleeping and waking, not upon her knees, but upon her bed, was all of prayer that preceded her conversion. Is it possible, that the Most Merciful, heart-searching God, could have said of her at this moment, " Behold she prayeth ?" She cannot tell. He heard an Ahab once: but Ahab wanted what he asked, she did not; she was determined not to have it. She cannot tell, but this was the moment when the messenger of peace appeared. In the destitution of her affections at this moment, Caroline fixed them with vehement partiality on the daughter of a clergyman in the adjoining parish. As all her feelings were passions, and passion is not very discriminating, she finds it hard to judge now, whether this new object of her enthusiasm was all she took her for; subsequent events have inclined her to doubt it; but she was a lovely creature, of great beauty, highly cultivated mind, and most endearing manners; a perfect contrast to Caroline in character, but alike in age, and though then living in her father's house, contemplating the necessity of entering upon the same course of existence, being the eldest of a large and unprovided family—a great favourite too—far more deserving than poor Caroline, for she was kind and grateful to the members of the family in which C—— resided. And here again she would bear testimony to the generous kindness of those friends, mortified as they plainly were, by the preference, or rather the exclusive affection these young ladies exhibited for each other. Nothing else was cared for, nothing else was enjoyed; the three miles that separated them, gave occasion for daily correspondence, and daily impatience of all that intervened. The devotion to each other was, or seemed to be, equal; and there was a further equality not very common in these attachments between females—which ever was the superior on the whole, it is certain that each one looked upon the other as something superior to herself, an object as much of admiration as of love; so at least it is remembered that Fanny always said, and Caroline always felt. If she be living, she may remember otherwise. Their mode of carrying on this romantic fondness was different enough. Caroline, as usual, run headlong into it, said all she thought, did all she wished, and committed herself in a thousand ways, in order to pursue and gratify her impetuous affection. Her friend was calm, polite, self-possessed, conciliatory; she knew the world better, and cared for it more; she never said, or did, or looked anything that was not proper; for time, or place, or circumstance; in short, Fanny was always doing right, and poor Caroline was always doing wrong—upon the matter of their mutual love.

Was Fanny religious? All who read this, will eagerly ask it.—No! let God have his glory, and the Holy Spirit the sole credit of his work. After the deep-felt experience of five-and-twenty years, and the thoughtful reconsideration of all that past, it is written without hesitation, Fanny was not then spiritually enlightened, though apparently religious; but Caroline thought she was, and that mistake was made the instrument of her conversion. Fanny had had an early disappointment, probably a blight of her affections, certainly of her worldly expectations. Her beauty and education had failed to procure for her, up to that time, what both she and her parents had expected from their charm; and what is not uncommon at five-and-twenty, the day seemed wearing away, and destiny taking its colour from the past rather than from the future. In short, the beautiful, fascinating, clever girl, had been in love, had been forsaken, and was in despair—of faith, or truth, or love, for ever after— her father was very poor and getting old, disappointed expectation lay behind, and anticipated dependence lay before. The world and Fanny " had long been jarring, and could not part on better terms than now ;" consequently she denounced it, she wished to leave it, she talked much of its vanity, she was or thought she was of a consumptive habit, and not likely to live many years; she talked much of death, and much of eternity, and much of God; I do not remember that she ever spake of Christ, of atoning merits or redeeming love. I believe she knew them not, she talked of the world's emptiness, levity and injustice. I do not remember she ever spake of her own sins. I believe her religion was purely sentimental. With Caroline it passed for more, she believed all, even to the consumptive symptoms and premature departure, many times shed tears alone at thought of losing her only treasure ; but these forebodings were, however, not realized. Caroline had not been in love, and had not been forsaken, and had received no injuries from the world, but she was out of humour with it too. She too was five-and-twenty, and thought the past was all, and she and the world worn out. The character brought with her into the world had now returned upon her, and under the auspices of her new friend, when they stole at midnight from their separate rooms to pass the night together; again—for the first time since she sat on the stile at seven o'clock in the morning, in " the Folly," at Tunbridge Wells;—she resumed the reading and enjoyment of Young's Night Thoughts—drinking deep of its melancholy, its pathos and its poetry without its religion,* as she had done at first. In the midst of their sympathy about the present evil world, by which was meant its sorrows, not its sins, one difference between the friends now made itself to be felt. Fanny expected something more, Caroline did not, and this plainly gave an advantage to her friend: both had, or thought they had, lost one world,—Fanny only had, or thought she had, the promise of another. Not a word of this difference, however, ever passed between them, for Caroline never spoke of her unbelief, nor confessed the total absence of religious feeling in her bosom. Religion was never

* Recollection of the two periods of her life, in which this book was her favourite, has given an abiding impression, that it is not, with all its piety and beauty, very wholesome reading.

once the subject of their conversation, as far as she remembers. But Fanny read the Bible, Fanny said her prayers, Fanny was exact in all her religious duties. This was nothing to poor Caroline; but Fanny was also very stoical, very patient, very meek, very submissive to her destiny, and determined to fulfil its duties, however distasteful; a very philosopher in practice as well as in theory.* Caroline noted this with shame and bitterness of soul, when having passed the night in sympathy of thoughts, feeling, judgment, liking, disliking, wishing and determining, without a difference, they appeared in the family circle, the one wilful, excitable, hasty and unsatisfied, the other all calmness, propriety and civility. On this difference she poured out her heart to her friend, continually bewailing her impetuosity and want of self-control, compared with the composure and philosophy manifested by Fanny, on all occasions.

Oh! what it was that turned upon that small spring! I should feel the want of words to tell it, but that words however multiplied can add nothing to the bare and simple facts. Most Merciful, most Inscrutable, it was thy doing! How can it do otherwise than surpass my telling. Let the story tell itself.

---

* When Fanny soon afterwards became a governess, I believe she did fulfil the duties and meet the difficulties and *désagremens* in a most unexceptionable manner, and retained her first situation till she married.

Friendship had looked through the cover of silence that slightly concealed Caroline's infidelity. Wanting courage, I suppose, to enter upon the hitherto avoided subject when they were together, Fanny took the opportunity of a short absence to write Caroline a letter. She deeply grieves that she has by some means destroyed or lost that letter, for it was the sole and single instrument of Heaven for the conversion of her soul. She kept it many years, and often read it, each time as her knowledge grew, with more astonishment at the wonder-working power of God—for there was not in it one word of gospel truth. The design of Fanny in writing was to tell her friend that religion was the source of all the advantage over her which Caroline had so often noticed, and so often envied—all that she called philosophy. The whole amount of the letter, dilated upon well and feelingly no doubt, was this, to the best of her recollection,—that religion was the only remedy for the ills of life, and alone furnished principle for the fulfilment of its duties; that she had religion and Caroline had none; therefore it was, as Caroline so often observed with pain, that Fanny was better and happier than herself, under similar feelings and circumstances of life. Caroline believes that it contained thus much of truth and nothing more, pressed home with kindly remonstrance and persuasion, abetted with arguments and proofs; she is sure it contained no mention of Jesus' name, of justifying righteousness or sanctifying grace; or any thing that believers call the gospel of salvation. But the statement was true, she had no religion—it was religion that was wanting in her—she who wrote it little knew how true it was; she knew neither the extent of the irreligion, nor the greatness of the need; nor the value of the remedy she proposed. The truth, the bare, bald truth, that religion was the one thing needful that she had not, struck conviction to her soul; it was the sword of the Spirit, piercing to the very bones and marrow of her existence.

But not without resistance. The first emotion on perusal of the letter was a paroxysm of grief and indignation; grief that the idol of her affections should condemn her, and indignation that she should presume to teach her; the next was a determined resolution that Fanny should not influence or persuade her. She would resent the impertinence; she would quarrel with her; she would break up the friendship altogether. What business of her's was it whether Caroline had any religion or not? With which brave but impotent intent she wrote a long and bitter reply that night, to be forwarded next day. The next day, however, brought no opportunity of sending to the parsonage at C———. The letter remained, and on the return of evening was re-opened. The resentment, as usual, had spent itself in tears and bitter words, and left only pain and mortification to herself; the expressions of that resentment were still in her own keeping; she put the letter in the fire, and began to write again. Now she would be kind, reasonable, indifferent, philosophical, superior to all such pretensions. She is not sure whether this second letter was ever finished, certainly it was never sent; and the third evening came:

> "But O what endless ages roll
> In those brief moments o'er the soul."

Before the third night arrived, the struggle was over, the battle had been fought and won, the strong man armed was vanquished, the banner of Jesus waved peacefully over the subdued and prostrate spirit of the infidel despiser of his word, the conscious hater of his most precious name! Has there been one moment since that night in which she has not loved it? "Lord, thou knowest." There have been many in which she has disgraced it. Caroline does not know that ever she has disowned it. She is sure there has been no time at which that name has not been all her hope and stay and confidence, for time and for eternity. What other could she have in a case like this? "Lord, save me, or I perish," has been, and is, from first to last, the sum of her religion, dated from that most wondrous night! the first in which she knelt before the cross; in which she prayed; in which she slept in Jesus; and died, and rose again to live in Him for ever. Amen and amen.

She can give but little account of the actual conflict. The battle was not her's, but God's, of which she seemed little more than a spectator, wishing victory to the opposer of the Spirit. She can recal the shame, the vexation, the wounded pride with which she first became conscious that there was a conflict; that her heart was moved; and comforted herself that nobody knew it, that nobody could know or ever should know, what was passing in her mind. Even her friend should never know that she had been for a moment shaken; the shame of that moment's weakness should never be revealed. More than this she cannot retrace, the work was done without hand, without time, without a process; and like him of old, she found herself in her chamber " clothed and in her right mind," clothed with " the garment of salvation," and assured of sin forgiven, with as little perception of the means as he, the less possessed than she had been, of the infuriate spirit.

Whether that evening or the next, she does not remember, her friend's letter was answered with a full confession and submission to the charge it contained, and the truths it urged: but Caroline has not the smallest recollection of the manner of it, or how much it disclosed of her altered mind. She understood too little of the revulsion to explain it probably. To others around her, circumstances prevented detection of the change, which she had not then the courage to make known; and which she could not have expected to be believed or understood, by persons whose religion had not the faintest colouring of evangelical truth or knowledge; whose whole creed was, the "Lord, I thank thee," of pharisaic confidence. The unwholesome atmosphere to which, doubtless, was attributable, the physical depression she had previously suffered, as the winter advanced, brought on alarming symptoms of pulmonary disease; she kept her chamber, and after many weeks of the most tender, the most feeling, the most unbounded attention from that generous family, so much fear was excited for her life, that her friends were sent for, and she was removed by slow journeys to her distant home. All that appeared therefore of the change, and became a subject of remark in the family,—as, her love for the Bible, and her attention to religious reading, was of course attributed to sickness, and the contemplation of approaching death. What was in her mind, meanwhile? Most naturally it was to believe that her conversion was the preparation for her soul's departure. She believed that she should die, and was well pleased to do so, for she knew that she was saved; there was no place for any feeling in her bosom but wonder, gratitude, and joy, that the brand had been plucked from the fire, at the very moment when that fire was to become eternity. There needed time to disclose to her, how unmeet she was for the companion of her Father's house, to which she had been called and chosen, and by how long a process the dross of such a heart, had to be burned out, by the sanctifying influences of the Spirit. Freed from the guilt of sin, she had yet no knowledge of its power. Her state of mind during that illness, may best be compared to his to whom it was said, "This day shalt thou be with me in paradise:" she saw nothing between her and the Lord who bought her, and the inheritance that he had divided with her. It was a presumptuous expectation, but it was the natural result of inexperience in the truth; it was justly grounded, and had her illness terminated as was expected, it would not have been disappointed. She would have been with Jesus; she says it and signs it now, that time and deep knowledge of indwelling sin, have modified without changing her views of the method of divine grace, the doctrines of the gospel—respecting, that is, the progressive sanctification of the justified believer, the work of the Spirit in the elect of God; she says it in the face of years of subsequent vanity, earthliness and inconsistency; in the face of accumulated sins of which the burthen is far more intolerable, at times, than those that preceded her conversion; she says it in the face of many, who reading these memoranda, may affirm that they knew her after this period, with few signs enough of conversion upon her; had she died then, her hope would not have been made ashamed, she was justified in Christ without the deeds of the law; she signs it now, and if the opportunity be afforded, should she ever live out her three-score years and ten, she believes that she will resign it on her death-bed, to the glory of the power of the free grace of God in

Jesus Christ; and the comfort of all who know themselves to be the subject of it. But He, whose precious gem she had become, had no intention to take it from the fire with all its base admixture of earthliness and corruption, infixed and indurated in a manner the most difficult to eradicate—by habit, by character, by circumstances, and by wilful opposition to the word, so long indulged.

It is not the intention here to pursue the ransomed spirit's history. It will be found, if God spare her to write it, in the regular progress of the memoir. There may be letters extant in which, being written at the time, the state of her heart is better exhibited than it can be at this distance. Her brother was naturally the first, to whom she specially declared what God had done for her; and with whom from that time forward, she was likely to hold the most confidential spiritual correspondence. His high and decided views of doctrinal truth, were likely to meet with all sympathy in the first fervour of the new-born soul whose history was a confirmation of all that he believed and taught. Perhaps he preserved her letters; if so, they will be the best witnesses to the truth of the present statement. Private letters are of all documents the most veritable of that which they disclose of the character of the writer. While every other testimony is but the portrait, which may or may not be like; they are the cast exactly moulded on the living form. If there be such letters, they should be here inserted.

Having no religious friends, it is improbable her feelings should be disclosed to any by letter but her brother, and those sisters, M——, L——, A——, who were already members with her in the body of Christ; but separated, as she thinks, at that time, from her. Hard, sterile, and unproductive was the soil on which the precious seed had thus been sown; the perfecting of Jehovah's work will be scarcely less wonderful when we come to tell it, than its beginning. Caroline never changed her faith, or revoked the profession of it; she never changed her purpose, she never let go the death-grasp she had taken on the cross of Christ; there was no season when that once abhorred name was not music in her ears, and balm upon her lips; but she was a graceless, senseless, and unruly child to her heavenly Father, as she had been to all others; and many, many were the years before she or any one else could find the fruits of holiness, on that wild olive-branch, engrafted as it was in the pure stem. It bears them scarcely still; we will hereafter tell it all. Suffice it now, to say, that the most immediate result of Caroline's change of heart, was, the happiness to which it had at once restored her; at peace with God, she made up her quarrel with all things. The zest of life returned; she no longer quarrelled with her destiny, or felt distaste of all her pursuits, or grew weary of her existence without any reason. The void was filled, she never after wanted something to do, or something to love, or something to look forward to; the less there was of earth, the more there was of heaven, in her vision; whenever man failed her, Christ took her up. She had no more stagnant waters, long as her voyage was through troubled ones; she was, with all the leaven of the older nature that remained, essentially a new creature to herself.

And Fanny—what more of her? We will tell all hereafter; unconscious instrument of all that God was doing, she disbelieved the work she had performed. Removal separated the friends, but for very many years did not divide their hearts; they were still dearest of all things to each other, but we must tell it here, for it proves the work of God. As the vital principle developed itself in Caroline, Fanny took offence at it. When Caroline wrote her a distinct statement of the change her own letter had been the means of effecting, Fanny laughed at it. She did not believe in conversion, in regeneration of the Spirit, or anything of the sort. She even said, her father held such doctrines, but she did not know how she had escaped the infection of his fanaticism; whenever the subject was resumed in their letters, it was an occasion of difference and dissatisfaction. They never met again, till an event occurred which proved that Fanny's heart was as diverse from her friend's for this world as it was for the next; that her denunciations of this life had been as little real as her early anticipations of another; the world might have her back if it would give the price. Fanny contracted a marriage, in a worldly point of view advantageous, but the sympathy that had seemed to bind the friends together was now dissolved; and every feeling they had in common proved to be, on Fanny's part, and by her own acknowledgment, as merely sentimental as Caroline believes her religion was. Caroline witnessed the transaction, and parted with her friend for ever, with a heart wrung with pain; several years longer, the form of friendship was kept up by letter, but the life was gone, the death-blow was struck. Once only again Caroline saw what had been the idol of her affections; it was not the thing that she had loved, or that she ever could love. Caroline herself was changed, and perhaps was as distasteful to her friend. Fanny, the intellectual, studious, poetic, religious girl, was . . . . if we survive her, we will tell what she was, and who she is; if not, she will read this, and she knows. A very short time after Caroline had visited her for the first time, and the last time, in her married home, a few unpleasant letters having been exchanged on the subject of religion, too vehement most likely on the one side, too scoffing and contemptuous on the other, the discussion reached its extremity; and Caroline, with that too hasty warmth, that has left so many things to regret that cannot be undone, desired that their correspondence should cease. It ceased, and they are strangers.

May eternal mercy grant to Fanny, the blessing she transmitted, and yet despised.

LETTERS.

LETTERS.

I.—TO THE REV. JOHN FRY.

Hastings, May 19, 1825.

My dear Brother,

I answer your letter something quicker than else I might, to tell you that a few days before I received it, I heard that Mr. ———, of Edinburgh, wanted just such a curate as you describe, to succeed Mr. ———; I shall subjoin the address, and your friend can apply if he pleases. I am just returned to my solitary home, and my goods being yet in their packages, I cannot even get at your letter to reply to it. What I imperfectly remember of its contents, is something about my own enigmas and something about the world's. And I remember thinking while I read it, how different an aspect every thing must be seen in from the hallowed stillness of your secluded dwelling, from that in which it presents itself to me. And I longed to sit down with you in that tall arm-chair, and Munchausen-like, tell of the wonders I had seen. But how, at this distance, am I to sketch for you the features of that world of which you inquire—the religious world. Whoever used that expression first, did not suspect that he described the thing it stands for, more exactly than if he had written volumes. The last term is that our Lord has chosen to designate his enemies; the first is that which distinguishes his friends; the both together is that strange admixture which is the distinguishing character of the present day. I suppose you will not understand me now, any better than when I said,—It is time to cease from man. Well then, can you not imagine how a person going always behind the scenes to see how the thing is got up, and to see the dramatis personæ disrobe themselves, &c. &c., might grow very weary of scenic representations? But this is myself again, and I am going to tell you of the world—few people can see so much of it really as I do—because I hold no settled rank in it, and move in no determinate sphere. One day the splendid carriage dashes up to fetch me, with two footmen to bang down the steps, lest one should not make noise enough: the next day I trudge off in the mud with my bookseller's apprentice to carry my bundles; sometimes I am everybody, and sometimes I am nobody, and I am equally amused with all; for all is life, and all is nature, and all lets me into secrets that those who walk a more settled and determined course but little wot of; and I note everything, and listen to everything, and lay it all up for future cogitation. And many a smile I have in private, aye, and many a sigh too, at the charlatanage of the deluding world. In respect to its present state, I should say nay to what you say, as it regards the taste of the public for religious truth. I should certify on no light grounds, that the defection lies elsewhere; there is appetite for the whole counsel of God, but they who are left in charge, have found in their wisdom that the food is not wholesome, and they *dare*—I speak *strongly*, for I have felt it strongly—even to tears; I have felt it under their pulpits—they *dare* deny it to the flock they have been sent to feed. Comes there a man in town or country, or on week-day or Sunday, who in simplicity delivers the whole of his message, and you will see how they throng his aisles, how they will steal forth like Nicodemus by night, to take of the desired but forbidden draught,—afraid to be blamed by their ghostly confessors if they are detected. Look at their faces while they listen to the unusual strain, and you will soon see if it be not welcome. Ask them when they go away, how they like it? They will speak of it as children of a birth-day treat—which to be sure if they had it often might disagree with them—so they are taught, so they believe; but they can relish it well enough. I do not speak of one class, or of two classes; I believe this to be the general aspect of things. I can set my eye on one pew, and say these people are of such a congregation—and on another, and say these belong to such a chapel—and why are they all come here? And many are the times I have whispered in the ear of those who sit satisfied, nay, absurdly devoted to some favourite preacher of a garbled truth, that there is more behind, and have been surprised to find how well they knew it, how much they could like to have it—but it is not good for them! The servant has grown wiser than his master; the messenger can amend his message—God can no more be trusted with the salvation of his people—Man knows a better way, and expediency is like to become the Anti-christ of our land. You question my term " magnificent preaching"—" Why not as well without the pomp?" you say. Our powers are of God; and if he have given the graceful mien—the deep-toned voice, and the overwhelming impulse of exalted feeling, and the resistless burst of eloquence, which in Athens held the lives of men, and in Rome the fate of nations, at its pleasure, to be the companions of his grace and truth, imparted to the minister of his Gospel, shall we say that they are useless? I wot not: though I would not over-value them. The great Lion of the day is ———; a man of most amazing powers of oratory: a person of taste, who did not like religion at all, might listen to him with rapture, for the thing is perfect in its kind. The Christian who cared not for eloquence at all, might listen with equal satisfaction—for he delivers his message fully, boldly, aye, and simply too, with all his oratory; for the wisdom of man is not mixed up with it. Then there is Irving, new to me, though passed the meridian of popularity. If ever you could conceive John Knox—if ever you pictured to yourself a blood-hot covenanter, preaching three hours together on the field of battle, with a highland blade in his girdle, and a bugle at his back, as willing to slay as he was to save; as willing to die, as he was to preach; fancy all this, and you have the man. But you cannot fancy it till you have seen Irving—I never could, but now I see it all. It was to me such a realization of imagination's dreams, that when I heard him first I could scarcely refrain from exclamation, so much did it seize on my poetic fancy. Common sense tells one, that to a chapel full of Holborn shopkeepers this is not the thing—and right feeling tells one, that this sort of excitation, under a sermon, is not to be allowed—and so I went no more: but knowing what it is, I would have gone from London to Edinburgh to have heard it once. At one of the great meetings, where he got up to make a speech, no longer restrained by the feeling that the gratification was out of place, I did really jump off my seat and clap my hands for joy—but one need be a poet to understand all this. Dear old Mr. Wilkinson still holds his post; the still small voice of truth sounding as it were from out some holy recess, where the tumult, and the cavil, and the disputation, are unheard or unregarded. You read his name in no printed lists—you see him in no strange pulpit—you hear of him in no company—but go to his church, and there you find him, the same words ever in his mouth—the words are few, and the ideas few, and there is little variety in either. He controverts no man's doctrines, he takes note of no popular wrongs or rights, he is like one who neither sees, nor hears, nor knows what is around him, he comes blindfold from his closet to his pulpit, to tell in one, what he has learned in the other—the most secret, the most mysterious, the most precious purposes of God to his own elected people: a tale with which none else can have to do, and which none else can understand. * * * * The man with whom, were I resident in London, I should probably settle down as my regular minister, is Mr. Howells, of Long Acre, a Welchman; not because he is better than some others I have named, but because some preaching is good to one cast of mind, and some to another; and amid the much I have heard since I have been now in town, I am inclined to think I should be, on the long run, most benefited by his. Howells has not a large congregation, but a very peculiar one—I should say he puts his fingers into other men's gardens, and carries off the fruit as it ripens—not in crowds, but here and there one. Popular he cannot be, because he is above the reach of the untutored mind, and above the taste of the vulgar mind. I never saw a congregation in which the proportion of *men* was so large, which it is easy to account for. He takes the learned of our religious world, but not till the whole counsel of God has become acceptable to them; for there is no equivocation with him. These are the luminaries of London. Others there are, the favourites of a corner, the Popes of a set—some true to what they know, but knowing little—some knowing all, but proudly withholding it on their own authority. * * * I spent a week at —— where —— holds the cure of 20,000 souls. The religious few who for years have been expecting anxiously his coming, are all forsaking his church, while the worldly sit under him at ease. When questioned as to his faithfulness, he replies, that in two years he will preach otherwise, but the people are not ready for it! What an awful responsibility! So much for preachers—but what are the hearers doing, you will ask—Who would not live in these days, to see two thousand saints at a time in Freemason's Hall, and all so occupied that they can sit patiently seven hours a day! Could the Christians of the days of Paul rise from their graves to see, how would they recognise their despised race amid the tramping of horses, and locking of chariot-wheels, and thronging of fine-dressed ladies, fain to leave their beds some hours earlier than they are wont, in the hope to get a seat. Placed in these scenes for the first time, many and curious were the thoughts that came across me. I thought of the caverns in which these despised hid themselves—of the sheepskins that were their covering, and the berries that were their food. And I said, How strange, how wonderful are the ways of the Almighty! To me the thing was new; I had never seen a crowd of that description, since the days I saw them at the opera or in the ball-room, and whether it was the recalled association, or whether the animating bustle had merely withdrawn my mind from the purport of the thing, I actually started when the language of religion first reached me from the platform. There was not much good speaking, little tone of piety, but most fulsome praises of each other. I remained discomforted and went away dissatisfied. This was not, however, the case the second time. It was for the Jews—the children of the school were present. I cannot tell you all I felt or all I thought while I looked at them. The helpless offspring of God's chosen people, sitting there as supplicants to the bounty of that gay Gentile crowd. Here all the poetry of my feelings was awakened, many good things were spoken, and I was very much delighted. Next came the Hibernian—see what a devoted saint I am become! There I went too, and I was pleased again, for I love the Irish to my heart, and the first feeling of incongruity was entirely over now. I had gotten into the full spirit of the thing. An old lady, deep in these matters, who sat beside me, said a thing that struck me. She was complaining of Irving's impolitic speech—I said, "It seems to me he is the only man amongst them who has stood for God, and for his truth." She replied angrily, "What is the use of that? They come to speak for the interests of the Society." I said no more, but I laid up the speech to think upon. What he had said really was a magnificent warning to the children of God, when the children of men come in to join themselves to their counsels—as fine a charge as ever I heard; placing a child of God on such a proud pre-eminence, that the great ones of earth seemed to dwindle into nothing as he spoke. The Lords and Right Honourables looked a little uneasy.

The last I went to was the Naval and Military —interesting from its peculiarity. Here more of the language of scripture was used than in the others; more mention was made of the Gospel of Christ, and more use of its words and doctrines— and the speeches came not from the church, but for the most part from the soldier or the sailor. So much for my devotions through the first week in May. What have I brought home with me from it all? It is fine, it is striking, it is interesting, and more so than I thought before I went. The purpose is good, the means seems to be legitimate, and the end must surely be what heaven designs by this strange change of circumstances. Well then, let it go on, and I would aid it heartily. But I have brought away this—religion is not the popular oratory—religion is not the crowded hall —religion is not the printed list. The children of God have need indeed to be warned, and if it pleases God, those words of Irving's shall go with me to be remembered whithersoever I am bound. And so much, my dear brother, for the sketch of London. Now of ourselves. You must pay double postage, but never mind, you may not get another letter for a twelvemonth. I have not read your Church History, but have it ready to read. I only reached home two days since. I know not what to say to V———; I hear strange things about him. I have no objection to subscribe to his work; but must see it before I recommend it to others. It was not true that I was worn with labour, but I was worn with bustle, too much eagerness, too much excitement. I must be quieter. Little do you dusty commentators know how we poets live and feel. I have just now found your letter. Why yes—we are tired of disputing about predestination—and as to the Second Advent, we think it is no business of ours! We had rather talk of Sierra Leone, and the Catholic Bill, and East India Sugar. Aye, truly, I shall enjoy your Job, but I have no light upon it, except that a friend of mine says that Job could not be happy in the end, if he had the same wife! * * * I do not despair to see Desford again some time. Love to all the party. I wish I had met John in town. After a most tremendous conflict, such as you would wonder to hear about, I trust that the dawn is again breaking upon me. Some time I may tell it all, but not now.

Yours affectionately,
Caroline.

II.—TO MRS. * * *.

November 6, 1825.

Dear Thing,*

I am always pleased to see your little notes, but this is a bad account you give of yourself: still I think that beautiful sea will do you more good than advice here. I believe I ought to have acknowledged your remittance, but I did not come home that day till late, and calculated a letter would not arrive in * * * till you were gone. I have been thinking to send a note thither for the chance of a parcel.

Now you bid me write by post. I suppose you must be obeyed, otherwise I am in that sort of mood in which I seldom allow myself to write; lest I should get into a tone of sadness, too nearly approaching to discontent, to become a child of God. These are feelings I attribute greatly to indisposition; and the indisposition greatly to the weather; of this one is guiltless, and there is no remedy but patience. It is, however, difficult, when one has cause of sadness, to distinguish one thing from another, and to be sure whether one is ill, or miserable, or wicked; and when once the

---

* This Lady, a few years younger than the writer, was her most beloved friend, with whom for twenty years she was on terms of the closest intimacy.

scale is bearing downwards, both sorrow and sin are ready to throw in their make-weights of sadness. I have been very well till the last week, however, and trust it may please God I shall soon be so again. The incapacity for employment is what I suffer most from on these occasions. I thank you, dear, for the inclosure, and for its machinery. It does its duty well, and is very useful to me. I am in all such matters now very comfortable, and for accommodation desire nothing better. I shall be very glad when you come back, for though I shall not very often see you, I shall be at liberty to think perhaps you will come, and that is something. It has been said, He that multiplieth riches increaseth sorrow, and as friends are part and portion of this world's good, I believe the more we have, and the more we love them, the readier access has disappointment to our hearts. But we must not be ungrateful; we must pick the beautiful flowers He scatters on our way, and not be impatient that now and then from too much eagerness we prick our fingers. I do sometimes wish my heart were as hard as a millstone, but I think it is a wicked feeling, and never encourage it. Among many things that teaze me now, is my publication; I want to give it up because it is too much for my health, and have always intended to do so at Christmas. But my publisher is outrageous, he positively will not stop. I know not what to do for the best: but I trust that God will guide me. I wish only to do His will, could I know but what it is. If the work were His, I should be ill-disposed to stop it, but I do feel unequal to its task; and surely if He takes away my strength, he means me not to continue the undertaking. Let me have another little note from you some day, dear, to tell me that you are better. I am thinking of going to —— at the end of the month; but am not certain: and only for a week or ten days. God bless you, dear, do not leave off loving me because it teazes you sometimes: it is not wasted on me, at least without return.

Very affectionately yours,
CAROLINE FRY.

III.—TO THE REV. JOHN FRY.

* * * 1825.

MY DEAR BROTHER,

If I were to date my letter from the comet, I suppose you know me too well to be surprised. I never write to you in a common way, because it is of no use, and everything with me now is questioned upon the *cui bono*, if it asks for time. But when I take a new peep into this old world, I feel impelled to send you news of it. So here I am—stumbled on a visit to * * * whose name cannot be strange to you. * * * How I came here, matters not much. I have been with them five or six weeks, and am soon to return home. * * * These people are most deeply interesting; just in that state in which one looks fearfully towards heaven to ask what it intends for them. All respect for established things gone; the bridle of prejudice broken—the deep truth of metaphysical scrutiny read to the bottom; the feelings exhausted by over action; and the conscience withal goaded into an almost morbid sensibility, ashamed of the past, and bewildered for the present, and vaguely anxious for the future. It seems to me that they know not what they mean, nor what they believe—sometimes I tremble for them as upon the point of making their peace with the world under whose lash they are writhing, by giving in to its habits and practices, and hiding their principles in their own bosoms. At other times the genuine seed of gospel truth seems to be so surely in their bosom, that I think they will settle into humble, subdued, and devoted Christians. I cannot get at them. At one time I hear them pronounce the Calvinistic doctrines to be dangerous, and always tending to carelessness of life—alas! they may have seen cause to think so—at another time they betray by some casual expressions, that its deepest secrets are in fact the strong-hold of their faith. If we hear a strong doctrinal sermon, and I say I like it, they say they do not; but I can perceive that they do! The most interesting person I have seen is * * Of him I should say, that if ever I have seen a humbled, subdued, heart-broken, deeply-taught christian, it is he. I was but once in his company, but there was something that responded to my own feelings in all he said and in all he looked, that I scarcely can explain or account for; and once I heard him preach, and felt the same. Of him I should not hesitate to say, he is come out of the fire purified. Of * * * I know not what to say: he is such a superior being, in intellect, in acquired knowledge, in goodness, in conscientiousness, in humility, in everything that is beautiful. I want to say the same thing of him; but then if I talk with him, he seems or affects to know nothing. I spoke of the sinfulness of sin: he said he did not know what it meant. I spoke of the love of God in redemption,—he did not know what that meant,—and yet I verily believe that he does know.

But how shall I tell you the beauty of this place. The trees such as you never looked upon; the garden with every thing in it, from the rarest foreign plant that money can purchase, to the commonest wild flower of the hedge, all botanically arranged; and yet so tastefully, and inartificially, you would almost believe they came there of themselves; then the library, with all the books in the world, just to make one sad, that life is too short to read them. I pass the interior of the mansion, because I care for none of these things. I love the comforts and and actual enjoyments of life perhaps too well, but its splendours I have no taste for, though, *entre nous*,

I have a little taste for the productions of the French man-cook. This, however, I at least shall learn here, if I knew it not before, which I believe I did,—that the abundance of this world's goods, adds little to the happiness of its possessors; and that I, a homeless, houseless, pennyless creature, am a happier being than * * * * with twenty thousand a year at her disposal. And one of her miseries is, that with all her means she cannot get her children educated; and about this I must have a word with you. Do you know any gentleman you can really recommend to the joint office of curate and tutor: he should have a wife, be a gentleman, and a scholar, and have some of the qualities of Job beside. The situation would be very lucrative, but very difficult; a good house would be provided him, the pupil would be sent into the house to him, at a high rate, and he would have the opportunity of taking three or four more. * * * you know is rector, but wants help. The pupil is a most desirable one in himself; I never saw a more pleasing boy; but, owing to a bad constitution, the enormous value set upon him, and the delicacy with which he has been reared, and the really good judgment and penetrating intellect of the father, and the womanly feelings of the mother, it is almost impossible for any one to give satisfaction. But with all this, there is such essential kindness, benevolence, and liberality, that it is quite sad that there should be nobody with sense enough, and Christian forbearance enough, to overcome a few peculiarities and difficulties, and gratefully and faithfully to perform the duties required, for which they care not what they pay. The boy now costs them about £400 a year, at Mr. ——'s; and they are wretched about the distance, and the treatment. I verily believe that if the living were at this moment vacated they would give it you, or anybody else who would preach the truth, and educate their boy. They asked me if you would take the curacy, and hold it with your living, residing here. I said, No, I do not think he would. Do not speak of this out of doors, but if you have any one to recommend, write to me directly, and as I shall leave here on Monday next, direct to me the following week at * * * where I am going to see Lydia; and after next week, to my domicile at Hastings. I am once more very near changing my residence to London; it depends on the turn of a die, which I leave in the hands of Providence to throw. I have no choice in it but to do His will. My heart is light upon the weightiest matters when once I can be sure of my motive; that is seldom, but this time I think I am sure; the advantages are so nicely poised, the results so impossible to perceive, that there is not a hair's weight to turn the scale, but what seems to affect my spiritual welfare, always deteriorating in my present residence. In this inclination I may err; therefore simply and heartily I leave it for the decision of heaven. How, I have no room to explain; but if I change, you will hear of it after Christmas; it will be to live somewhere in London. Love to dear Martha, and all the family, whom some time I hope to see again.

Affectionately yours,

C. FRY.

IV.—TO THE REV. JOHN FRY.

London, 1826.

MY DEAR BROTHER,

I have much less communication with you than I wish, but I am so overwhelmed I know not how to help it. Many times a day things occur of which I say to myself, " I should like to tell John this ;" but I am busy and they pass. Your domestic sufferings too, have perhaps lessened your immediate interest in passing things; and I have felt it would be ill-timed to tell you anything of myself or of the world. Do not think I have taken no part in your family interests. I was thinking of writing to you about the girls in particular, but the sound reached me of schemes in hand, and I thought I had perhaps better mind my business, and wait till I was consulted. Now I know all from Lydia, and do trust that providence has devised the scheme, and will perfect it to good. For myself, I am going to say nothing, because I have too much to say. If ever I see you again, I may say it all. Should I ever have courage to tell the whole of my spiritual story, I believe it will be a picture such as has been rarely drawn. Suffice it now to say, God is all truth, all love, all wonder, overwhelming wonder. Years now have gone wearily over, since one bright beam has been upon my bosom; the hold I have maintained has been upon a twig that seemed withering in my hand, every moment ready to break and leave me to destruction. I have looked about, but there was none to help; I have waited, and it is come back; and my bosom is too narrow to hold the happiness that has come into it. And this is all now; I will tell you more hereafter. I am requested to send you the enclosed. Have you heard that we are all in an uproar about the second Advent? If so, you must be curious to hear more; they started it at the Jewish anniversary; but at the Continental Society it was a concerted thing; they embodied it in their motions, and identified it with their society. As you will have all the Sermons and Reports, I need not tell you the nature of them; but we are all wild about it; and there will be a battle as fierce, if not as fatal, as Armageddon itself. With all my heart I wish your sober head had been amongst them, for though I love the subject, I fear the party. There is * * * * a most exalted and devoted creature; his bosom bursting with love to God and man; but the veriest lunatic out of Bedlam. Then my poor friend * * * whose past excesses and present defections, his indiscretion, and versatility, bring mischief upon every cause he meddles with, though he never means but right; and then * * * the most splendid and wildest genius enthusiasm ever lighted, all boldness, truth, and zeal, but rash, confident, unchastened by experience, and hurried on by popularity. And last, though in honour he should be first, there is the Presbyter—my only hope is in his massy brain; but, alas, men go mad with too much brain, as often as with too little. And so they are off, the sails are swelled with talent and popularity, but I fear there is no ballast in their hold. I wish I may be wrong. They are determined to proclaim the immediate coming of the Lord in glory, to the world in general, *nolens volens*; and to the Jews in particular, their immediate restoration. They are extremely happy to produce your interpretation of Greek and Hebrew, and I imagine you will find an increase of notice of your work; but in the interpretation of passing events they outrun you far. I scarcely yet know what to think of them. I fear the beautiful subject they advocate will be identified with a party, and wrecked by their violence. * * *'s piety and sense is all my hope. And after all, if it is indeed the Lord who has awakened them to announce His coming steps, we have nothing to fear for them or for their cause. My penetrating eye was perhaps too busy, when, through a splendid array of talent on the platform, the heart-rejoicing truths they poured upon our ears, I read the characters of the men I knew, and said doubtingly, "Is this anything?" I wait with anxious expectation to see what it is. A party will soon be in array against them; and nothing else will be talked of this year. Irving's book is very beautiful; how just his interpretation, time must reveal. For my part these things have been so long the familiar belief of my mind, that I heard * * *'s sermon without finding out that it was not like other sermons, till I heard next day how much offence it gave, and how strange it was. I should like to hear your opinion of these spirits. There is no one in our world now, who stands so high in general estimation as * * *, he has lived down all critics, and outstood all censure. You have no idea of the value our churchmen have for him, and the warmth with which he is looked for, and received everywhere. I am a little proud of my discernment in having liked him from the first. Ask Lydia about him. Among other apparitions, there has been a very lovely one in the form of a Swiss Malan: I heard him preach in French, a sermon such as English ears hear not too often. What amused me, was to mark the satisfaction with which some persons swallowed in French, a dose of Calvinism, that in English would have sent them out of the Church. Excepting from old Wilkinson, I never heard so exclusive a sermon, and not often from him. It was plain, his mind beheld no unbeliever while he preached. In truth, it was a heavenly morsel to those he meant it for, and their language has words of tenderness and love, we know not where to look for in our own.

The inclosed has been written a long time, and waiting the chance of a frank. As it is exactly what you ask for, perhaps I had better forward it, and let you pay double postage, which I cannot now avoid. It is a sketch of the party, such as may help you to mould your dealings with them. I have nothing to do with the breakfast, nor indeed did I know, till afterward, that the Prophets were assembled here; —— is the very focus of all their machinations. I had a mind to tell you to be primed and loaded, in behalf of these *enfans perdus,* who are like to have no Millennium at present; if I am rightly informed of the fire that is to be opened upon them. The * * * will charge furiously, out of spite to Irving, who has drubbed them out of the pale of common sense. But I do believe that the feeling of the Christian community,—I mean of those who commune with their God in secret, think of these things, and say nothing,—is with you; and I cannot help saying to you, Come forth and help them. Do not let every blunder-headed pamphleteer, brow-beat and abuse them, without a knock in return. You will see my judgment of the party; of the cause you will form your own. At any rate, you need not fear that the world will at present sleep upon the question. They have immense talent and popularity on their side. I look upon * * * * to have unlimited powers of mind, deep religious experience, with all the characters of a broken and contrite heart, loved of God and accepted. But of man he cannot be—

wild, strange, eccentric, imprudent—perhaps more literally mad, than I would admit to an enemy of religion, or of himself. I will receive Job with great pleasure. I do hope sometime to have a holiday with you, but for this summer I am disposed of, there being a strong inducement for reasons I cannot explain, to pay a visit to the Abbess of C—— House, which will take me to Clifton in August. I beg you to be informed that six numbers of my magazine are ordered monthly for his Majesty's Library. This is by favour of the new bishop, Dr. Sumner. I have not time to add more, but shall be happy to communicate with you upon all these matters. I did not know you were to stay at Desford. I have heard your plans imperfectly. All is right, and nothing signifies; it is gone as a tale that is told.

Affectionately,
CAROLINE.

V.——TO MRS. * * *

July 25, 1827.

MY DEAR FRIEND,

You will not, I am sure, await my answer, to be certain that a request which comes from you will not be refused. If it will please you so to oblige your friend, it cannot but please me to do so small a matter for you. I think, however, it must wait my return. I can do it while I am with you perhaps, but now I am so little stationary, I scarcely know where I shall be. I spend the greater part of my time in the open air, and am then too much fatigued to do anything. I feel quite sure, were I to let you send the books, &c., it would be unavailing—evening being the only time I am at leisure, and that will not do for painting. It shall be done to the best of my capabilities, on my return. I thank you, dear, I am as much better as possible in health, and as light of heart as one can be who carries her greatest care about with her. It is beyond the reach of earth's medicament, but still not without a remedy. My mind is in the position of the Psalmist, when he says, "I wait upon the Lord." If in the issue I be refused, I know that my will must alternately lose itself in his. As it is, I am never happy, nor can be made so by anything; for the joys of heaven itself are overclouded; but except when my health fails, I can be cheerful and active, and take of the good that Providence daily and abundantly bestows, I hope with a grateful, if not a gladdened heart. I write to you now from Southampton, but return to Stansted on Monday; I have been here ten days enjoying my greatest pleasure in its kind, tossing on the wide waters. Yesterday I went round the Isle of Wight, a scene the most exquisite I have ever enjoyed—the steam-vessel keeps close on the shore, and by the rapidity of its motions, presents a new picture every moment. This sort of amusement never fails to brighten my cheeks and elevate my spirits. I am not sure about my future movements, but I shall be at Stansted a fortnight. If you do not get any answer to the advertisement by the middle of the month, I think it would be well to repeat it. I saw some advertisements lately which I thought would do, and I wrote to Mrs. * * * to inquire about them : because, being on the spot, I thought it would be less trouble to her than to you; but I have yet heard nothing. I like all that you tell me of yourself, dear: I like that you should tell it me. While the interest of every thing else is waning fast, so fast that I sometimes wonder what is to occupy the other half of my three-score years and ten, this is a subject of which the interest deepens every moment. These bright returnings are worth the darkness that precedes them, were it not for the sin that belongs to it; but I am persuaded that it comes of our own fault, of our wilful preference of something else to him. He sees it, and leaves us to make trial of our own devices. "He is wedded to his idols, let him alone." What we are when let alone, you have amply proved, and so have I, too well, I trust, to try our schemes again. But certainly you need not fear that He will take your rejoicing from you. It was God, in some sense, who cast Jonah into the deep : but the separation began not with him; it was Jonah's doing, not his, that ever he came there. That second chapter is a beautiful picture of the darkness and lifelessness in which we have sometimes found ourselves. I say *we*, for in this we seem to have been alike. But I think we are alike in our present feelings—but that my rejoicing is silenced by circumstances extraneous to my own salvation; spiritually I have been at no time so happy as I am now, and from much the same feeling as you speak of. We shall talk of it together. God bless you. I am quite tired, and have written myself sad.

Very affectionately yours.

VI.—TO MRS. * * *

Milton Street, Dec. 8, 1827.

MY DEAR FRIEND,

I was so pleased to find a letter from you on my return: it seemed long since I had heard about you. Meeting, I grieve to say, appears distant, as you are ere this off to Brighton, and next week I am off to Bristol; I cannot consequently accept your kind invite for Christmas, unless I should return anything of time before my pupils want me: I shall stay at least three weeks: I sympathize, be assured, in all you feel, and wish I could be with you. St. Paul says, "affliction though good is still grievous;" and I suppose he knew. Be not therefore as one is apt to be, depressed because of your depression; I mean by reproaching yourself with it. I believe the Christian's appointment is not to be happy—always—but to be peacefully content to be otherwise when it pleases God. What frets me most is, that you look thin and ill; I wish I could nurse you. For myself, I am brave. I have had ten days of absolute enjoyment at * * * a scene novel enough. To sit down, Lady * * * and myself, every day with four and twenty men, all staying in the house; men distinguished too for various kinds of talent, and for no common degree of pious devotedness to God and his truth. I certainly felt considerable fatigue from the effort of listening and understanding the deep matters in question; but this is not so bad as the excitement of playing an active part oneself to amuse the stupid! It was the excitement only of deep thinking. I would not wish its continuance, however; the whole party began to knock up; they dispersed yesteday, and I came home to-day, with a head full and a heart full of good and holy things, that ought to last me for some season. I really have never seen a fairer display of christian principle and feeling—and that unity of heart which in such disjointed company, nothing but christian love could give; I must tell you about it when we meet. I think upon the whole my heart is lighter than it's wont. The quiet respectability of my house continues to be very valuable. I believe I shall go to * * * for a day with Mrs. * * * and will take to your house Mrs. G's book; if not, will leave it for you here with Mrs. G——.

to Sir Thomas Lawrence, and am to have another this week: so we are in a fair way to finish; so much for self; but I would rather talk of you, dear thing; you write in so much sadness, I long to come and cheer you. But it must be, dear, that we learn these lessons. He whom we follow, little as it might seem He needed it, even He was made perfect by suffering. How should we be perfected without it? Your cup is in many respects so full of this world's good there is more to dread for you from too much prosperity, than from these intervening hours of sadness; it is necessary, doubt not, that your heart should feel desolate amid surrounding abundance, while others have fulness amid surrounding desolation. It is the same beneficent and careful hand that mixes a bitterness with the draught of prosperity, and sweetness in the cup of destitution, and both to the same end. It matters little which we drink, for all will soon be over. I feel persuaded that the fashion of this world is about to pass away, and all that we need care for is to be ready; or, if not, the three-score and ten are telling out. Write to me at Bristol, if you *like*, for I am always glad to hear of you. I shall be at Mr. John H———'s till about the second week in January. Give my love to * * *, and kind regards to Mr. * * * Good bye, dear thing.

   Very affectionately yours,
        CAROLINE FRY.

VII.—TO MRS. * * *

September 29, 1828.

MY DEAREST THING,

My heart reproaches me for not writing to you; and though the time approaches when I trust to see you, I think I must try to compound a letter. The more so that I hear you have been again in trouble, dear, with dangerous illness in your family, the ingredient of bitterness, which it seems the will of Providence to mix in your else full cup of prosperity. I am grieved, but little surprised to hear of poor * * *'s increased illness; I thought her very ill; for though strangers are apt to say, and even Doctors are apt to say, that certain feelings are all nervous, and might be resisted, I never believe them in cases such as hers. I hope she is recovering, as I have heard, and that you, little, kind, busy darling, are freed from your anxiety and not injured by your nursing. Write and tell me so, if there is time—but I believe there is not —I think to leave here the beginning of next week, and to reach home before the end of it. This is a sorry subject with me; I grieve and am ashamed to say how painful it is to me to think of coming home. There is sin I fear, as well as painfulness in the feeling; for I ought not to hate the home that heaven has assigned me; I did not always do so; the time has been when I was entirely satisfied with it, and thought I would not change it for another's home if I could ; and professed before God that I desired nothing but to be able to keep it. I wish that this feeling might return; for it must be wrong that I now dread always the time of my returning, sicken at heart, whenever I think of it ; I catch at anything that promises to put it off. I believe it was this made me give ear to a journey to Edinburgh previous to my return ; but some increase of indisposition blighting the spirit of adventure, and some facility of returning to town in company has decided me otherwise, and I shall come home next week. I have had a most prosperous journey ; every thing since I left Bristol has turned out well, every facility of circumstance for health and enjoyment has been afforded me, and there have been no reverses ; I have seen a great deal to interest me by the way, especially in Ireland, where I was detained by pleasure, not by illness ; and in this delightful seclusion, with my most precious and beloved friends after years of separation, I am as happy as I can be, who for years have ceased to know what it is to feel entirely happy. The worst part of my summer history, is, that with " all advantages and means to boot," I am not better. From the time of leaving Bristol, I travelled to a certain point of betterness; for forty hours I think I was well—that was at Holyhead ; since which I have travelled back to where I set out : my hysterical feelings have terribly increased ; my walking powers are not amended: and I have nothing in prospect for my return, but the same confinement, joylessness, and uselessness, that preceded my departure. I have again had medical advice, and received a multitude of directions for things possible and impossible, of which the former half, I suppose, will lose their charm, for want of performance of the latter; but I shall try. I believe, however, that the better charm will be, by heaven's grace, to make up my mind to accept as unseen good, what seems evil; to submit to idleness as a proof that God has nothing for me to do; and to joylessness as an evidence that enjoyment would do me harm. It seems that this would be greater wisdom than to contend against feelings which have resisted the most favourable circumstances. My Doctor's most imperative prescription is, that I shall do nothing mentally, or bodily, that can be left undone. What would you do with such a prescription as this, dear little activity? Not observe it, I believe, for all your faith and perseverance in medical directions. I am very reluctant to leave this spot; but for one reason, I should like to stay here a twelvemonth. I feel the want of my own church; the cold and comfortless Sundays that bring no sermons, and scarcely any services to cheer and gladden the heart. The country is beautiful, but not so beautiful as Ireland. The county Wicklow exceeds all I have seen in Wales or England for picturesque beauty. I was better there, but never well except upon the sea. Dear Thing, be at home when I return, and keep a warm corner in your heart to welcome me, for I shall need some pleasure amid the abundant sadness I shall feel, and there will be none greater than to see you again. Do not write unless you can do so before Sunday; do not forget to love me, and to let me be,

Very affectionately yours.

VIII.—TO MRS. * * *.

Monday, October, 1828.

MY DEAR FRIEND,

I was very happy to find your letter on my arrival on Saturday; I should have told you so before, but I had no senses that night, and yesterday only got up to go to evening church. Here I am however, as well as I may expect, considering that I was in bed all the day previous to my journey, and so unwell on the road as to be obliged to stay two nights at Oxford. But I scarcely yet know where or how I am. Come and see me as quickly as you are able; no fear of finding me out, and my heart will rejoice to see you. Poor dear! Do not reproach yourself for sadness and ingratitude; what you feel is merely the result of physical exhaustion, the after-misery of too much anxiety and exertion. Treat it as such, and not as moral, far less spiritual defection. Humour yourself and rest yourself, and believe that God knows you are but dust, and judges of you according to your feebleness. No, dear, I do not think you fickle, but it is a hard matter, when we know ourselves, to believe that anybody can love us long; and as day by day we find out that we are nothing, of all the great things we have thought ourselves, there is an involuntary apprehension that others will find it out too, and cease to care for us. Happily there is no fear of this from Him whose love is best, for He knew all at first. I write in haste; God bless you, dear. My kindest love to * * *. Come soon.

Very affectionately, yours.

IX.—TO MRS. * * *.

January 31, 1829.

DEAREST LITTLE PRECIOUS,

To have your note to answer this evening, is a blessing to my idleness; for idle, miserably idle are my hours day by day. My cares with you, dear, did me no harm, they only for a season diverted my mind from the weight that oppresses it, and made me seem the better that I am not; as I always discover when the temporary excitement subsides. And so I am neither worse nor better than before I shared your painful tasks. You tell stories.—I may know or I may not know, for friendship's eye is keen, and conscience is treacherous; the nature of the sins that weigh upon your heart, and those which blacken my own, may or may not be of the same nature; for I have never shocked any eye but that of Heaven with the exhibition of them. But of this I am quite certain, if sympathy can be secured by the measure of sin, of sorrow and of self-reproach, I can sympathize with yours, for I defy them, yes, I do defy them to exceed my own, whatever difference of character they may bear. But we know that we are pardoned both. The memory of these sins with God is blotted out: thence is our joy:—with us it must go to our graves, thence is our sorrow; and so far from believing in an experience, all of sorrow or all of joy, I believe the exquisiteness of the one will, in every mind, be proportioned to the agony of the other. And be our assurance what it may, and it cannot be too much, there will be these returns of bitter self-reproach. Satan knows his opportunity too well to miss it. Whenever the spirits are depressed by outward circumstances, the nerves shattered by disease, or the enjoyment of spiritual things overclouded; he comes in to disturb what he cannot destroy; he brings to mind the former things which he but knows too well. Too well he knows the secret things of the heart where once he reigned, and he lays them bare before us whenever opportunity serves, in hopes to drive us from our hold on Christ. Thus he is emphatically called in Scripture "the accuser of the brethren," and he has more witness to bring against them than any other, because he was a partner in all their crimes. And because he may no more accuse us before God, he accuses us to ourselves, that we may judge ourselves when God will no more judge us. This is your case at the present moment, and it is often, very often mine. Thank God! experience has taught me to recognize the countenance, and the language of that accuser: though still he comes to tell again his oft-detected lie,—"Too wicked, too wicked to be safe!" Bid him get behind thee, dear, whenever he tells thee so; and appeal to Jesus, for he hates that name, and flies the very sounding of it. As to your thoughts of chastisement for past sin, I do not think we may look for it with emotions of fear. I think the chastisements of God upon his people are prospective; retrospective never. Do you see what I mean, dear; if I had yesterday a cankered wound in my hand, the careful surgeon may come to-day and cut it off. Not because it was diseased yesterday, but that it may not be so to-morrow: if he saw it cured, he would not cut it off. Exactly in this point of view, I look upon the chastisements the believer has to anticipate. No punishment but that which is remedial; if the sin which last year broke out into action of offence before God, be this year existing unabated in my bosom, ready to break out again, then chastisement must come; the bitter remedy must be applied; the painful cure performed, because by any means, or all means, I must be made holy. This is all my idea of punishment for forgiven sin. The sin of yesterday will not be punished, unless it be to prevent the sin of to-morrow. Our Father will spare it if he can; there is no wrath in his bosom for the past: and if my view be right, I see in it no ground of depression, but rather of rejoicing, of encouragement. If we hate the sin more than its consequences, which I believe we do, we shall rather hope than fear, to see those consequences doing execution upon the sin. It is very different from punishment, resentful, retrospective punishment. Never think of that. What is past of sin is forgotten; what remains of it in the bosom is remembered to be eradicated. Oh! you dear little creature, you think your heart is worse than any other; and well you may, for it is the only one you ever saw. But I could show you one to match it, if indeed it be not worse, which I suspect it is. But of the heights of joy, and of the depths of anguish, I could almost say of hell itself, you can tell me nothing that I do not know; and I am sure that one state is as safe, though I say not as desirable, as the other, and it is in the latter state that faith is strongest: if it abide at all in the former case, it participates so much the nature of sight. Whose faith think you was strongest, the disciples' on the Mount, or Jonah's in the deep? I conclude the latter. Be comforted then, and if you be sunk as far from light as he, do as he did, and it will soon be day. But now, dear, if I have written you comfort, I pray you write me some—for I am as sad as you, as low, as joyless, though not exactly now in the same frame perhaps; and nobody comforts, nobody counsels *me*—well, I must *wait* too. I am glad for the recovery of your party; as for the prints, they have been in my way ever since; but I could not remember to send them. Nor shall I now, unless you ask for them when you come; yet have I kept them carefully. When shall you come? not soon? Do not come on Thursday, for I shall be out all day—

Your's, affectionately,
CAROLINE FRY.

X.—TO MRS. * * *.

March 19, 1829.

MY DEAREST THING,

Your sadness is so much on my mind, and your dear little mournful face, I cannot help writing to you. Yet what to say? Only to repeat the still-repeated tale; for ever true, and still to be believed, when all without us and within seems to belie it. This is the case with me, and it may be with you. I cannot see that God is good, I cannot feel it, but still I can believe it. I have not joy, I have not comfort,—how then can I give it to you? But I have faith, and with that, dear, I would try to encourage you. Your position is full of painful circumstances, and well I know what is the sickness of baffled hope, and seemingly unanswered prayer. All I can say to you is, to remind you of the strong faith, the vivid joy, so lately granted you; when your mountain seemed to stand so strong that nothing could move it. I knew better, because I had tried all this before you: and I knew that trial and much casting down must follow. When the disciples were on the Mount, they would have built tabernacles to remain there; but only for a moment were they on that height, to prepare them for the depths of temptation and affliction they had to pass through. So Paul, when he had been in the third heaven, and because he had been there, found it needful that he should be humiliated and afflicted to prevent spiritual pride. Your case is similar. You had so bright an enjoyment of God, so full a taste of the freedom which his entire salvation gives, to enable and prepare you for all the trials of your faith, and all the depressions on your spirit that have come upon you since, and may be still to come; and you will not mistrust in darkness Him you have beheld in light. It were but a little matter to trust him and love him then. The excellence and reality of your faith will prove itself by loving and trusting him now; by believing that all is good when all seems evil; by hoping when there seems no ground of hope; by giving praises in the midst of sorrow. This, dear, is the best I can say to you: because, to say that you have not cause for fear and cause for sorrow, is not to speak truth; and though I may truly say I yet hope to see your fears removed, it is a more Christian tone of consolation, to say that God will support and bless you in the midst of trouble, than that he will avert it,—the which he has certainly not promised, though frequently he does it in answer to our prayers. And may he so to yours, dear, or rather to ours, for I pray for you daily. I wish you would soon write and tell me how you go on. And particularly do not let Satan harass you with thoughts of self-reproach, as if, if you had done other than you did, or had been other than you were, things would have come out otherwise. That is a favourite lie of his, to harass the grieved spirit. That it is one, be sure. The salvation of any one soul, cannot depend on any human agency; what God means to do, he puts it perhaps upon some honoured agent to perform, but not in a way to be hindered by their unworthiness, or defeated by their unfaithfulness. To think this, is to take salvation out of God's hands into our own, and does him much dishonour. * * * * * * * Good bye, dear. It is a great effort to write even this scrap, for my spirits are so bad, my mind so gloomy, I think it best to abstain from writing to my friends, lest I give unfit expression to my feelings.

Very affectionately yours,
CAROLINE FRY.

XI.—TO MRS. * * *

Nov. 28, 1829.

MY DEAREST THING,

I was wishing much for the postman to bring me one of the well-known notes that always come in so welcome. There is no perceptible reason why I should not come to you next week, if I am in the least degree worth your having. This only I am inclined to doubt. I have not been so well the last week, and my spirits have been low beyond what I can account for by any known cause. I was so much better in this respect, the only thing really painful in my illness, that I cared little comparatively for the rest; but this week I am quite down again, with little relish or desire for anything; and scarcely able to control my tears. Under this circumstance, I should say to anybody's *ask* but yours, I will come if I am better, but to you I still say, I will come if you like me. I believe, however, that the close weather may be the cause of my being so unwell, which the lapse of a week may make a change in. How I want to see you I cannot say. I feel great hope that your anxiety for Mr. * * * is gradually subsiding, and will be removed. For poor * * *'s case I feel anxious, but not despairing. You, dear thing, are in the hands of Him who loves you, and has set his seal upon you to secure you for his own: harm cannot come to you, though sorrow may, and even in the midst of it you will be as Paul, "sorrowing, yet always rejoicing." I want to gossip with you sadly, to cheer and to be cheered. If I know not how my writings can comfort you, dear, as little do you know how it comforts me to hear of it; for in the great sadness of my spirit at times, I have the feeling of being useless to everybody and worthless for anything; everything I have done seems wasted and amiss, with a hopeless discouragement ever to do more. To believe, if I can believe it, that one hour of anybody's sadness has been lightened by my means, is a real medicine to my own. Under some such feeling, after receiving some such commendations, I penned the few lines I have enclosed; no, not penned, this is the first *penning*, but jumbled in my head. They come to you, because they mean what they say—they ask a prayer; and perhaps where people mean what they say, as you do, about my writings, they may win one; so here they come: at least they will divert your mind for ten minutes. I have received a letter from Mrs. H. M—— to-day, with an account of my poor friend's death, which did not take place till last week, and a message from her death-bed; it was most happy. God be thanked I do not mourn her death, she was too miserable for friendship to wish to keep her. But a thousand recollections of by-gone days, life's broken promises and abortive hopes, have come to me in the reading of this letter, and perhaps not raised my spirits. In sadness or in joy, still,

    Very affectionately yours,
        CAROLINE FRY.

> The thanks be to another—look you there
> Upon the midnight's solitary star;—
> It is not hers; the light she sheds on you,
> She borrow'd it—she soon may want it too.
>
> But oh! if ever on a night of yours,
> The poet's lay has scatter'd moonlight hours—
> Shed one bright beam upon a doubtful road,
> Or ting'd with silver streaks one parting cloud:
>
> If ever, by the glimmering of her light,
> You 'scaped the snare intended for your feet;
> Or from the altar of her hopes have won
> A spark of fire to re-illume your own:
>
> Then think upon her when her light grows dim,
> When falls upon her disk no sunshine stream;
> Think when she wanders, from observance gone,
> Perhaps in darkness, and perhaps alone.
>
> It may be that in all her hours of wane,
> None pays to her the sunbeam back again;
> Nor any star begirts with grateful light
> The clouds that hang upon her bosom's night.

Go then to God—and if before the throne,
There comes the thought of ought that she has done;
Leave there the thanks, and leave the praises there —
But Oh! remember, that she needs the prayer!

XII.——TO MRS. * * *

Nov. 1829.

MY DEAREST FRIEND,

It is never any trouble to me to get your notes, no matter what brings them. I enclose you the letter you desire. They will see by it my opinion of the miracles, and also of the party that have promulgated them; and if what I think might be of importance to any, I wish it were proclaimed from the house-tops. Yes: I too have heard Mr. * * * since his *ocular demonstrations,* and I heard him say that the regeneration of the soul by the Holy Spirit, does *not* make a man the temple of the Holy Ghost, but these miraculous gifts do: that not to believe them *without proof,* is not to believe in God! Would you take the authority of such a bedlamite as this, even for what he says that he has seen? I would not. Dr. Chalmers did say that of Irving, but it was three years ago—antecedent to any of these flights that he has taken. I am grieved exceedingly that Mrs. * * * has followed this party: but I am not exactly surprised. It is to be observed, that all the adherents of Mr. Irving have believed these miracles, and not one individual that I have met with beside. I certainly do counsel you, for yourself, not to trouble yourself about them; but if it does occur, as in spite of ourselves it sometimes will, that we must speak for others' sake, then it is needful our protest against them be plain, firm, and decided. I am resolved for my own part how to act. I will keep out of their way as much as I can: when I cannot do this, I will refuse to discuss their doctrines; but whenever compelled to speak, there shall be no mistake as to what I think about it. Of course you know, or will know, that * * * and the girls are going,—actually going, to Scotland, for the avowed purpose of seeing these wonder-workers. Mr. * * * has a right to please himself in the objects of his travel, to be sure; and that is no business of mine—but girls, young girls! Alas! dear, there are more kinds of revolutions in the world than one; and if we live long, we shall see more things overturned than the thrones of the Bourbons. I am just returned from a dinner party, where I was obliged, *à contre cœur*, you may believe, to take part against a disciple of prophecy; because, with no very deep knowledge, as I fear, of Christ crucified, he chose to propound, that every man who resists these views of the Advent, wilfully denies the word of God; in short, that they are essential and indispensable. Now is not this enough to make one, if it might be, deny one's creed?

Thank you, dear, I know you wish me happy, but I am too miserable to say words about it. My head has been very bad during the cold weather, but is better again this week. Write often.

Very affectionately yours.

XIII.——TO MRS. * * *

February 15, 1830.

You are such a sensitive little darling I really do not know how to deal with you, much as I am accustomed to hasty people. Oblige me, dear, at least by reading my note again when you are cool; you will surely perceive that you mistook everything in it: that it was not intended or calculated to lower you in your own opinion, or sadden your heart. You will see that I said your note had not caused my silence. And when I spoke of your unsanctified words, thoughts, &c., I had no idea of making a charge against you, but to assent to that of which I thought you complained; which I thought you knew; which I thought every Christian knew; which if I had said of myself, I should have expected you to assent to; and which I should not have contradicted had I heard it said of any saint alive. I did not, my precious little thing, mean to say that your character was more unsanctified than my own. I declare before God I do not think so. You have many advantages over me, in natural disposition, and the greatest advantage I have over you is in experience; I see your faults because I have committed them; I know the fallacy of your words, because I used to say them; I perceive your mistake because I have suffered from the same; and I warn you of dangers, because I fell into them myself unwarned. Far be it from me to tell you, you are better than you think. I believe you are worse than ever you knew or can know. But I meant to tell you, and I thought what I had said would have that effect, that you were not to be cast down by the discovery of faults that every saint must discover at every step of his progress heavenward. My dear thing, do you repeat every Sabbath on your knees before God, that there is " no health in you," and yet feel surprised and pained on the Monday to discover that you have faults, or to hear that others have perceived them? The time will be, and perhaps not long first, that you will never feel ashamed or sad, but when you are commended. I would not for any thing have said what I did, if I had thought it would sadden you; even what I remarked of your manner, I should not have said, had I not understood you to complain of it; and though true, I wished you not to distress yourself about it, as if it were an evil really in your heart. I must have been very awkward to hurt when I meant to heal; but, dear thing, you must not attach too much importance to what people write in moments of such intense suffering as I am under; it affects our expressions, and often makes bitter what should be kind, and is really meant to be so. You think too well of me a great deal, which is an evil in our friendship, because you expect better from me than is in me; and attach importance to opinions that are not worth a straw, and when we differ you are fretted, as if I were not just as likely to be wrong as you. I will tell you something Mr. Howells said yesterday. Preaching on the words of St. Paul, "Of whom I am the chief," he remarked, that Paul does not say he *had been*, but that he actually was, at that time, the chief of sinners: although he was perhaps, the greatest character, next to Christ himself, who ever lived on earth. He added too, that he believed the words should be taken literally as true, that not only did Paul think himself to be, but that he actually was, the chief of sinners. Now dearest, be comforted; Think as ill of yourself as you like; but do not be surprised, do not be cast down by the discovery. Read my note again, and see how different it is from what you thought. I love you very dearly, I am quite as much hurt as you can be when you say we do not understand or suit each other. I do not believe it. Your kindness and affection have been of great value to me in my great sorrow, and will be so still; nobody has contributed more to my comfort than you have done since I knew you. If I said you cannot help me, I meant at this exact moment;

because I must stay at home; and your occupations necessarily keep you from me. You are my own little precious, and though these may seem terms of which I am prodigal, I never will use one of them unless I mean what I say. With regard to pain you have given, dear, you did not mean it; I was never angry, though I was pained;—you did me no wrong. I have written with difficulty, but I could not forbear. My head-ache is intense; I can hardly describe the state it was in last night from the excitement of going to church in the morning: where, by the by, I found out how much that which is good may be exceeded by that which is best. You know I have been pleased, and yet in hearing Mr. Howells again I wonder how I could be, so much is he superior to everything else! Now as you construe everything to your own disadvantage, you will remember that I said you would not like him. I meant no depreciation of you or him in saying so; I feel very curious to know how it would be; but I think his irregularity would put your mind into utter confusion before you had time to compass his meaning; some of his astounding propositions would so overset you at the commencement, you would not sufficiently recover yourself to enjoy the rest;—this is what I meant.

I meant you to have this by the first post to-morrow, but I have had so many visitors; and now I am so tired I cannot write more, and my dinner is come in. Dear little Thing, you can do me good even now—you can pray for me—and I believe *that* is a greater good than most that we can ever do for each other.

Very affectionately yours.

XIV.—TO MRS. * * *

Hampstead, Monday, April 26, 1830.

My Dear Thing,

How much the few added miles has really separated us, I feel every day. It was not, however, an uncounted cost. You, as my dearest and kindest friend, I considered the greatest loss: but I must of course feel the loss of my London society generally: and do so very much. But if the sacrifice is only what I calculated upon, the gain is much more; for I *am better* beyond my expectations. The exhilaration I feel in wandering about this beautiful heath, is more than I have felt since our summer excursion; and even my home feelings are much improved. I have felt even an inclination some days to resume my pen and *enlighten* the world again; and have really had the long unknown sensation of wishing I had something to do: a very different sensation, I assure you, from that I have so long suffered, of wishing I had power to do something. So far, therefore, I am satisfied and grateful for the change. I have no pupils yet; but I dare say they will come; when it pleases God to send them. I cannot be anxious upon a matter which has been managed without my foreseeing how it was to be, for these twenty years past; during which I have never had anything, nor ever wanted anything. I have never known how any year's expenses were to be provided, but they have been. This is ground enough for reliance. But not to claim too much for my trust in God, I must acknowledge the efficacy of one great care to absorb all lesser ones. * * * * * * * * Enough of self. I should not have suffered your former letter to have remained unanswered, dearest, had I known how to reply to your expressions of sadness. This I did not, having no clue to the cause, not even enough to judge whether the trial were some external cross, or some internal struggle with your soul's worst enemy. In this uncertainty, I feared that if I attempted to speak, I might say exactly the wrong thing, and wound where I desired to comfort. Your situation necessarily exposes you to many external difficulties, but He that is for you is greater than all that is against you; be mild, firm, and faithful, and you will pass safely through every storm. To external conflicts, your own character eminently exposes you; but here too you have no cause to feel: the battle must be fought, but the victory is sure; you began it not in your own strength, and therefore cannot lose it by your own weakness. Go on in the strength of the

Lord, and fear no evil in the issue; nor any thing in the way but sin; the contact, the approach, the semblance of sin: fear that increasingly, as you would save yourself from those returns of misery which are its genuine consequence. But I am talking at random, and may well leave off. I have promised to see the * * * if I am at * * * while they are there; then I shall make] you go with me, and show you to them, for I think they would like you, and you would like them; though under all circumstances, formal visiting would hardly perhaps be available. God bless you, dear; it does grieve me not to see you, but I know it cannot be otherwise: write soon.

Very affectionately yours,
CAROLINE FRY.

XV.—TO MRS. * * *

Monday Evening, 1829.

MY DEAREST FRIEND,

I was very sorry to miss your visit in town; as for writing, I deferred it till my return home. Thank you now for your various communications, all kind like yourself. The cap is very pretty, and I am infinitely obliged; but have you not cheated yourself in the outlay? If not, I certainly cannot complain of the expenditure, and am be-capped for some time. I am less surprised than grieved that you are ill; for I thought you seemed so; send me a better report, and do not be downhearted, dearest; lights and shadows are perpetually passing over this transitory scene. Things look cheerless sometimes, we scarce know why; and then the sun breaks out on them again; and all seems well, though nothing is really changed. Thus it must be for a season, but all will pass, and endless serenity is beyond. Yes, dear, I did enjoy, for novelty's sake, my little stay in London, and the convenience it afforded me of doing business and seeing folks. Perhaps I enjoyed the associations of its sights and sounds with by-gone, but unforgotten misery. And certainly I enjoyed the comparison of its turmoil with my quiet home, its insipid society and empty converse, with the vivid, deep realities that form my delights apart from it. It is well to look upon the world sometimes, to learn how blessed we are to have escaped its barrenness. What bliss do men forego! What trash do they take up with instead! This is the conclusion one comes to everywhere, be it town or country. Let the Christian go where he will, his greatest happiness is that which he takes with him: and if this is true of all, how doubly true of me, whose temporal as well as spiritual happiness is independent of place or circumstance, —is that which the world did not give and cannot add to. I am very glad to be at home again.

Ever affectionately yours,
CAROLINE FRY.

XVI.—TO MISS * * *

Hampstead, June, 1830.

My dear Girl,

* * * * I have heard this story before, but things are so diluted in the retail of society, I am glad to have it from the *manufactory*, I was going to say; but that is to prejudge the case. I have also been often asked before what I say to it. I generally answer that "I say nothing at present, but that I do not believe it." I will not put you off with so brief an answer; I am not likely to let a thing of this sort, perhaps of any sort, pass by me unconsidered, though I do often refuse to discuss them with my *young friends;* thinking it best for them to hold their tongues, whatever it may be for me.

I have a very decided opinion upon this subject, which I can have no objection to give when seriously asked, reserving to myself the right to change it, if ever I see occasion. According to Mr. Erskine himself, two things are to be considered in estimating the truth of any report, viz., the character of the narrator, and the credibility of the narration. I confess that to me, the former consideration weighs all against the reception of this story. The party with whom it originates, and among it is at present confined, is certainly not marked with any character of sobriety. They are pious and talented, but they are not sober-minded; they love novelty better than their daily bread. The simplicity of divine truth, and the equal dealings of divine providence, are not to their taste; they have mystified the plainest doctrines of the gospel; they have made war upon every thing common and received; they have quarrelled with their mother-tongue, because it can be understood. Having thrown the whole church into confusion, they have called their own uproar, a "sign of the times;" and denied salvation to all who will not run with them to like excess of riot. Such a party is exactly the quarter from which one might expect such a story, and the last from which one would receive it. Then the character of these miracles, so much in unison with their own excited feelings; their expectation of the Redeemer's coming; their love of His appearing; the readiness with which enthusiastic minds always expect what they desire, and imaginative ones fancy what they expect; every thing identifies the offspring with its parentage, the wonder-workers with their wonders. Pious people are not always wise, and clever people, by reason of their temperament, are peculiarly liable to extravagances where their feelings are interested. So far from considering the people as credible witnesses, I own that any thing coming from them at this moment, would wear to me a suspected character: Then the probability of the narration! You know that I expect as fully as they do, the events of "the last day;" but the more I believe of this, the more I am upon my guard against the "Lo here! or Lo there!" with which the levity of men anticipates the majestic walk of Deity. I know that God can do what he will, and will do what he has promised; but I am accustomed to adjust my faith to the promise, not the promise to my faith, as is the fashion now with some. Though it is true the Scripture nowhere says that miracles shall cease, I am equally sure, it nowhere says that they shall not. We can only judge therefore of what God meant to do, by what he has done, and it is certain they have ceased for many centuries. Whether God recalled these gifts for some good purpose of his own, or whether man forfeited them by unbelief, I do not know,—for the same reason; the Scripture has not declared it. If the former, I doubt not God will fully manifest his purpose, to restore them when His time is come; and I can wait till he does so. If the latter, I must have some evidence that the faith of James Macdonald, and Mary Campbell, is more than the faith of Luther and Latimer, of saints and martyrs, of men of God both dead and living, who, with equal zeal and sounder minds, have followed Christ, but worked no miracles, before I believe that increase of faith has brought back the gifts.

There is one who says, "If I testify of myself my testimony is not true;" but these people not only testify of their own gifts, but give the credit of them to their own faith, which they represent to be more than all the faith that has been in exercise for sixteen or seventeen centuries. Perhaps you will say, "But here are facts, how can you account for the delusion, without supposing wilful imposture in the witnesses?" This I cannot, neither can I explain how Papal Rome performed her well-attested wonders, nor how Joanna Southcote's absurdities deluded 40,000 people; nor how Prince Hohenlohe made the lame to walk. All must stand together till these new miracles have some better ground to stand on, than the honest credulity of those who think they have witnessed them. Respecting the recoveries, I am not prepared to say how far the senses may be the dupes of the imagination. I have seen enough of this, to believe much more; and without a miracle, we see every day, the "speculations and anticipations of physicians," baffled by the recovery of the patient, from a seeming death-bed; and that often by no means but strong mental excitement. As for the tongues, I can imagine nothing easier for man or woman, than to utter what neither themselves nor any one else can understand. And the Chinese characters! I have been told there are 8000 in the language; she must be an unlucky wight indeed, who could not hit upon something like some of them; particularly if she is familiar with the outside of a chest of tea. I must really wait the interpretation of their tongues, and the use to be made of them, before I treat this part as any thing but a gross absurdity, calculated to discredit all the rest. To tell the truth, if the Spirit would constrain some of these people to hold their tongues, rather than to talk, I should be much more disposed to admit a miracle: the gift of silence would be an extraordinary blessing to the Church at this time. Mr. E * * *'s letter is not the writing of a sensible man. His talent and piety we all know; and it is sad indeed, that men who have been distinguished in the Church, should occupy themselves with turning the heads of silly women, by over-excitement of their pious feelings. Respecting the young clergyman you speak of as having propounded these things from the pulpit, I truly wish he had been older. * * * * Till you are forty, dear child—which I believe will be some days yet—I entreat you to have nothing to do with these things. Believe that the Lord is at hand! Love his appearing; watch and pray that you enter not into temptation; whether he come at the second watch, or the third, be you ready; be sure that you have oil in your lamp, and then wait in quietness, till the footsteps of our Lord himself arouse you; but if any one say to you, "Lo here! Lo there!" go not after them.

CAROLINE FRY.

XVII.—TO MRS. FRY.

Paris, Hotel d'Angleterre.
Juin 11, 1831.

MY DEAR MARTHA,

My letter has no chance of a welcome, unless it comes from Paris, therefore I have not written before; and therefore I make haste to write now; for we have been long on the road, and do not intend to stay here long. The road, indeed, had as much interest for me as the capital: all was new, all was changed from the moment we set foot in France. I was pleased at Havre, and at Rouen delighted; but with nothing more than with a delightful passage of ninety miles up the Seine, from one place to the other, amidst the most enchanting scenery. However, my brother will listen to nothing short of Paris, and I suppose him in so much hurry to hear of that, that I must not pause to tell you by the way, that I am quite well, quite happy, too happy almost for this passing world. But it is God who has given me all, and what he gives, is blessed, is safe, and may be taken fearlessly. Well, then, of Paris—what of Paris? I think, as a whole, it does not equal my expectations; it does not equal London; if things so unlike may be compared at all. But there are things in it which exceed my expectation. As contrasted with London, you miss the air of wealth, of studied luxury, niceness, and abundance; the splendid equipages, the magnificent shops, and the crowds of well-dressed people. My first impression of the streets was of meanness, neglect, and inconvenience. But then where in London do you find the picturesque; here it is everywhere. And the public buildings—these exceed my expectation— so many, so magnificent, so tasteful. But above all things, and most above my imagination, is Pere la Chaise. Perhaps I never saw anything that so satisfied me. I thought it would be beautiful, but artificial: this it is not; it is a forest of tombs; it is impossible to give you any idea of what it is; art has done all it can, and nature has outdone it. Wealth has adorned its sepulchre, and glory recorded its deeds; but the aspect of all is death:— the air is still as the grave, wild, ruinous, and romantic. I never have seen anything so impressive. Of much that I have seen with pleasure, and shall hereafter be glad that I have seen, perhaps this alone I shall think of hereafter with a longing wish to return to it. After all its boastings, Paris derives its chief interest to me, from the events with which every part of it is identified; the important past, the overhanging future; every street, every palace is historic ground, so closely associated with all that one has thought, felt, or read, for thirty years past. I never can disunite the spot from the deeds that have been done in it: and thence feel intense interest everywhere. As to all that people find attractive in this vain capital, I see nothing in it; I feel not a wish to stay, nor a wish to return to it again: though I shall always be glad to have seen it. The *maniere de vivre* is pleasing only for its novelty. It is very amusing to dine a few times at a table d'hote, and taste the savoury varieties of a coffee-house dinner; but it is adverse to the habits, tastes, and feelings of our English nature: it is all show, all outside, all frivolity and nonsense. And the people—they are so ugly, so unnoble, and withal have such ill-shapen heads, I am already tired of the sight of them. There is not the slightest appearance of evil working at present; but it is impossible to traverse the courts and galleries of these magnificent palaces, without asking one-self what murderous deeds are to be done there next. To those who think that Bonaparte "is not and yet is," there is something very striking in his unfinished works; the monuments of his greatness standing as he left them; half-built, the scaffolding still round them, as if they waited his returning. The most exquisite building, to my taste, is St. Geneviève, now called the Pantheon, desecrated by tombs of Voltaire, Rousseau, and the so-called great. We have been to St. Cloud to-day, which is really delightful. I suppose nobody will be so foolish as to compare the gardens of the Luxembourg and Tuilleries with the Regent's and Hyde Park; but there is an effect in the artificial alleys and close shaven trees, and formal avenues, which I did not calculate upon: far enough from the cheerful beauty of our plantations, there is still a touch of sublimity in them—dark, gloomy, unnatural, they seem the work of other ages, and of other beings: consequently excite more interest than I anticipated. This is a poor sketch, written in haste, and at random: but we are out all day, and tired enough by night. Accept this fare, and excuse this unworthy epistle. It is the most I can do. Perhaps it is more interesting to you than if I had filled it, as I might, with thanks and acknowledgments for all your kindness, and pleasant reminiscences of Desford festivities. My beloved husband cannot forget it, and will not forego the wish and hope to visit it again: it has made so great an impression.

Kindest love to my brother, and whoever of the party are still about you. You must enjoy, I think, a season of tranquillity, after the distraction we imposed upon you. Excuse all else.

> Ever affectionately yours,
> CAROLINE WILSON.

XVIII.—TO MRS. * * *.

Keavil, 1832.

My dearest Friend,

I think I promised you a letter, and I think you wish for one; if in this last I err, it is a pardonable offence, since it only assumes that you think of me absent, and desire to know what I am doing. Indeed, dear, I am doing nothing but enjoying myself, and giving thanks,—wondering thanks, to Him who fills my cup so full, and gives me so much capability of tasting its sweetness. Thus far all has been prosperous with us, and all delightful; though we have not yet reached the point of attraction, the Scottish Highlands. But how much there is to delight one everywhere, when one is in the mind to be delighted: when no clouds without or mists within, obscure the charms of nature's prodigality of beauty. I was immoderately happy at Cambridge, where I had not anticipated much pleasure; with Scarborough, I was, as I expected, greatly pleased: we took a lodging there for five days, and greatly enjoyed the interval of repose. Our voyage thence to Edinburgh was most favourable; with the exception of two hours, I remained all night upon deck. But Edinburgh—I suppose you have seen it—if not, I shall not describe it, partly because I cannot, and partly because all descriptions are tiresome. Be it enough, that I lost my senses at the first sight of it, and have not quite recovered them. We sojourned here six days, and now are staying with my beloved friends in Fifeshire. Dear things, it is a melancholy pleasure to see them; and if one had not cause enough and sense enough of gratitude before, we well might learn it here; in comparing our health, and vigour, and cheerful capacity for enjoyment, with the blighted helplessness of these sweet loves, who, deprived of much that was most dear, have not power to enjoy what is left.

Tobermory, Aug. 2.

O dear! I never had time to finish this letter, and I found that if I had, I could not tell you when we should be in England, so I have carried it in my pocket till it is nearly worn out; still I am anxious to acquit me of my promise. We have had no letters since we left home, having ordered them to Glasgow, where we shall not be till next Saturday. It is impossible to tell you all we have done and seen since I wrote the above. Our journey has been most successful throughout; it has been without accident or impediment. You know Loch Katrine and the Trosachs, and perhaps you know the yet greater beauties of Loch Lomond. We spent last Sunday in Inverary, the most enchanting of places. We were at Staffa and Iona yesterday, and to-morrow really start on our way homeward; we think to spend the next Sunday at

Glasgow: and if we do, I will try to hear your favourite Dr. Wardlaw; indeed we have been so fortunate as to hear a good sermon everywhere, except at Cambridge, the school of divinity. On Monday or Wednesday, nothing occurring to prevent it, we intend to embark for Liverpool. There I hope we shall not be detained at all, but proceed to Bangor. * * * *
I do not know what will become of us beyond Bangor, we shall probably be tired of moving, and stay at some place in Wales till our time is out. I do not feel any expectation of meeting with you; but am wishing that at least you should know where we are. To accomplish which, we have made two attempts to buy a pennyworth of pens, the purchase has supplied a stick; with which I finish. The Laird of the place has just been, I do not know why, to ask us to dinner; and at six in the morning we start for Oban. All these little towns are so pretty, I know not which is best—accommodations generally good, and conveyances procured with facility: supposing you can ride in a cart and walk over a mountain. The weather, except a little too cold sometimes, has been delightful, we have not had an hour's hinderance from it. * * * I must make free to say, no Highland lass can better get up a mountain than your humble servant. Indeed the air is so exhilarating, you gain strength at every mile, instead of losing it. Farewell, in haste. If you are in Wales, let me hear of it at Liverpool, or at Bangor, should

this letter reach you in time to do so. Tell the world of our well-being; this is my first and only letter since I started.

Ever affectionately,
C. WILSON.

XIX.—TO MRS. * * *

January, 1833.

DEAREST FRIEND,

It is quite time for another "how d'ye do;" but I have heard that you are well again, else I should have inquired before. Lady * * * says you will not come and see anybody: so to see you I must not hope. It has not appeared practicable for us to come to you before going to Bristol, otherwise I was not unmindful of your kind wishes on that head. Now it seems as if we should go on the Saturday of next week, or on the Monday of the week following; and we think to return within a fortnight; if you have anything to send or to say, make it ready. We shall of course see Mrs. * * *, if she is at home. I dare say you will hear some report of our well-being from the S——s, who have just left our near neighbourhood. Tell me of her health, if you know, when you write, for I feel really interested about it; her's is such a dreadful complaint; I can only wonder how so much pain is endured as it is. I do not bear bodily pain myself, which makes me feel more for others. What a mercy to have none to bear; that is the burthen of my song; but I do not mean to be talking of *myself*, I must refer to your note to talk of *you*. Dear thing, I understand it all. More consciences are stained with " flagrant sin," than we know of: and doubtless what you say is true; the stain remains within, when it is blotted from the book of heaven, still the sad memory is a cure for worse things than itself, most bitter as it is. It is a perpetual antidote to pride, an ever-ready reproof to discontent: a good help to penitence and self-renunciation; and above all, it is that which, in its very bitterness, makes the heart to run over, in its fulness of gratitude for redeeming love, and preferential grace. Mr. Howells said, if he were to define salvation in few words, he would say it was " deliverance from ourselves." Now it is when we see ourselves in that abominable, detestable light, in which the memory of gross transgression places us, that we perceive the full value of this deliverance—this salvation. When could David have felt it as he did when Nathan said to him, " The Lord also has put away thy sin." It is true there was a " nevertheless"— —which followed—as I believe there generally is on sin indulged—a " nevertheless" of temporal evil, incident upon it. But how is it lightened still by that first sentence, " The Lord has put away thy sin." This has been written a day or two, and never got finished; never mind. I do not think we shall go before Monday. Will you be so kind as to give me again the receipt for making Scotch woodcock, for some of my former cooks took it off with them.

Ever affectionately yours.

XX.—TO MRS. * * *

January, 1833.

Dearest Dear,

I should not have treated you with such neglectful silence, but our Hampstead visit being put off and still uncertain, on account of our friend's health there, I knew not how to answer you: and still I do not know, but hope to do so on my husband's coming home. I only know now that we always like to come to you, and that we have some reasons for going out next week,—but this hereafter. I am so glad you are better. No, indeed, dearest, I shall not tell you that having Christ, and being therefore rich in hope, you can want nothing more. I know that when sure, quite sure of the pardon of sin, we *do* want more—we want to be rid of it. Such is the beautiful design of God. We are safe in being justified; but we are not happy, but in proportion as we are sanctified; the former satisfies our fears, but our desires are restless for the latter. As the former is the first act of divine love, it is naturally the first thing a believer seeks to be assured of; and when he has assured himself of pardon and justification in Christ, he very often fancies for a time that he has the whole of salvation, and is sanctified. But this does not last; he finds out as you do, that he wants more; he wants holiness and cannot be happy without it. But then what a comfort that the one is secure as the other, although a slower process; that the same blood which bought our justification, and bestows it at once, bought our sanctification,—the other half of one and the same salvation,—and must bestow it ultimately. This is a thought full of gladness when the sense of pardoned sin still wearies and torments the conscience. For that other source of bitterness, who can feel for you as I can? Who has suffered from it intenser anguish? I am bold enough to believe *no one.* I remember a poem in some late number of somebody's magazine, written under a temptation like that you speak of, of intensest anguish, by reason of unanswered prayer: and well it recals to me the agony of the time at which I wrote it. Yes, dear, I can feel fully for you; but, after the issue of all my own sorrows, can I despair for you? I know what Satan whispers at such moments;—either there is no God that answers prayer, or that he breaks his promise, or that we are not of his children, to whom he made them. But Satan was a liar from the beginning. He used to tell me all this at times, and bid me give up the rejected suit. But I used to plead these lies before God, as a reason why he should vindicate his own truth and glory in disproving them; and I still went on, though sometimes I could do no more than pray that I might not give up praying. I do not tell you not to grieve; for I should have thought ill of one who could have told me so: but I do tell you not to despond. I reproach myself now with having done so.—I wonder how it was I did not always believe that God would hear me; that I did not always know He would grant the prayer at last; and sometimes I think if I had prayed with more confidence and assurance, I should perhaps have been heard sooner, for that is an important word, "Whatsoever ye ask, believing. I wish we were nearer, that I might break your loneliness as you used to break mine. How little that word has to do with numbers. How lonely I have been, when every hour of every day was passed in company—compared with now, that the greatest part of all my waking time is passed literally alone: though still at times I wish it otherwise.

Our going to Hampshire is still postponed, and our going to Bristol not likely to be possible before this month is out: and my husband does not seem to think we can fix to come to you just now.

Ever affectionately yours.

XXI.——TO MRS. * * *

April, 1833.

MY DEAREST FRIEND,

I am only reconciled to seeing so little of you, by the fact that I see as much of you as of anybody. Your information disappointed me, inasmuch as I was in the act of asking you to name a day that you could spend with me. I now regret that I so long delayed it; for which the only reason was the prolonged coldness. Though I knew *you* might think it worth while to come and see me in any weather, I could not like to ask it of your party till summer-like evenings should make the distance of little consequence, so I waited on, and now it is too late; we are going to town till Tuesday; and then you will be gone,—you do not say how long. Let me know the first of your return, and promise to come before we go from home, which, if we can let our house, will be at Midsummer; whether for the Rhine, or Scotland, or elsewhere. * * * * * * * * The book I return with thanks and commendations, it is very good. As I was going to observe just now, it will give the H———s much pleasure to see you, and show Mr. ——— anything in Bristol he may wish, except the manufactory, which is burned down, and which was remarkably well worth seeing. I am sorry you are ill, dear, but change always does you good; I am a little fretful not to see you. I am rather bustled at last in preparing my book, which I shall hope to present to you before you go; if they do not disappoint me. May it be blessed of God to the good of somebody, which is my first wish about it: for I cannot but recollect that I am now receiving much, everyway, and rendering very little, except in gratitude and praise. So I pray that God's blessing may be continued on my works. Thank you, dear, Mr. Wilson has had a cold, but is recovered, and I am quite well; I am still susceptible, as I used to be, of cold, taking it very often; but with my general health and spirits, it never signifies as it used to do, and is soon over. One's ailments are trifles when one is quite happy, they seem nothing when I remember how every little addition of illness used to overbear me.

I suppose poor Emma ——— will feel a good deal the loss of her child; it is her *first* sorrow, which usually falls heavy. It may please God to bless it to the restoration of her reason: there is nothing like a painful reality to dissipate delusions. Farewell, dearest, the peace of God be with you on the way. Let me know of your return.

Ever affectionately yours.

XXII.—TO MR. H. * * *

Blackheath Park, Feb. 30, 1835.

My dear Sir,

It gave me the most real pleasure to get a letter from you: hearsay reports are never satisfactory, and I have thought about you much oftener than I have been able to get intelligence. It was very thoughtful of you to write yourself. That you are already better, gives the fairest promise for the future. " Study to be quiet ;"—that must be your text—and " Hope unto the end." Hope and quietness are a compound of wonderful efficacy in the cure of diseases, bodily as well as mental. But we are such silly children, or as Howels used to say, such " fractious brats," that, when we cannot walk, we do not choose to be carried, and mightily fatigue ourselves with kicking. Sickness seems to be the one bitter among your many sweets; the extent to which you have suffered it amongst you is really remarkable; but I am sure you accept it as good, and I cannot help thinking of every one, that the more suffering they have had, the less there is to come, assured that it is strictly measured to the necessity,—of course I speak of the children of God; He who is so prodigal of all good things, is parsimonious of inflictions where He loves. We call our trials much and long, but that is in earthly language ;—terms will have a very different meaning by and bye; I suppose we shall sometimes wonder at the ideas of length and greatness we have attached to such mere instants of duration endless. I can believe no small part of your trial consists in your separation from your dear babes: but they are kept for you. Poor ———'s is an affliction indeed. All God's people must suffer a good deal before they can be fully able to administer to the need of others. Thank you for all your kind thoughts about us, we are all well—always well. It has pleased God to give us the sweet and the bitter separately, while others have it mixed, so now the land overflows with milk and honey; and what is not always the case, I have so much of peace within, together with prosperity without, that if it were not for a certain earthly remembrance called *sin*, I might sometimes fancy I am gone to heaven; as it is, I can only hope that heaven has come to me, with some bright glimpses of its eternal promises. I have been very busy getting a new work to the press, and other matters; I meant it for something to be read in families, but my books do not always turn out what they are meant to be: and if people prefer to read it in their beds, which is very likely, I cannot help it; you will hear more of it about the 1st of May. I must write, whether the world will read or not, for mere want of something to do. * * * How sad a close of poor Irving's sometime brilliant promise! When we think of him as he once appeared, "a giant prepared to run his course," now extinguished in his own darkness, dead in his mischief, a blot removed from the Church of Christ below, we hope made white in heaven, but unable to efface the evil impress of his footsteps here, surely it is a lesson; a warning not to venture on unbeaten paths, to walk humbly, simply, safely, in the vulgar track, as these spiritual aspirants deem it. The first steps in error seem so trifling, so little dangerous,—only for the sake of inquiry—only for pure love of truth, perhaps for love of talk, oftener than anything for love of novelty. May not this awful exhibition of the issue, be a message from heaven to give notice of that snare, the favourite artifice of Satan in this restless age. I look upon it that poor Irving was as much the victim of his own ambition as ever was hero dead on the field of battle. "Let them that think they stand, take heed lest they fall." I should like to hear from you again; our united kindest love to Mrs. ――

Ever yours sincerely,
CAROLINE WILSON.

XXIII.—TO MR. H * * *

Blackheath, Feb. 1, 1836.

MY DEAR SIR,

I hear often that you want a *long letter*, though I am at a loss to guess what you want it to be about. When I received the pamphlet you were so kind as to send me, I thought it might be a challenge to a controversy, and read it in expectation of finding whereof to doubt and so whereof to write; but as it merely goes to prove that whereof I have never doubted, I can only express my full approbation of the same. If, as I believe, baptism is the rite of admission to the external church, as circumcision was, I cannot entertain the smallest doubt that it should be administered to infants. If it were, as I believe it is not, a rite of admission to the invisible fold of Christ. I should consider the subject farther. But then what am I to write about? Of you and yours I should like it to be; but then I know nothing at all about you. I never see, scarcely hear of you, and so much are we apart, we have scarcely a word in common to make talk about; and thus there is but one thing left to talk of, my own individual self, a subject I never liked. Once I thought it intrusive to talk of my own sorrows, and now I think it will be sickening to talk of my own joys. Mistaken perhaps in both cases: since it is all one story of Divine love and faithfulness. But *you* at least have learnt this story through; you know what it is to be kept through storms and sadness, and in the worst of times to be enabled to hold fast your faith, and to be raised from shipwreck. And you know that in the brightest days, amidst flowers and sunshine, and all surrounding joys, there is one joy that so much exceeds all other, one good so far more precious than all the rest; the very light of earth seems but as darkness by the side of it; in short, I need not tell *you*, that what in adversity was all, in prosperity is all still; yet this is pretty well the whole I have just now to say. Year after year goes on, and no shadow comes across my path— no sickness within my doors, or care within my bosom; while the vision of eternity is like an horizon that grows clearer and brighter as the calm increases; I know it cannot be always thus: and whenever a change comes, it will not take me by surprise; but while it does not come, let *God* have the praise of his *un*measured, *im*measurable goodness to the most unworthy. We are looking forward, though not yet quite with certainty, to a change of residence; for one, if it be granted us, which will add yet more to my already full cup of pleasure; such a sweet house upon the heath, now building, to be ready about Midsummer, a very *Poet's* spot: which, by the blessing of God upon my works, I shall myself be able to furnish and complete; then if you do not come and see us, you are people of no taste at all. But I wish you would not wait for it, but come soon and see what it is to be; it is so few years since you furnished, perhaps you can give us some hints for convenience, and economy, and so on. I should like to know how you like your house and neighbourhood, with all the etceteras of place. It might be as well, by-the-bye, against you want another letter, to remind you, that in these days of exchange and barter, the surest way to procure a commodity is to give an equivalent,—letter for letter; long for long; and short for short. With kind love to your happy group, Mrs. H. in particular,

I am, my dear Sir, ever yours,

CAROLINE WILSON.

XXIV.—TO LADY * * * *

Blackheath, April 1, 1836.

MY DEAR LADY ———,

I was much pleased to hear from you, though you are very bold, methinks, to brave my scorn: Not like Hastings!—monstrous! That is, you do not like the influenza, and the rain, and the cold. I should not wonder if a little sunshine make you change your mind. Until the last week, we have had incessant wet, with a thermometer scarcely above the freezing-point—enough to extinguish all difference of place. But I am afraid the secret of your dissatisfaction is in your health; I have known many who cannot be well at Hastings; whereupon I intend to forgive you, and very disinterestedly advise you to come home. By the way, were you ever anywhere that you did *not* wish to come home? If not, Hastings is acquitted. I, who love to be abroad, find the desire for home returns on every cessation of pleasurable excitement; by which I judge that though pleasure wanders, happiness stays at home; for when we are most happy, we least desire incitement to pleasurable feelings. What these last are to be made of, nobody can decide for another; *you* want a little more *couleur de rose* to mix up yours; *my* farthest remembered pleasure was the earliest primrose or the first blown snow-drop; and by the returning strength of these first tastes, I think I must be near upon my second childhood. I have delayed my letter some days, because I wanted to tell you we are beginning to move. * * * What children we are; six months ago, I thought I was too happy to want any thing; two months later I took to wanting that house, and have been teazed and troubled about it ever since; so wise it is to let our hearts go after the things that do not signify! Rain, rain, no hope for Hastings; but, however dirty you find it, I can assure you, though I have not been there, you will find —— dirty also. Hail, and snow, and storm: this is our portion as well as yours, without the waves for compensation. I ought to write you a budget of news, but we do not gossip in these parts, and know nothing about any body. The only thing I am sure of, is that I shall be glad to see you back. I am afraid your poor child will scarcely have found her flowers. No doubt, you are going on upon a rather *rough road*. I should not, as you know, have been acted upon as you were, for the very thing that moved you disgusted me; but I think it very likely that change and interruption would have done the child more harm than can result from continuance for another year; which, if you think so, will reconcile you to many disagreeables. * * * * * * * Come, here is more news than I thought of, provided you did not know it all before. Have you not found it very difficult to write one letter to a person, though very easy to write a dozen; just as persons who meet seldom know not how to make talk, while those who live together are always talking. On this account, society would be better if we saw fewer people, and saw them oftener—would it not? I can only inform Mrs. S——, that her house has not disappeared; the green palisades went down and came up again yesterday. I cannot guess when you will get this letter, because it is too full for postage; but observe, that I finish it this 1st day of April, and am, my dear Lady ——,

Ever affectionately yours,
CAROLINE WILSON.

XXIV.—TO MISS * * *

My dear young Friend,*

* * * * *

* * * * * The impression you have received, and the resolution you have come to, are, I trust, of God; and if they are, He will confirm and bless them to your abundant happiness now, and to your everlasting joy. The disposition to religion I observe in all of you, is very pleasing to me. Still more pleased shall I be to know, it has become the " one thing" for which you live, (and it alone is worthy) on which you set your heart, and from which you seek your happiness. For, believe me, dear, what by experience you cannot perhaps have learned; the differences between the godly and the ungodly; the believing and the unbelieving; the regenerate, and the unregenerate, are not *shades*, but *contrasts*; not parallel or intersecting, but continually diverging paths. To enter and to tread the narrow, but joyous way of life, needs only such a determination as you express; but it *does* need it. May yours, dear girl, be true and permanent; and do believe, that if ever, *on that*

---

* The letters, of which the following are extracts, were written to a young lady of considerable talent, and of an imaginative character—but displaying, with great anxiety, to learn the way of truth and peace, some morbid feelings on the subject of religion, and erroneous views of the duties it enjoined.

subject, I can afford you light or help, or comfort, it will not be put to the account of idle gossip or scribbling.

March 17, 1838.

* * * If angels in heaven rejoice over every soul recovered, can it be that there should not be joy in the heart of one—unworthy, and of herself incapable, when allowed to perceive that she has been in any measure the medium of renovating grace. If my young friend remembers how dear to Jesus must be the souls of his redeemed: and how dear to me should be all that is dear to Him; it will not require more words to convince her, that her's was a welcome letter. I can confidently commit her to Him, who will not leave to unfruitfulness his own engrafted bud, or let its fair promise fail. Every station has its peculiar duties; every individual his peculiar gifts; there is not one so lowly or so ill-endowed, she cannot do something for the love and service of her Redeemer God; nor one so high and gifted, that she may be excused for thinking anything her own, that she should withhold it from Him. And why is that imperious yoke so easy, that burthen of obligation so light, so blessed? because it comes of love, and is achieved by love; Jesus claims it, as the requital of his love to us, and receives it as the offering of our love to Him. But there is more in it than this: if there was not, that which you contemplate as difficult, would be impossible alike, to you and me.

In that blessed Redeemer's service, not one thing is required, that is not first bestowed; not a service for which strength is not given, nor a grace that has not been promised. We serve a Master, who gives us all for nought: and we repay him only with his own. Whatever God requires of you, ask of Him; and for knowledge of what He requires, ask Him; and for the will to do it, ask Him; and for the love that sweetens all we do. The teaching of His Spirit and His word, will be more to my young friend, than any thing *I* could tell her, who know only what they have taught me. The distance between us, that *she* thinks so great, is only this. I have had time to prove and know, and what she has called upon simply to believe,—the sufficiency, the all-sufficiency of Christ for time and for eternity. I would exhort her to lose no time in trying Him, to waste no years in bargaining for the cost, or in tampering with her blessedness, by unwholesome compromise, and wearisome indecision . . . I am glad to think how short is the time in which she has '*done nothing.*' If the gift of one heart be more acceptable to Jesus than another, it must be that which is given to Him, before it is seared and indurated in the service of this ungodly world; and if there is one child of God more blessed than another, it is that one, who has not to look back on wasted years and mis-spent feelings, or forward to the conflict, with earth-bound affections, and long-indulged sins. . . . May our Heavenly Father, who has so early set His name upon her, bless her abundantly with the hallowed influences of his Spirit, that she bring forth fruit a hundredfold, to His great glory, and the happiness of those around her. I shall "thank my God on every remembrance" of her, and I desire to be considered her affectionate friend, &c.

I would have you, while you thank God for the measure of grace, that made you distressed on that occasion, bear in mind what is said in scripture, of those whose heart condemns them in what they do. The evil of all these worldly amusements and compliances, is difficult to tell, but easy enough *to feel.* As a voluntary act, it is taking part *with* the adversary of your soul, *against* Him who you say is "for you." If He is for *for* you, my dear young friend, protecting you from evil without, and struggling with you against the evil within, is it not ungenerous, unthankful, to throw your own weight into the opposing scale? To go, where the thoughts of Him must leave you, where your love for Him must be chilled, where your mind is unfitted for prayer at night, and disabled from devotional services the next day; and the imagination filled, for days and weeks, with unholy images, with which the thought of Him *cannot, must* not be intermingled! We deal not thus with earthly loves, and I trust and believe the time will come, when you will refuse these things, not because you *may* not, but because you *cannot* thus tamper, with the grace and mercy of one, who *did not tamper*, who did not calculate how small a sacrifice would do, or how *little* obedience would be accepted of the Father, when He gave Himself up *for you.* Yet, this is the way we all set out, when we begin or mean to begin, to give ourselves to Him. It is " May I not just do this?" " Am I obliged to do that?" " What! give up all?" " Let me first bury my father," &c.

O my friend, it is pitiful work, which you will one day weep over, with mingled love and shame, that your Lord should so long have borne with and forgiven it. But *He does* bear with and forgive it all, and if His forbearing pity will not shame you out of it, I know that the terror of His commandment will not, and therefore I am not afraid to tell you, that the way to overcome the world, and resist the temptation of the flesh, is to increase your faith, to increase your love to Him whom that world has crucified, and for whose sake that world must be crucified to you, and you to it. Do not make resolutions, and weigh out words and actions as Papists count their beads, and fret your spirit to know when you have done enough. This is the service of the natural heart, adverse in all things to the mind of God,—the heart that loves sin, while God loves holiness; and is for ever busied in the adjustment of adverse interests. Try rather to love what he loves, to will what he wills, to choose what he chooses; and delight in what he approves. This is the subjection of a child. To this end pray much for the increase of your faith; and avoid only such things as unfit you for earnest heart-felt prayer. Think much of the sacrifice, the life and death of Christ, and give up only those pursuits, that preoccupy and indispose your mind to such reflections. Read much —of the Bible most; but of other religious books also; and abstain from such occupations as make this impracticable or distasteful. Above all things, try, pray, labour to increase your love; for love is the fulfilling of the law. If you ask me how? why, we know how earthly love is begotten and encouraged. Not by determining to love, but by thinking, speaking, hearing, of the One beloved; of what He is; of what he has done; of what He offers or promises to do for us or to be to us;—of the qualities that deserve our love, and the benefits that have earned it of us: Such love will settle many difficulties in point of conduct, by closing our ears against all who would depreciate the object of our affections and our hearts; against all that would be likely to weaken or divert these from Him.

Try then in this manner to increase your love. May He, who only can, give you grace and power to make the attempt honestly, and all the rest will follow. Make the tree good, and the fruit will be good. Beseech Him to take your heart, and then you will freely give him up the sinful cares and pleasures of this poor passing world. With Christian interest in your welfare, &c.

Your trouble about prayer is common to all Christians. A mournful evidence of our fallen, perverted, helpless, senseless nature—a ground of deepest self-abasement and self-abhorrence, not of discouragement, or despondency, or distrust of Him who is touched with the feeling of our infirmities, and does for us all we cannot do for ourselves—who *maketh intercession* for us. . . . . Christians, I apprehend, the most advanced, are not without the same difficulties, as to what they ought to do, or rather ought to think and feel under certain circumstances; and whether what they actually do feel is right or wrong; and they can do no better than you did—throw themselves on the grace and sympathy of One who knows *all*; how much is sin, and how much is infirmity, how much is to be forgiven; and how much is only an added claim to paternal pity and support. Farewell now, and may the God of peace and love be ever with you, and deal with you according to his great goodness. How great it is, if ever we know, will be the most amazing of all disclosures!

In Him, and for His sake, consider that you have a friend, of whom you may ask anything she may be able to impart.

These feelings are not peculiar to yourself, though perhaps peculiar to individuals of your character and temperament. Remember at such moments who it is, that is at your elbow; and in whose strength you, even you, may overcome his suggestions; and be the stronger for having known what it is to "endure temptation." You recollect who it was that said, "Get thee behind me, Satan!" Give the same answer, and his power is gone. Don't fancy you are the only child of light that passes through hours of darkness. A perpetuity of joy and peace, is the hard-won victory, (if ever it be attained on earth) of many hard-fought fields and vanquished enemies, aye, and many wounds received, and battles lost—efforts foiled, and expectations shamed; you cannot have them yet; but accept with gratitude and confidence every interval of such accorded you. God knows when to send the rain, and when the sunshine; you must have both in spring-time, if you would have fruits in Autumn. "Remember that we are but dust!" is the prayer I say the oftenest; I know moments when it is my best comfort to believe, that somebody I know not is offering prayers on my behalf. You are afraid you may have given offence. I wish you to believe that this cannot happen, and therefore need never be calculated upon. It is a very common thing, my child, for persons of a nervous and sensitive temperament, to fancy that people do not like them,—that they misjudge them—are unkind to them; when nothing of the sort really occurs. I have suffered so much from this through my whole life, (being only relieved from it in a measure now, by not so much caring whether folks like me or not, possessed as I am—for this world and the next—of happiness, that mankind can neither give nor take away,) that I can assure you, that nine times out of ten, these are mere fancies; and for the tenth, it does not become a miserable sinner, to be over tenacious, since nobody can think so ill of us as we deserve, make what mistakes they may upon particular points. If they knew as much of us as we know of ourselves, would they bear with us at all? We may believe generally that a wish to please will be successful; but it is absolutely indispensable to our own peace of mind, to be satisfied with the conscious intention, without a too watchful anxiety about the results. The former may be the growth of love to our fellow-creatures, and should be cultivated as such; the latter, I apprehend, is more nearly allied to self-love, a source both of sin and suffering. It has been so to me, and therefore I tell it you. Do you know a beautiful work of Fenelon's, entitled "Lettres Spirituelles"? there are excellent remarks in it, on this and other similar subjects, that would be useful to you. In the meantime, my dear child, put your intercourse with me beyond all such questions. It had no other origin, but the expectation that my experience might help your inexperience; and my better knowledge of the human heart, might help you to understand and direct your own. Farewell now, may God direct, bless, and sanctify you, always.

I believe you are wrong in thinking, that you dwell too much on the promises. The promises of the Gospel are not to *find* us consistent Christians, but to *make us such.* In all examples of our Lord's teaching, the promises come first. They did so in Eden; they did so in his own Sermon on the Mount. Peace was the announcement of his birth, Peace was the last behest of his departure. At the *time* that you dwelt exclusively on the promises, suited as they were exactly to the then condition of your soul, I apprehend that you acted under the Spirit's guidance. That same Spirit may now tell you, it is time to act, as well as feed upon these precious truths; do not distrust His teaching.

I don't know if I ever asked you, what sort of reading you indulge in? Your metaphysicopoetical head might happen to like what would be exceedingly bad for you. I know by experience that the poetical may not feed on poetry, nor the metaphysical on metaphysics. The existence of evil in the presence of Omniscient goodness, is a subject that has puzzled all heads, but those that were too wise to knock themselves against it. *You* must absolutely not think about it, nor read about it, or about anything of the sort. Repeat the Psalmist's words, " I am not high-minded, I do not occupy myself with things too hard for me." Fare you well now, my dear child; be fearless and commit yourself to God; wait the manifestation of his purposes, resting yourself in hope; you do not, you cannot, know yet how good he is. Shall we ever know?

Let me persuade you, at this season, not to write or read, as far as you can help it,—not even to think, overmuch; and not to use long and forced exercises of devotion, all equally detrimental in your present state of health. As many *flowers* as you like, whether lilies of the field, or lilies of the garden, or any other of God's works; which, next to his word, are most wholesome study, nay, to some minds, at some seasons, they are more so.

Now I hope I shall not offend a sensitive young lady such as you are; by calling you what in this instance I cannot but think you show yourself to be; a foolish and unreasonable child. You are twenty-two, or thereabouts; the Sun of righteousness has barely risen upon you, begirt with mists of ignorance, inexperience, disquietude, to say the least; and you talk of having "nothing to do *but*" to do that, my child, which, if you number three times two and twenty years, you will not have done; but instead of sitting down in despair at your own failure as now, you will be amazed and thankful for any measure of success. Come now, listen, and I will tell you how it is with you; for it is a plainer case than you ever made out to me before. You are trying to heal yourself; you are impatient of the great Physician's slowness; and instead of waiting upon his sure, impalpable, and often imperceptible medicaments, you charge him with failure or refusal, and betake yourself to nostrums of your own. Shall I tell you what you are like? Why, for all the world, like to certain country people, who being taken in ague or typhus,—no brief disease, as they might know, *if they were wiser*,—on the first return of the hot fit or the cold fit, decide that the quinine or the bark are useless; and betake themselves to the "wise woman," for a charm to be rid of all at once. Yes, dear, and there is a conjurer always ready to take the Great Physician's cases out of his hands; and profess to do by miracle, what He, with power supreme, hardly does in a whole lifetime; a long struggle against the inborn disease of a body dying, and a soul once dead in trespasses and sins. I know not who—unless the aforesaid conjurer set *you* upon attempting the keeping of Lent after the manner you have hinted; the entire cause I doubt not of your subsequent depression; and enough to cause it in a less nervous and irritable temperament than yours. I don't believe that *unbelief* either past or present has had anything to do with this, in the way of origination; but believe me, it is not of the good Physician's prescription,—this that you have been taking. He never bade you to sit up late and rise early, and exhaust your body, and stimulate your brain, by extraordinary exercises of prayer and meditation. It was short, the prayer He dictated—" after this manner pray you." It was simple, the remedy He proposed: "As Moses lifted up the serpent in the wilderness, so must the Son of man be lifted up, that whosoever believeth on Him should not perish, but have everlasting life." You want quietness and simplicity and child-like confidence and expectation. You require to let yourself alone, to renounce yourself and forget yourself, while you fix your eye on Christ, the author and finisher alike. You'll win no race, by counting your own steps, and watching the stones you stumble over; men win by looking at the goal. Dear child, you are born in iniquity, conceived in sin, the whole head is sick, the whole heart is faint, there is *no* good thing in you. You know nothing, you deserve nothing, you are worth nothing. Are you content? Then throw yourself into your Father's arms, and leave your cure with Him, and trust his promises, and wait *his time*. Moses kept sheep for Jethro, for forty years after he was appointed the deliverer of his people. Joseph lay seven years, guiltless, in Pharaoh's prison, before he sat next him upon his throne. Abraham had only a burying-place in the land of promise. Did God not keep his word with all three? And so He will with you, in His time, not in yours. He must both mix and administer the drugs, and if they be slow and bitter, you must lie still, and quiet yourself as a weaned child. You think too much about your symptoms, I mean spiritually, which must always make a *hypochondriac*, physically or spiritually. . . . And you forget that it is not for the ore to tell the refiner, when the dross is burned out of it. . . . I *will* pray for you, but I *will not* ask what you bid me, I will not ask that the new-born babe in Christ may start at once into a perfect manhood, and be forthwith put into possession of its inheritance. I will ask, that it be nursed with tenderness, and humored, and corrected, and controlled; fed with milk, quieted in its tears, borne with in its petulance, and protected in its helplessness, until it gain strength to fight (like a true soldier of Jesus Christ, clad in the whole armour of God) its own way, through hosts of vanquished enemies, to the throne, where the Captain of our salvation has fought his way before us. I close in haste, and have said what I meant imperfectly. Remember, that "in returning and rest, shall be your safety; in quietness and confidence shall be your strength."

Such reading as this work of Luther's is very good for you. Convictions deep as yours; such perceptions of the profundity of nature's darkness, are only to be reached by the strongest lights, the deepest truths, the highest, fullest privileges of the gospel. It is only by the truth of its doctrines, that any soul can be saved, but every soul has not the like consciousness of their necessity. Many a one has been saved by the electing love, and justifying righteousness of Christ, without experimental evidence, that they could not be saved in any other manner; such as others have had, who feel that they must receive these truths or die. For you, dear child, who are, I conceive, among the latter, it is most necessary that you should have a clear, distinct perception, of the perfectness as well as pricelessness of Christ's work: so that you may have done with *yourself* altogether, and be absorbed in Him. . . . Coldness would be no coldness, if we could feel the absent warmth; darkness no darkness, if we could see through it. Wait it away; trust it away; believe it away: that is, wait, trust, abide in faith, till it is gone. Sit in darkness submissively, patiently, hopefully, till you see light. You know the promise, "Who is among you that feareth the Lord, that obeyeth the voice of his servant, that walketh in darkness and hath no light? let him trust in the name of the Lord, and stay him upon his God." If you cannot see, if you cannot feel, this is the time for trust. And of one thing you may be sure—as long as you receive any single message from God: as long, that is, as you find in Holy Writ any word that suits you, that meets your case, or calls to you by any name, or appeals to you under any character, to which you can answer as your own —God has not done with you, has not forsaken you, though His face may be hidden for many moments, and His comforting presence withdrawn. . . . But now we are upon this subject, believe this, dear child, she you speak of is not too proud to value human testimony: she is too humble, I *think* she is, to be exalted by it; for she is one who carries by her temperament, so great a weight of sin, the utmost inflation of the b eath of praise, could not more than suffice to keep her head above water; besides, to borrow a less grave figure from your last, people who remind us of our "talents," are little else than duns, calling for ever for payment of our debts. And as to the use made of them, the good we have done with them, alas! my child, there is one at least, who can bless God, and does with all her heart, for every the least mention of it that reaches her ears;—she needs it all to keep her heart up, and enable her to do any thing. Christians who rest all their hope of commendation at the last, upon that sweet gentle word, "Let her alone, she has done what she could," are not likely to grow high-minded. Once established in the truth, that all our powers are debts, not riches, and we can no longer be in danger of undue exaltation, by either the possession or the use of them.

The book is gone to press, and will or may come forth in March. It is called "Christ our Law," and will suit a little lady very well, I dare say: taking her prepossessions into the account. I wish the Giver of all grace may give her so much, as to take all the comfort of its doctrines to herself: then they will indeed be enough, and she may take them,—of that I have no doubt; all may take them who can love them, choose them, delight in them, *submit* to them, for that is nature's difficulty after all. It is not the exaltation, but the abasement, of the creature, that is really resisted in the gospel-scheme. There is no humbling like that of consenting to be nothing, desiring to be nothing, liking to be nothing, that Christ may be all in all; but then we expect by union with Him, to become everything in Him! Pure as he is pure, holy as he is holy, happy as he is happy.

My new work, (Christ our Law) is just out. If you read it with attention you may discover, that the case in which you suppose yourself, is an impossible case; the position in which you contemplate yourself, an impossible position, which no one ever did or can in this world occupy. God has laid no "perfect rule down before you," by which your salvation is to be won or lost. He has not "denied" you "the liberty of choosing" life rather than death. What you call the necessity of your nature to desire, is, *in fact,* what no one naturally does desire, and if you do, it is not of nature but of grace, a strong evidence, that HE HAS "chosen you." The fact is, my child, you neither are nor can be lost, by virtue of your descent, and therefore cannot be called upon to consent thereto. If you are lost at all, it is because you deserve it, by actual not original sin, and because you refuse to accept the only remedy provided for either, the sure and priceless remedy for both . . . . You destroy your peace, and your soul's health, by metaphysics. "Read my book," as Abernethy used to say to his patients, and try to become as a little child, that you may enter into rest; there is no other way. Seriously, you speak nothing but the truth when you say, that your "mind is overrun with fallacies, you see nothing rightly." The Spirit of God will be your better teacher, but he uses means, and I need not affect modesty in saying that "my book" may throw some light upon your mind, being written with the express intent of disentangling the thread of divine truth for the benefit of the simple.

Who, and what is your habitual ministry? Don't neglect any opportunity of hearing the gospel preached. It is God's specially appointed way, both to convert and to sustain, to heal and to mature, and I don't know anybody to whom it would be so likely to be essentially beneficial, as yourself . . . . Be sure I shall not blame you for excessive reading. It is exactly what I advise for your character of mind. Nothing is so bad for you as dwelling exclusively upon some one—or some few—trains of thought and feeling.

I differ from Miss S's opinion (with regard to the distribution of Tracts) wholly, as it regards the poor, though but partially as it regards well-educated youth. The last may be induced to take up more solid reading—the first cannot. The mental powers of the latter are in our hands to be strengthened or weakened by the aliment we supply; those of the former are not so. We must give them what they understand, or they will take in nothing. Tracts for the poor, are not on the same ground as novels for the rich, but as story-books for children, which nobody in their senses would think of prohibiting. . . . God never enjoins any more than he imposes; an hour's, nay a moment's bodily suffering, unless to a further beneficial end, any more than a physician gives a draught, because it is nauseous, or prescribes an indulgence because it is agreeable. What he does not for us, we may not do for ourselves. For admitting that our Heavenly Father may sometimes send pain and privation, merely as a punishment, without a further end; (which yet as to his children may be questioned,) it is wholly out of our province to imitate him there; no man is at liberty to punish himself, or do penance for past sin. With regard to fasting, there are scriptural reasons, why it should not be spoken against; but practically I cannot give an opinion with regard to it, as I never fast, simply for this reason, spoken out of a heart, honest I believe in its own desire after the increase of spiritual affections, the subjugation of its sins, and the entire conformity of its whole being to the mind and will of God;—I never fast, because I never find the occasion when my soul could be benefited by doing so; when my devotions would not be more hindered than helped by it, and my mind more dulled than cleared by abstaining from customary food; and I consider that fasting is intended as a means to an end, and should never be used as an end itself. Where indeed it is found to be a furthering and help to the growth of the divine life in the soul; where it leaves the mind more able and more disposed to spiritual exercises, and detaches the heart from earth and self; to lift it up to God in prayer, praise, and high and holy intercourse with Him—in that case fasting is a righteous act to a most righteous end—to any extent, not injurious to the body's health; for this I believe to be never designed or permitted of God.

I consider that all persons careful for the truth of God, should bestow their support on the evangelical societies, and withdraw it from those Societies which are suspected of Tractarian influence, for they will be true to their principles, if we be not to ours.——As to submission to clerical authority, against your judgment, I say "Not for a moment." Call no man master upon earth in the concernments of the soul; whether of your own or others. Then as to your deeper, nearer, and more vital interest, my dear child, the evidences of the new life within you,—which you say are all you have,—are all you want,—is not one in particular God's own evidence;—that I mean, which he has specifically chosen, "Because ye love the brethren?"

I remember, early in our correspondence, advising you not to read metaphysical books, or to discuss metaphysical doctrines, and now I press on you more earnestly than ever that advice. I would have you put the subject of your difficulty quite away, as beyond your reach and quite unfit for the peculiar character of your mind, rather than try to satisfy yourself upon it. "If any man would be wise, let him become a fool that he may be wise,"—is a precept good for all; but where there is a natural disposition to cavil and object, it is peculiarly indispensable to the study of divine truth. Believe, submit, obey, without questioning, is, I am perfectly certain, your safety and your peace; the simple acquiescence of a little child, in an authority it may not doubt, on subjects that it cannot comprehend. It is likely that time will remove your painful doubts, if not, submission will take out the sting; they are not so unusual as you suppose, but have been aggravated in your case by the circumstance that you have lived too much alone, *mentally* at least, and thought too much by yourself and of yourself; I don't mean in the sense of self-love, but of self occupation and seclusion. Now, I do advise you, to do, think, feel, and seem, as much like other people as you can: in religion especially, try rather to be common-place than curious; take the plain letter and abide therein, and God, I do not doubt, will give you light and peace. It is not necessary to understand God; it is necessary to believe Him and adore! . . . Meantime, without the said key, be not too sure which of us two understands your mind the best, or is least disposed to blame you for that which has sorely tried it. I think I do understand you; I only want you to learn to understand yourself.

———

Now to your kind inquiries, I have only to answer, Quite well; a grateful word it should be to all who can so say. I am sorry that you speak of "troubles:"—yet who has them not? and who should desire not to have them? Assuredly not pilgrims and strangers, who seek a better country, but are terribly disposed to sit down and rest themselves, on any pleasant spot they come to by the way, till some rude impulse comes from behind, to drive them forward—Is it not so? It has been necessary or rather right, that we

* * * * * * * * *

This was a sore message from the All-wise disposer, when it reached me first. Yet so beautifully does our Father win his wayward children to the way he means them to take, that in a little while we have become more than reconciled to the change. May it be so with you, dear child, the stern realities of life will make you perhaps less a poet; but it is possible that they will make you also by so much the happier. Wise, most wise, loving, always loving, amid the changing phases of providence, is He who rules over all. My child, you need not be afraid, "He will do, as he has done," but He does not require that you do not grieve. Where is the benefit of adversity, if it be not felt? What are the gains of chastisement that is not grievous? Remember all, feel all, and yet consent to all; you are, I believe, about five or six and twenty; that is a long time; a large portion of three-score and ten, to live at ease in luxury and love, supposing that it ends there. But it will not do so; a few days of storm, a few long wintry nights, losses, pains, separations, and there will be time left still for half a life of domestic peace and love, when He who takes, thinks fit to give again. Take hope as well as gratitude in aid of submission for your support, under the really great trial that is upon you now, which those who know more of life than you do, will not be likely to under-rate on your behalf.

"Any thing," you say, "may be borne for a time," and nothing is borne for more than a time; not only is this true of the universal limit of all sorrow, but it is true of all feeling, in its own nature; it wears itself out, and the greater its poignancy the shorter its duration. If it were not so, there are feelings, that would very soon come to be not felt at all, for the physical capability would fail. If God take away much; if He empty you of *all* else, it is only to fill you with himself. Take courage; be hopeful, be confiding, and don't quarrel with yourself, because you are not a *block of stone!*

XXVI.—TO MRS. * * * * *.

1838.

My dear Friend,

It was much pleasure to us, to receive both your own letter and Miss ———'s precious one; to hear first that you had reached your home in peace; and now that the promise of recovery is confirmed. The very thought of your trials makes us ashamed of having thought any thing of our own; but the light weight and the heavy one, are proportioned by the same hand; and fitted to the strength that is to bear them. I never had reason to think my precious husband's life in danger; though in the multitude of my sad thoughts upon my bed, it sometimes would occur, that I might never see my pretty home again. Still I never really thought the complaint dangerous, so, what were my cares to yours? If your present happiness and gratitude are in equal proportion, as I doubt not, you must feel that indeed. I am so habitually persuaded that evil, greater or less, never overtakes the child of God, but as a message from the Most High, I go naturally in the smallest reverse into investigation of the cause, if so I may find out the cipher by which the message can be read. Doubtless all Christians do the same, and by the Spirit's help are led to judge themselves aright; mine was a gentle hint; I wish to understand and take it, that there be no necessity to speak louder. Yours, my dear friend, spake fearfully, and perhaps you have deciphered it aright. It is so common a mistake, that whilst vanity of vanities is written on all besides, and we should be ashamed to set much value on riches, or beauty, or high station for our children, learning and talent have been exempted from that sentence; and may be pursued without risk, and coveted without restraint. But whoever thinks so, will be sometime undeceived. Every good gift of God has its value, and it is equally a mistake, to suppose that the lesser gifts are to be despised or undervalued; but greater or lesser, the things of earth are earthy, and may not be too anxiously coveted or eagerly pursued. If beauty lasts but a season, learning serves us but a season more, and both may be blighted in a day. There is no doubt your dear child will recover her mental, together with her bodily powers; and you will take graciously the parental warning; neither to overtask her powers, nor to regret that she is not able to do more. You have fair promise of a great blessing in them, if they grow up as they are now. . . . . . I feel it is useless now to talk of seeing you here, as we so fully anticipated to have done before this time; still you will keep it in mind; and like an honest woman, let us know when you are able to discharge your just debts.

Very affectionately yours,
C. W.

XXVII.—TO LADY * * * * *.

The Windmills, Blackheath,
Dec. 19, 1839.

Dear Madam,

If you were well acquainted with the habits of our excellent friend, you would not be uneasy for the safety of your letter. It is not the first time I have received a similar " writ of discovery," and generally can do no more than assure my appellant, that Mrs. —— *never answers* letters. In this occasion I am happy to have procured from her an acknowledgment that Lady ——'s letter is *in a drawer*, which *will be* looked over, and that she will communicate to you the result: for which last, however, I decline to be her sponsor. This lady, like many other valuable things, is a curiosity. Though living in near neighbourhood, and entire friends, I have not seen her for a twelvemonth. I leave her to make her own apology; but feel obliged to an incident that has procured me the favour of your Ladyship's letter. The subject is one on which I feel deeply, painfully, perhaps with too much hopelessness, that any thing we can do will stay the mischief; yet we ought to try, if only to shelter some buds of promise from the blight that has come into our Lord's own garden, checking every symptom of restored vitality. Personally, I am averse to controversy in reading, writing, or conversing: as one housed and sheltered and secured, is averse to put to sea again and bide the storm. I was long entreated before I wrote the "Listener in Oxford," and have read as little and thought as little as possible upon the subject since; not from indifference, but contrariwise: from painful susceptibility to the mischief; less painful to my mind, in its bolder outrages than in its hidden influence. We know the lazar-house, and may shun it, but who shall set landmarks to the infected atmosphere that surrounds it, and say, "here all is safe." I see nothing safe. Persons one has depended upon, Christians and Christian ministers, who have no idea of taking up the Tractarian views, have so lowered their tone in spiritual things, as really breaks one's heart with sadness! I live much at home, and out of society; but still I meet and feel the chilling influence every where. It is a real refreshment, to receive a communication such as yours, from one unchanged in the profession of the gospel. Your ladyship is perhaps a better judge than I am, respecting the plan proposed. I have heard that much good has been done by the association that leaves religious tracts monthly at the houses of the rich in London; they read from mere idleness or curiosity, and because they do not know where they come from. I will gladly do anything I can do to promote the success of such plans as you may devise. I take the liberty of inclosing the only thing I have written further upon the subject, in the form of a review, for a monthly publication, of an inferior order, but for an important class of readers, for which I wrote it by request.* I find it more wholesome, and how much more pleasant, to write for truth, than against error; but we must do what we can.

My brother, for whom you kindly inquire as my father, is still in the exercise of his ministry at Desford, though a good deal reduced in capability by recent severe illness. With many thanks for the pleasure you have afforded me, I am,

Your Ladyship's obedient servant,
CAROLINE WILSON.

* Review of " The Church in the World."

XXVIII.—TO LADY * * *

The Windmills, Blackheath.
January 9, 1840.

MY DEAR MADAM,

It is indeed curious that I should send you the review of yourself, without the remotest suspicion that I was doing so; I received the work, as you must know from the author; and though I inquired of S——, to whom I owed my thanks, he kept your secret entirely. I did in fact attribute it to another person, a gentleman. Need I add the secret is safe with me, and I think you do right to let it be supposed of masculine origin. I should much like to see the proposed paragraph added to the very useful little Tract, which last I take the liberty of retaining. The only freedom I have used, or found the least opportunity to use, is in drawing my pen through your own correction, which seemed to ask the reader to choose between two phrases. Am I right in judging, that while "the baptismal font," is *nothing* in *any sense*, the "water of baptism" is a Scripture term for vital renewal by the Holy Ghost: and that therefore the former expression is rather the safest for your purpose?

You do injustice to your style of writing, to suppose it incorrect; but in that or anything else, I beg you to command me at all times. I feel, or apprehend a time approaching, when those who will hold fast the former things, and openly contend for the pure faith of Christ, will be " left as a beacon upon the top of a mountain, as an ensign upon the hills," abandoned altogether of the host; but they will be rallying points to the scattered flock, round which the few will gather close amid the general dispersion; and dear and precious they will be to each other, beyond anything we have known of in our late triumphant progress. I have thought, and so have others, that this may be God's purpose, to bring out of all parties a people for himself, and unite them to each other by the defection of their own separate churches; thus making Puseyism itself the instrument of producing a *unity* in the *Church* of *Christ*, far other than their arrogance demands. For the present, I can only say, " Blessed be His name!" for every individual whom I find *safe*. To you, my dear Madam, I cannot but perceive there is a nearer and more painful interest : the evil has touched your home and your domestic affections, and mixes fear for those you love with jealousy for your Saviour's glory. Still, be comforted, these things are terribly *taking* to the young, unchastened heart; but many are gone out from us who will come back: and many are hesitating who will yet not go. All means must be tried, but the most powerful is *prayer*.

The above was written before I received your Ladyship's second letter; for it, I must reserve my answer till a future day, being busy, yet un-

willing to detain this. Meantime, in some haste to terminate this unworthy return for your kind communications, believe me, my dear Madam,
Very sincerely yours,
CAROLINE WILSON.

XXIX.—TO MR. B * * *

1840.

It is reported that Mr. B—— wants to know why Mrs. Wilson thinks it *more a sin* to go to the * * * church concert, than to go to Westminster Abbey at the Coronation Festival. Mrs. Wilson has not said it is SIN to go to either. The inexpediency and impropriety of the one festival appears to Mrs. Wilson to bear no proportion to the other, though both may be, and have been questioned.

Westminster Abbey is at all times a place of pomp and ceremony more than of devotion. The Queen's Coronation is a thing of rare occurrence, and certainly the appanage of the royal ceremony left nothing of association with church worship in the appearance of the place. A very different case in Mrs. Wilson's opinion to the desecration of parish churches, and common places of worship, by the same persons and in presence of the same populace, who are to occupy the same seats for their habitual Sabbath service; which, if it have *no* effect upon the mind, the setting apart of buildings for the purpose can scarcely be necessary at all; but which in Mrs. Wilson's opinion, is calculated to bring *the church* into contempt, if it do no worse. However this may be, as to the celebration itself, Mrs. Wilson is sure there is a great difference between the act of an *individual* going in a crowd to Westminster Abbey, at a season of national rejoicing, to an entertainment so sanctioned and appointed as that at the Coronation; and the act of those, who having consecrated both themselves and their churches to the service of God, do for their own purpose, get up such entertainments, and affix *names* to it, that ill become the printed lists of this world's pleasure-makers, however innocent the occasion, in the face of their congregations, to the distress of the tender conscience, to the offence of many, to the misleading of more, to the triumph of the worldly, who know better what a believer's profession requires of him, than he sometimes knows himself. *All this* is done on the present occasion. We leave the parties to measure and divide the evil-doing.

XXX.—TO LADY * * * * *

Bath Hotel, Bournemouth,
August 13, 1840.

DEAR MILADY,

Your much expected and more desired letter overtook me here; no unfit spot to enjoy the thought of your enjoyments. I need hardly tell you how much I am delighted with your description of yourself. Those are delicious moments, when the worn and jaded spirit that the world has tired, finds the fresh zest of young existence *can* return, and we be *sixteen* again, in the enjoyment of what neither wears nor ages. I am so happy about you as I cannot tell; my love for you was never so well proved, to myself, as when I first heard of your departure from the Hospital, by the fact that pleasure was my first sensation at the news. *Self* spake afterwards, and said we could not spare you: but I thought, I *knew* that you were right, and doing most wisely for yourselves, and though I could spare some better, I have never brought myself to the exact point of being *sorry;* if I had, your letter would have shamed me. Now if I were not the happiest of beings I should *envy* you; most fully I do indeed enter into *all* you speak of, and since the place is what you expected, and the *church* what you expected, I do not regret the sort of unseen leap you took, although I did, and read anxiously on, till your description came to the Sunday. Truly has God cast the lot into the lap for you, and as surely will He bless it to you. Your dear child will retain, I trust, unspoiled, those natural and innocent tastes which alone will bide the test of time and sorrow, and whatever else advance of years may bring. In early life I knew no other pleasures, and though I have tried many others since, and loved them, and worn them, and loathed them; the time seems fast approaching when these will alone remain. To find they do remain, in all their freshness, is ever and anon a great delight to me,—as it is just now to you—fancying always in society I am five hundred years old, and had better be off the stage, —yet, turned loose upon a heath, I discover that I too am sixteen. I was under this blissful impression when your letter reached me. We travel at a sort of venture this year, scarce knowing where we would go. From Southampton we drove to Lymington, to pass a quiet Sunday. It is what may be called a stupid, uninteresting little place; but the *air* has something so peculiar in it, as makes it a pleasure to exist and breathe: there is a good clergyman, a comfortable little inn, and we passed a most *pretty* Sunday. More *rapturous* sensations waited for our arrival here. Had you not left our world, I am sure we should persuade you to come; I have enjoyed nothing equally for very many years. It is a new watering-place, easily accessible in one day from London; and to us poor Southrons a great discovery; beyond the smell of gas, the noise of engines or the taint of smoke; beyond the regions of donkey-driving, and almost of carriage wheels, with the very best accommodation that can be enjoyed at an Hotel. We have found no place where the sea could be so enjoyed within doors and without; you can walk miles by the water's edge, with the most beautiful cliffs above you, and when tired of that, you may strike into the woods and lose yourselves in impervious shade. I have been in a fit of poetry ever since I came here—now ten days since—and had there been no seventh in the ten, it would have needed only continuance to be as bright as yours; but alas! the Sabbath brought nothing but blight upon our paradise. Whatever the first Eden was, it ceased to be when God went out of it, and there has been no Eden since, till He in His grace shines on it; and though next to His word, there is no pleasure like the enjoyment of His works, the one has no zest without the other. Yes, I mean to be quite sure we shall come and see you next summer, because if we do not, it may be still *the next*, and never get farther off; anticipation, however, is not one of my faculties, and if I lose some pleasure by this want of forecasting, I also escape much pain. Much I should like to see you *now*. We leave here on Saturday for Weymouth, thence pass at the beginning of the week to Lyme; and thence on a visit to my sister near Bristol. We expect to reach home about the 10th September, there and then to miss once more our friends at the Hospital, the very name of which now grates upon the ear. Self must have its say, and since I cannot after your letter regret that you are at C———, I must wish C——— were not where it is; too far for us, though not for you. This last, I well believe; It is a knot more easily cut than disentangled, that holds the Christian and the world together. Great indeed is the manifestation of divine love to those, to whom is given both the power and the will to do what you have done. I wish—no I don't wish —for God has done for me abundantly above all I could ask or think; but if I did wish at all, it would be for exactly such a home as yours to end my days in. By favour of the new freedom of the press, I hope you will write to me from time to time, if only to convince us that you are not too happy even to remember,—as I shall else suspect. Perhaps you will not like to write again till we reach home, or if you should, the letter will be forwarded, without troubling you with a new address. With all love and gratulation to Sir J——— and the young naturalist, believe me, what you know I am and shall be,

     Ever affectionately Yours,
      CAROLINE WILSON.

XXXI.—TO LADY * * * * *

The Windmills,
Nov. 6, 1840.

DEAREST MILADY,

If I forgot you at all other times, I should think of you in a gale of wind: but it is not so. The supply of letters is very short this season, and perhaps my correspondents do not suspect it is owing to the dryness of the weather. Yet is it true, both in fact and in philosophy; and you may not expect letters in fine weather. My mornings are devoted to my books, broken in upon only by charitable and domestic concerns; my afternoons to exercise and visiting, my evenings, to my husband; consequently the only time for letter-writing is a wet afternoon; and if there are no wet afternoons for six months together, what but absolute dearth can be expected. This is the simple truth, worth a hundred thousand *excuses.* But I did want very much to hear from you, and to have the beautiful impression of your felicity renewed. It is a strong word, perhaps, for such an attainted world as this. I should not apply it to any sort of happiness, but the enjoyment of God in his works, or in his words. Most earnestly I trust that you will long retain it unembittered. You do not wish *now* to take Admiral F———'s vacated honours, I am sure. However I laughed at the romance of C———, I never doubted the blessing of God would attend upon your leaving the Hospital, because you did it in His love. How many restless and joyless members of God's family might have peace, if they would go and do likewise: if they had courage to cut the knot they cannot disentangle. I want to see you *dreadfully;* I must beg you not to fall out with C——— till we have been to visit you. I feel a wonderful persuasion of coming next year, wonderful for me, for I do not like *next-years.* When I was single, I said if I ever kept house I could have no *salt beef,* because I could not provide for *next week;* it seemed too long. However the beef comes ready salted, and pleasures innumerable have come ready sweetened and prepared; and found me ready to accept them and be grateful to the Giver, baiting nothing of enjoyment for lack of expectation. Now what am I to tell your felicity-ship, of this working-day world of ours! Nothing now, for the sun is come out, and I am off, and you must wait the next rainy day.

Thursday, March 2.

To resume.—Great part of our *friendly* population are away at Brighton; and we are enjoying our uninterrupted homeliness, a little disposed, in one sense, to walk disorderly of late, that is, to walk away to Mr. M——— on a Sunday. I suppose you are not beyond the reach of " rumours of wars," &c. It has occurred to me, whether it might be that *a war* would break *your peace.* I hope not, for one who has served his country so long and well, may justly claim the remainder of his years to serve another master, and enjoy his better wages; not that any body believes we shall have war, except the students of prophecy, who are all alive; and they prefer revolution, I believe, which seems nearer at hand. If God's time be come, we have no interest in wishing it postponed; but till we see the sign of His coming, "Give peace in our time, O Lord!" is the heart's natural prayer; and I do not like out-running God's judgments, to go before his wrath. It seems as if we were less patient of iniquity than He is. Indeed, with all I have seen, and learned of his goodness and long-suffering pity, it is the greatest trial of my faith, to believe that there will *ever* be an end to it. But He has said it. Now how much love will you please to deliver for me, to Sir ———, with some to the country lass, for whom my respect increases. Mr. Wilson would, I am sure, wish me to say for him all manner of fine things, both laudatory and congratulatory. Do write often, and whenever it rains you shall have first turn..... Farewell. I have not told you that we are well, but we are so, in mind, body, and estate,—to God be the praise! Shall you come up or down this winter? Or do you scorn us utterly?

I am ever affectionately yours,
CAROLINE WILSON.

XXXII.—TO LADY * * * * *

February 1, 1841.

My dear Lady ————,

I am afraid you have thought me long in writing. That you may never think otherwise than the truth about it, allow me to say that in the daily division of my time, there is none properly assigned to letter-writing; which therefore has to abide the chance of wet weather, indisposition, or other accidental opportunities. Some reason I had for delay, in the expectation of hearing from Seeley of your MS. As it has not appeared, I conclude he thinks, as I should expect to be the case, that it does not require correction. I have considered fully and deliberately all you say upon the painful subject of our correspondence, and feel I agree with it wholly and without reserve. It was early days in this mischief that I wrote my work; and it was framed more to defend the healthy, than to cure the already infected. I doubt it is in many cases necessary to give the poison and antidote together. But the more I deliberate, the more I feel assured I am *not the person* for the undertaking you propose; however, if your machinery were in motion, I might occasionally assist it. I will say nothing of disinclination to controversy, that would be a bad reason : but I plead unfitness; I am, if truth be told, too much a woman to play with such dangerous weapons safely; apt to be sharp when warmed in the conflict, and to wound when I do not mean it; and a great deal too sensitive in my own nature, to brave the wounds I may receive for reprisal. Beside, I am unfavourably situated, by the great goodness of God; out of sight, and almost out of hearing of the strife, except by remote effects. I live in a small circle of like-minded friends, and never meet Puseyites, unless some youth from college strays this way, or non-sense-talking girl; so that I really know not half that you do, of the actual workings of the system, and the phases under which it must be practically viewed and dealt with. If I may form a judgment from your letters upon the subject, no one would be so competent as yourself to meet the mischief and treat it in its *home* characters. Why not take out of those letters you speak of, what may be injurious to Dissenters, and so publish them? For my own part, I refuse to fight on any ground but the Word of God. I love the Prayer Book, and I approve the Homilies; but I can make no stand there; because, if Tractarians can prove their opinions in any degree upon the authority of the Church of England, I then demur to the Church. It is human. If the church is with them, the church is wrong. Such is my real mind upon this subject, that if all Christendom, past, present, and to come, should be brought to give countenance to these errors, it would not move me—to *anything but grief*—for there the Rock of ages stands, unmoved, immoveable, the same yesterday, to-day, and for ever; the same whether they will hear or whether they will forbear; the same to me, if not a foot beside were found still standing on it. I care for the church only because, and only as long, as she herself stands thereon. Meantime, she is but the superstructure, with all her excellence;— not the foundation. I will abide by and defend, but may not build upon her: I will argue *for* her, but not *from* her. Still I do think with you, that Puseyism is purely sectarian; and that Puseyite ministers break their ordination vows. The various modes you mention of meeting the subject, seem all good; but are they not occupied already? I see advertisements of publications almost daily, which seem,—for I do not read them,—to take up the subject in almost every form. The difficulty of getting the already biassed to read, is certainly great in all such cases; but that is a state of mind so uncandid, they would hardly be benefited if they did read. Nevertheless, I do not disapprove of your plans and suggestions,—quite otherwise: and would promote, as I might find opportunity, though I cannot originate or undertake anything; so at least is my present impression; leaving it open to the all-directing Hand to employ me as He will, if He should judge otherwise, and make manifest His pleasure to me. Do not let this, or my slowness in replying, deprive me of the pleasure of hearing from you, and hearing all that you are inclined to say, and doing all I can do, to assist *your* endeavours. I am sure they will do good, for your heart of hearts is in it, and God will bless your talent to His own use. No wonder you find all errors intermixed in this. It has been said, that Adam was the first Pope; if so, he was the first Puseyite; and it belongs by inheritance to every *natural* man; it is the religion of fallen humanity, and therefore has more or less been as it were the *colouring matter* of every device of the Father of Lies for the separation of the church.

Yours, &c.
CAROLINE WILSON.

XXXIII.—TO LADY * * * * *

March 12, 1841.

MY DEAR LADY ———,

The first paragraph of your letter makes me ashamed. I am not the busy, useful, industrious being you take me for, and I am not sure I did right to say I had not time for letters. There is a sense in which it is true, but it does not apply to my correspondence with you. Having *nothing* to do, but what I please, from my first waking hour to the last, I found nothing so easy as to fall into a habit of getting rid of time without knowing what became of it; and you know how soon the mind falls into the habit: and when a day has passed, in writing *nothings*, and saying *nothings*, and doing *nothings*, what a brain full of *nothings* will surely remain. The withdrawal of all intellectual impulsion and compulsion from without, would soon have reduced my sometimes overwrought, and therefore weary brains to this condition, if I had not made laws to myself, that such and such hours should be so-and-so employed, and should not be intruded upon by trifling occupations; among which, I ought not to have reckoned my correspondence with you, as correspondence in general, because your letters are both good and useful, as well as pleasant, and leave other than useless thoughts upon the mind. I make it a law to write for several hours every day, then I am a devotee to air and exercise, whether to tread the earth or dig it; and Blackheath, you know, is neither on the top of a lonely mountain, nor in the heart of a wilderness; and I am not in the habit of being either "engaged" or "not at home." Enough of self: but you will perceive how mere a fid-fad I might become, if I did not say to myself, "Those letters must wait for a wet day, and not break in upon my hours of study."

Your last letter deeply interested me. You will be struck as I was, with the remarkable coincidence of our thoughts, at probably the same moment: so much, that I am induced to inclose the extract of what I had written a day or two before I received your letter: coming, by so different a process, to so similar a conclusion. I was writing upon the incarnation, quite irrespective of anybody's views of doctrine, but, intent only upon my subject, wrote myself into the conclusion, without any premeditation, or design of proving it, that a Papist or Puseyite *cannot* believe the deity of Christ. Thus, while you were inferring from their language, &c., with which you are familiar, that they *do not* believe the doctrine; I, who know nothing of that, had by a directly opposite process, inferred for the doctrine itself that it *could not* be so believed. I enclose the extract, as it stands now, in a work I am writing, but may be many times altered before it reaches the press. Your observations will not certainly induce me to *weaken* it. I inclose again the Review, which I do not want, or can get again. I wish the Semi-Puseyites could be made to see the danger of their concessions, and the folly of their talk: where every inch of ground they yield gives standing-room for the assailants. Verily, if our ministers had been bred soldiers or philosophers, they would have learned better wisdom; if indeed there be no treason in the heart. In lack of both, a little memory might serve them. Cannot they, who are so anxious to *restore* the formularies of the church, remember what that church was before they were disused? Oh! I fear the leaven is in the heart—" members one of another," but not as " the body of Christ." I am not sure if I ever saw, or only heard of, your son as the favourite pupil of my brother; he, I am sure, will be gratified by what you tell me of his fidelity to the truth. Never, I believe, was there a moment in which *trimming* was so dangerous, so ruinous; and though it is a *light* word, it has a deep, a deadly import. The evangelical church itself, even as distinct party, has become unsound; and we witness the strange anomaly of an ultra-calvinist contending for baptismal regeneration. I read, with peculiar interest, your mention of God's dealings with yourself;—fitted indeed to give a just and painful accuracy to all your views and thoughts upon these matters, adding in some sense knowledge to your faith, even in respect of errors and corruption, which we know only by deduction from the truth that opposes them. To the "why" of a heart that must so long to be at rest, we can only answer, who is the Lord of hosts so likely to employ upon the field, in difficult and dangerous times, as the one who has *seen most service*. Certain we are, that whatever he requires, he bestows; the battle is not ours, but God's. With all Christian interest and regard, I am, my dear Lady ———,

Sincerely yours,

CAROLINE WILSON.

XXXIV.——TO LADY * * * * *

April 23, 1841.

My dear Lady ———

I hope you have not left town, seeing your letter dated a fortnight back; I have been absent from home, and only found it on my return. It has pleased God, since I wrote to you, to send a cloud over my dwelling-place: occupying for some time my thoughts and feelings: by the death of a sister, at my house, very unexpectedly, and with painful circumstances attending. I have since been away, for the refreshment of our spirits from the shock. I go so rarely to London, partly for lack of a carriage, and more for lack of inclination, that I have almost entirely lost my sometimes numerous acquaintances there, and do very seldom either go or stay therein. A more determined country-mouse does not exist. I loved society once, but I don't now. I loved nature always, and better now than ever. I never go to London with my own good will, although so near it: and generally in the bustle of a day's business; I can scarcely therefore hope for the pleasure of seeing you. Perhaps we must all feel a measure of satisfaction in the outbreak at Oxford; it promises a crisis; their submission is affected, and will issue in defiance, perhaps separation, which may serve the church, while it loses them. I think they can only fortify themselves now by isolation;—by becoming *a party*, and making proclamation of war. This will do good, for all except themselves: however we may feel for those within, we cannot, we must not, regret to see the *cordon de santè* drawn rigidly round the dwellings of the infected. I am told by a student from Oxford, that a Newspaper is to be substituted for the Tracts. We do not expect, of course, that they will be silenced. With all kindness and respect,

Sincerely yours,
CAROLINE WILSON.

P. S. On re-perusing your note, I perceive you have not seen No. 90. It exceeds credibility in evil daring. I am told Newman is a lost man: in intellect and spirits confused and crushed; I am inclined to think the best issue would be their absorption in the church of Rome; it would save numbers who will ever follow a separate banner. I perceive too, that I have not thanked you for kind wishes, and expressions of interest; and promises of prayer that availeth much, and is never undervalued by those that know their need. Neither have I said how much I should like to meet you, while yet acquiescing in the inutility of a brief and tumultuous morning call. You have not mentioned when you expect to leave town.

XXXV.—TO LADY * * * * *

Blackheath, June 19, 1841.

My dear Lady ———

I did not think I could be so long, without acknowledging your last kind enclosure; so very kind when you had so much to do. I was glad too to find that you are satisfied, that all is doing that can be done, to meet the painful need at present. I think so too, and every day see fresh advertisements. There is one from Mr. Goode, who is likely, I think, to vindicate spiritual truth faithfully. I dare say you have heard, that a gentleman in London has printed and sent by post Bishop M'Ilvaine's charge, to every clergyman in the kingdom. This is truly, as you suggested, to make a good use of the new *freedom* of the *press*, given us by the reduction of postage. I hear much of the Bishop of Chester's last charge, no doubt it will be printed; all this is good; and I have heard, I am not sure with how much truth, that a Tutor has been displaced from Baliol College, Oxford, for introducing Puseyism into a lecture. On the other hand, I hear anxiety expressed, do you, who probably know more—participate in it? that a Conservative government, will fill the bench with Puseyites. If this be so, what are we to wish for? I believe it can only be that God will do his own wise and holy pleasure in all things, without reference to our choice in any matter. Charlotte Elizabeth, who knows and cares so much for Ireland, thinks a change of government will put a stop to much of the good doing in Ireland,—Is it so?

Your extracts, printed and in manuscript, are very excellent, and very sad; as confirming our own sad impressions of the real, the final, and the fatal bearing of these views.

I hope you are enjoying your release from the bustle of London life, still surrounded and occupied by those you love. Leamington has not escaped the Oxford epidemic, I believe,—what has? I was going to say, who has? but thank God, there are still a few, and the gladness of one's heart, as ever and anon one meets with them, is a compensation, some compensation at least, for the perpetual and heart-breaking *change of tone*, detected everywhere around us. Would this be recovered, even by the annihilation of the party, as such? I am afraid not. The confusion of mind about regeneration in baptism, is undermining all truth in the evangelical party,—quite apart as they think and intend, but not really so,—from Tractarian views. Oh! how much poison people swallow without detection or suspicion. Well, we can trust God with the care of his own truth, and we may pray Him to take care as well of our valued and endangered church; most of all that our own hearts grow not cold, on the abounding of iniquity and error, so as to cede the lonely and forsaken standard. Let me have the pleasure, *some day*, of another letter from you; for believe me, I value them highly, and am, my dear Lady,

With sincere esteem, yours,
CAROLINE WILSON.

XXXVI.—TO LADY * * * * *

December, 1841.

DEAR MILADY,

With all thanks for your obliging inquiries; I have not gone down during the late gales, which is all that can be said, for I do not find I like it much better than I did last year: but having no harbour of refuge out of the house, I was obliged to betake myself to walking up and down between two baize doors that have been put up in the passage. I observe you make no allusion to anything in my former letter; but I conclude you received it. Thank you very much for yours, as bright as ever. Why do you thus endanger the tenth commandment? It has been a beautiful season everywhere—saving the winds—which yet were nothing like last year's and did us no sort of mischief; a hard frost last week, and now again warm as spring. This was true when I wrote it. I dare say there was much of truth in your judgment of your young neighbours,—but the line is narrow, an error on one side is nothing compared to an error on the other; and, I believe you know I always thought you a little too lax in the reading for young ladies; did I not? Whether so or otherwise, as applied to the present question, we know, dear milady, there is much that is attractive in mind and person, that is nevertheless contrary to purity and simplicity in a young female, and much, how much! that is pleasing to the natural mind, which is nevertheless contrary to godliness. I do not advocate a vacant mind, but, if there were nothing good to fill it, which cannot be, it is better than a polluted one. You will perceive therefore, I concur with your pastor in the principle, though there may be extremes in the practice. If one sin, aye or one sinful thought be spared them by this abstinence, they will not be the losers, will they? What have I to tell you? We are losing our friends the ————, who leave Blackheath at Christmas. I do not know what Mr. Wilson means to say to Sir ————'s delightful letter: pious curates are scarce since they all turned Puseyites. I know one sound and useful man, who has a curacy of £100 a year without a house, and would be glad indeed to get a better; particularly if where he could take in a couple of pupils: the Rev. Mr. ———— of ————.

This letter has been a week in getting itself written, and here it ends. With all love and affection, &c.

Ever yours,
Caroline Wilson.

XXXVII.—TO LADY * * * * *.

December 18, 1841.

My dear Lady ———,

I am so much obliged to you for writing again. I had become quite unhappy, because, having let time so unconsciously pass after the reception of your former letter, I did not know where to address you. A few days only before the coming of your last, I had sent to inquire if Seeley could tell me your present abode. Thank you very much for relieving my difficulty. I received your former communication on the eve of leaving home for our usual summer ramble, and did fully intend to answer it while out; but I did not do so, and then it was too late on my return, as I believed, to find you. Now my long loitering book is done, and gone out of my hand, and I am quite at leisure: and believe me, very happy to resume a correspondence on which I set great value. To answer your kind inquiry first, the Blackheath fire was not within reach of us, and occurred during our absence. The people were strangers here, but it was a very distressing scene. I have read with great attention the sermon you kindly send; I do not think the language of page 18, 19 can be admitted at all, without so much concession to Puseyism as throws all into their hands, though the preacher does not so intend. Is not this the whole secret of our danger and our ruin? (that men see not the issue of their concession) for ruined we shall be at this rate by our advocates, if such they are; I mean our peace-makers. "We have the Scriptures," but we are not left to our own "unassisted and erring judgment," &c., &c., to deduce the truth from them. True, but what is to help us? Not the Holy Spirit, who wrote the Book and can alone throw light upon it; but "a complete rule," composed alas! by other erring judgments and dim lights; but capable of a *completeness* which the Word of Inspiration wants! And how, after all, does this infallible authority end? Just as it always does: in the "I have said" of the preacher. The Bible is judged by the church—the church by the preacher—and the preacher, as he always must and ought to be, by the hearers; and if some recusant, sitting in the corner of a pew during the sermon, chooses, by his own unassisted and erring judgment, to decide that "Our own church *does* teach and enjoin things that she is *not* prepared to deduce and prove from Scripture," there is an end of the *complete rule*. The Scriptures only can decide the controversy, and we end where we had better have begun: in deducing the truth "afresh" from the Book of Truth. I do not so speak in verbal criticism upon this sermon, but merely to show what I am strongly convinced of, that there is nothing between the full exercise of private judgment on the written Word, and the infallible authority of an individual head—a Pope—even the apostolic priesthood will not do, because they will not agree. You may place an equal number of them on either side of your dinner-table: produce a certain text from the Bible, and ask them what it means; their interpretation shall be not only different, but contrary. On which side of your dinner-table is the authority of the church? And verily you shall fetch the Prayer Book and not help them: for the one half will say the church teaches baptismal regeneration, and the other that she does not. We cannot, because we *ought* not, to have peace on such terms as these. It can be so achieved only as it has been before; there can be but one of two infallibles—Christ, and Antichrist.—He who is God; and he who shows himself as if he were God. I am convinced there is no medium; and our ruin is, that well-intentioned, peace-loving men, do not perceive this. Is not the real panacea contained in Mr.———'s last page? Excuse me all this.

The only passage in my writings I now recal upon the subject you desire, is found in the "Listener in Oxford," pages 175—178. I know you have the work, else I would copy it. I think some part of it is to the purpose, but I will think farther, and remit anything else to you that I find, or that occurs to me to say of it hereafter. Your little Tract is *very* good to its intent; I shall be happy to distribute it. But what has become of *your own* book? I never heard more of it. There are some sad little attractive-looking children's books in circulation, by N——'s sister, that need to be exposed. I am going to do something in it by a Review, perhaps: but I have " fired my periodicals," and can do little more, I fear. We were this summer at the Isle of Wight, and looked in upon poor ——, one Friday, in the chambers of his imagery. Thank God! indeed, we may, that that misleading is over. It was sad to see *Christians*, true Christian people crowding to his chapel; and declaring that he still *preached the gospel;* so completely had he preached them into forgetfulness of what the gospel is, as they once heard it from himself. But he was too honest a man: and all who are so, must do as he has done; I am afraid we shall not find many. We have been pleased to find Dr. Arnold of Rugby taking so strong a position against them: on the ground that the church is not the *ministry*, but the *members*. I am afraid I have given you some proof herein of a fit of idleness, by all this idle talk. You seem to have a great many children: have you not? I cannot think how you can find time to write: and yet I hope you can; for it is a great pleasure to me. I am, my dear Lady ——,

    Most sincerely yours,
        CAROLINE WILSON.

XXXVIII.—TO LADY * * * * *.

December 5, 1841.

My dear Lady ———,

Very kind you are, to indulge me with such a family picture; blessed in you, and a blessing to you, I am sure. By the help of the night-lamp too, I discover how it is you find so much time to write, in the midst of all your patriarchal cares. I have ransacked the far places of my memory in vain, to recal a single impression of an interview I once had with you; my sister tells me it was at Tunbridge Wells, thirty-one years ago; but so full of bustle and of change, has been to me the tread of time in subsequent years, I find earlier impressions fairly trod out of my poor brain, while they are distinctly remembered by others. Great is God's goodness to the creatures of his hand, whether he blesses with many or with few; for I cannot help contrasting the full casket of your treasures, with mine—full too, yet made to hold but one.

Excuse so much of self, a sign the book is done; which you must allow me the gratification of sending you when it is out. I can hardly tell you the name, as that is the last thing decided upon; but I am sure that Christ is the subject; I have written it under more than usual discouragement. Many even of my own friends,—and of the public many more,—who would once have welcomed, and rejoiced in the truths it contains, will now disrelish, dispute, and perhaps reject them. "Who hath believed our report," is the altered language now of those who remain unaltered, whereas they were once upon the popular side. So at least, I think it will be more and more, for what I call the *out and out* evangelical doctrines; the full entire Gospel; such as a now almost extinct generation of pious ministers, in and out of the church, preached it, and bequeathed it to us; but left, as I fear, few successors to themselves. But may we not regain by opposition, what we have lost by amalgamation? It was not popularity *produced* those men, though it finally embraced them. God knows his own purposes, and we know that they are good. It should suffice us. Thank you for all that you enclosed, especially the very nice "Mother's Thoughts," which I do like very much; S—— has not sent the MS. to which I have full leisure now to give attention, and at all times would do so at your request. I felt much pleased by what you said of Archdeacon ——, not having read the —— ——, but knowing it to be Puseyite: but when I repeated it to a clergyman, one of the *truest* I now know, he said it was impossible to take out of the book, the false views that pervade it throughout. Is this so? I shall like very much to see your letters. It is easier to write in some cases than to speak, but it is a pity, when differences *must* be controversy,—too much the case just now. I hear we are to have a triumph at Oxford as to the poetry chair, in which I feel great interest, for the sake of the craft, as well as of the University; but most for the honour of the church and its religion. If I had known Mr. —— to be your son-in-law, I might not have ventured to criticise his sermon.

What is true on one side, is true on the other; and while there are many who are of Israel, yet are not Israel, there are some of every party who are not under its condemnation; and will eventually be proved to have miscalled themselves. I am sure you may hope this of all your dear children, who are now differing from you. Christ's sheep do often lose themselves, but He can never lose them.

With the best wishes of this best season, believe me, dear Lady ——

Sincerely and obliged, yours,
CAROLINE WILSON.

XXXIX.—TO LADY * * *

January 22, 1842.

Dear Milady,

The month of January is arrived, and I must inquire after the ponies; to whom I beg to make the compliments of the season, and if they stand so much my friends as to bring you hither, I promise them every manner of civility, excepting that of being run away with by them. Whether I will ever give them an opportunity, must remain doubtful, till I see them; though I am by no means *so bad*, as I was in that particular. Of course you can feel no surprise, at the precedence herein given to your favourites; before I express either sorrow or hope about dear Sir J——'s gout, &c., my thoughts being simply intent upon seeing you; and my purpose in writing to know when you will come,—much more important than the coming of the king of Prussia. You must really give us as much notice, as you give yourselves, because if we have not to fit up St. George's Hall, I am sure there are friends, who will desire to be engaged to meet you, and don't be niggardly of time. We have beautiful weather now, but I could have wished you here at a better season, for such a house as ours. We will do what we can to keep you warm: within if not without. Mr.

Wilson said I should tell you he left Staffordshire, when quite a boy, therefore knows not your present world. O fie! it was not Mrs. B——, but *your own* letters; and I shall not be satisfied till I *ask the ponies*. With the best wishes of the season, and every season to yourself and Co.

Affectionately yours,
CAROLINE WILSON.

XL.—TO LADY * * * *

February, 22, 1842.

MY DEAR LADY ——

It may seem strange, but it is true, that at this moment I have it not in my power to comply with your wishes. I never make but one manuscript copy of what I write for the press, and that is in the printer's hands. The proof has passed through mine, and is in his hands also. I cannot send for it, because I do not know in which sheet the passage is, and I am as utterly unable to recal my own words, as if they were any body's else. I think the inclosed extract has not been altered as far as it goes; but there is apparently something before, and something between, which are necessary to perfect the extract. In the former, it is, I know, a direct mention of Socinianism, something to the effect that they are consistent, in that, not believing the divinity of Christ, they do not pretend to trust their salvation to him. The latter omission is something to the effect, that He who judges will do it individually, not by communities, because in the soundest community there may be dishonest hearts, whose pure creed will not save them, and in the most unsound, there may be *wrong-headed* people, who neither understand nor intend what they profess. These are not the words, but the purport of them. I have every reason to expect, that the work will be out in a few weeks. If you can wait, the earliest copy shall be forwarded to you, if you will kindly tell me how and where; and then make whatever use you please of it. I am tempted to send you the inclosed, which will appear in the ——— ——— next month; but you will please to keep the secret, as to the writer entirely to yourself. We are much comforted, by the choice of the new Bishop. It has been told me, that he selects for his examining chaplain, the most pious young man in the University. Is the new Irish Bishop one of your family?

With pleasant anticipations of your coming packet, believe me, my dear Lady,
Ever Yours,
Caroline Wilson.

XLI.—TO LADY * * *

February 28, 1842.

My dear Lady ——

I have read your interesting document with critical attention, but I find nothing in it that can be objected to, according to my own estimate of divine truth. The sacrifice of truth to unity is the ruinous device of the Evil One, that needs to be scrutinized and exposed; because it is so well calculated to catch the simple and unsuspicious under the loved and ever lovely name of peace. There is a remark worthy of all observance, in the volume of Ridley, just issued by the Parker Society: either of his or Latimer's; that unity in anything but the truth, is not concord, but conspiracy. My dear old minister, William Howels the only *pope* I ever was in danger of acknowledging on my own behalf, was used to remark, that the Scripture direction is to be "*first* pure, then peaceable," which might never be reversed, to give precedence to the latter.

Your paper will be read with interest, and I doubt not with the blessing of heaven, by your children's children, perhaps for many generations. Dr. ——'s share in it is very good.

No doubt you are a subscriber to the Parker Society. It bids fair to be a rich mine of gospel verity to strengthen and invigorate our rapidly enfeebling hands. Of course, whatever be the pretext for a declaration of war, justification by faith *alone*, and regeneration by the Spirit *alone*, is the ground on which the weary conflict must be maintained, and all be lost or won. Satan cares as little about rubrics and formularies, apart from these, as the lowest churchman amongst us. The party, I had very nearly said *his* party, at Oxford, have not hesitated to say that high-church and low-church does not signify: it is the *Calvinism* that must be exterminated, a name that in their tongue I have no doubt stands for what we mean by *the Gospel*—the perfect work of Christ.

I shall take care of your paper, till further orders, and beg you to believe me,

Your obliged and affectionate

CAROLINE WILSON.

XLII.—TO LADY * * * * *

March 24, 1842.

DEAREST MILADY,

We have been much too long without communication from you, and with you. I find by experience the proverb must be reversed, " no news" is very seldom " good news;" but generally contrariwise. I suppose the old enemy must occasionally be contended with: and it is encouraging to hear you speak cheerfully of the winter past, notwithstanding your sick-room labours and anxieties. It shows you are yourself better, and more comfortably situated, which greatly tends to lighten your affectionate toil. It has been a very fine and cheerful winter: and having had few storms without and none within, I find myself in very good keeping. We look to your coming with great desire: and however it may be delayed, you will surely come at last; so I mean to think, as pertinaciously as I thought to see you at C—— last summer; I never found castle-building a bad practice. I write to you rather the sooner, for for that I expect to be from home all next week. Mr. Wilson is going to spend it with his relations in Worcestershire, and I am going with him for the simple purpose of not being left behind. You will observe by the papers, the death of Mrs. H——'s brothers. The first, and younger, was a very sudden but most beautiful death; leaving a wife and family; the second, occasioned no doubt, by the former, a single man, and the last brother. I dare say Mr. H—— will have written you the account of it, as I know he corresponds with Sir J——. It is truly such a death that one might long to be allowed to die.

Thank you for the sermon: and yet, I almost regret when you make me speak about this. If your pastor were an unknown man, I should hear with simple satisfaction what you say about him, on his account and yours. But Mr. —— is not unknown, and the more favourably you speak of him the more uneasy I grow on your account. If by *unprejudiced*, dear, you mean indifference to the empoisoning leaven, that is so rapidly corrupting the pure stream of gospel-truth, so full, so blest of late years in our church, and throwing into confusion the minds of God's own people; speaking merely of that modification of Tractarianism which would disown its name, and so be only the more dangerous to the simple-minded,—you may ask no such thing of me, dear friend; I am not one to stand indifferently by, while the strong-holds of our faith are assailed on the one hand, and betrayed on the other, and undermined on all; you know me too well to think so. But a *candid* opinion you *shall* have upon this or any other subject on which you ask it; so, candidly, I find nothing amiss in the sermon except two expressions, "Alms at God's ALTAR," page 1, and "Opportunities of receiving the Body and Blood of Christ," page 8; a mode of speaking better understood by me, perhaps, than by many to whom it was addressed. So, leaving criticism, I think, or rather *we* think, for we read it together, and made the same remark; it is very poor, and does not effect in us the only purpose for which it seems intended—to make the coin bestir itself in our pockets; the sad and urgent FACTS of the case being known to us before through other channels. Now all this will vex you: and I do not like to vex you; but, if you really are so *innocent* as not to know why *I*, an *out-and-out*

Evangelical, a Low Churchman, a Calvinist, anything or everything that you may please to call it, do not like Mr. P——, just ask Mr. P—— how he likes *me*, and perhaps he will bring you to a better understanding of the difference. Or ask Sir J——, if you like, why when all is making ready for the battle, the fleets do not lie *pêle mêle*, one amongst the other.

Mrs. W—— is so urgent upon me not to forget her kind remembrances, pray consider them as sent. She has moved to the Heath again, and is quite well. I am afraid there is no more news, except that the B——s are likely to lose their second daughter, Georgiana. Mr. L—— has now a religious curate, who is doing some good in the parish. So much for gossip. Love to Sir J—— and the young ladies. I shall come and see you some day, in spite of Mr. P——, but not till after your visit here: in *May*, I cannot give you longer. Tell Miss Fanny we are all "solfa-ing it;" and I expect when next we meet Mr. Wilson will sing *a second* with her in great style.

Ever affectionately yours,
CAROLINE WILSON.

XLIII.—TO LADY * * * * *

April 13, 1842.

MY DEAR LADY ———,

The long-expected book has come at last. I have inscribed the lowly offering to yourself, and put it in S———'s hands to transmit as soon as possible; for I take it to be too heavy for the post. Meantime, I lose not a day to enclose the extract you desire; and have added another, of the same import. Do with either what seems to you good.

Indeed, indeed it is a serious thing to write a book, or say any thing that cannot be unsaid—revoked—recalled—however we may change. Most grateful above all persons I have cause to be, that by a peculiar providence, I was withheld from the public exercise of my talent for scribbling, till the truth of God had taken full possession of my mind; and thus escaped the guilt and misery of its unhallowed use; and all the regrets that might have been helplessly suffered, in seeing my own foolish words remain in action on the minds of others. I think often, with mixed gratitude and horror, on what I should have written, had I written once.

Thank you much for all the contents of your packets; I like the Tract very much, as I do everything you write or say. I wish this sad, sad subject lay not so near to your personal feelings and affections. Without any such interests, one has enough to do, to keep one's mind in peace about it; and I am sure it must sadly intrude itself on yours. But I may write no more now, lest I detain the inclosure, which you want. The book I hope will soon follow it, and meet with some acceptance in your experienced judgment. It will be too strong for most, I know that; but so many like to read my books, who like not the whole truth as it is in Jesus, I had a mind for once to force it on their attentions. Excuse haste, and allow me to be,

Ever faithfully yours,
Caroline Wilson.

"One class of persons we know there is, who profess not to believe, that the Crucified was God; and there is so much of consistency in their creed they do not profess to trust their salvation to him: whatever value Socinians set upon Christ's death as man, they do not consider it that perfect and sufficient atonement for sin which it can be only as he was God. But there is another class of whom I think with more wonder and some doubt; who do profess to know the infinite character of the one great sacrifice and satisfaction made for sin, and recognize in the blood of the covenant the blood of God; yet make so light of it, take at so little its efficacious value, one scarcely can think that they believe it. Grosser than his who thought the gift of God could be purchased for money; baser than his who parted with it for one morsel of meat, is the estimate of Christ's atoning blood, by those who think its efficacy can lose or gain, by administration of their own poor polluted hands; or aught that they can add to it or take from it. I do not make myself their judge to decide a question, which may decide their everlasting state; I believe by Him who judges, it will be decided individually; not in communities or communions, whether held together by error or by truth. In the truest communion there are wrong-hearted ones, whose pure creed will never save them; in the most unsound there may be wrong-headed ones, who do not understand or intend their own profession; and so may escape its guiltiness. God knows, but when we see this precious blood postponed, its efficacy made dependent on names, and forms, and places, and ceremonies; ordinances, institutions, works, sufferings, merits, or whatever else man's wit can substitute therefor, or add thereto; and men profess to find more safety and repose in these than in the sole value of the death of Christ: the doubt forces itself upon me, and I return it to every such a one, and bid him lay it deeply to his heart, —whether he does indeed believe the Crucified was God."—*Christ our Law, p.* 50.

" Let us lose ourselves, and renounce ourselves, and forget ourselves in contemplation of the glorious mystery: (its Incarnation,) if only we be lost in shame with it for our low estimate of its cost of our redemption; thinking, as we do sometimes, to dispense with the Saviour's merits; at other times to purchase his merits with our own; nor that the lowest price; for while many are thinking to obtain salvation, or to procure the benefits of Christ's death, by obedience to the law of God, depending for acceptance on prayer, and penitence and baptism and church-communion, and other their good works, because these are ordained of God, and commanded to be done: not a few are merchandising for the same precious purchase with a still baser coin—with forms and fantasies of their own devising, which God has not commanded, and for which they can produce no law at all, but of their own making. And oh! the depth from which our thoughts have fallen from contemplation of that high and holy theme! even to behold no inconsiderable number whose supposed merits, proffered to Almighty God, as substitutes or make-weights of the Atoning Sacrifice, are things in actual opposition and contradiction to his word. Do *these* believe that the Crucified was God? We ask again and leave it."—*Christ our Law, p.* 59.

XLIV.—TO LADY * * * * *

May 10, 1842.

My dear Lady ———,

I shall be very much pleased to receive the book you promise me; that or any thing left for me at Messrs. H———'s, in Mincing Lane, finds its way to me in a few hours. I am not at all likely to be from home for more than a few days till July, and perhaps not then. I *will* give you a candid opinion of the letters; but I say beforehand, that there can be no reason to withhold them. The words of a tried and experienced Christian, who has seen so much of life as you have, must be valuable, at least to those who are entering upon it; and may be very strengthening to those who are equally advanced, and drawing near, as you are, to the longed-for shore. Sure I am, at least, they shall not be by me objected to on the ground you speak of. It is the wisdom of the world, not of God, to withhold the truth, and make compromise with error, because the one may do harm, and the other be mixed with good. The former position is *never* true, in the latter, the harmfulness of the error is all the greater for the mixtures. Of the works, of which you ask my poor opinion, I have read none, except Father Clement, very long ago; a pretty clear clear proof that I do not *like* them, but that is wide of the question whether they are lawful. I should not say unlawful—but I doubt their efficacy, and suspect their general tendency. For the very young I disapprove them wholly, and who else will read them? That is a foolish question perhaps, because a great many others *do* read them; and it is not impossible that just that number may derive good impressions from them, which they would not get, because they would not seek, in better reading; I mean the idle readers of a certain age. I do not know, but I so thoroughly distaste the things, I am afraid lest it warp my judgment to condemn them wholly: had I a family to bring up, I should *certainly* make no use of them. But should they not at best be judged of individually? I apprehend some of those you name to be much worse than others: and if they are to be tolerated at all as a medium of conveying religious truth, it must be with a strict limitation as to their character and bearing in other respects. * * *

Your next problem, my dear Lady ———, is a more difficult one; I fear beyond my solution now, not wishing to detain this letter. There is just that difficulty in the very front of it, which so often meets me, and puts my wisdom at fault. People ask their way without saying where they are going; and I may direct them to York, while they are bound for Exeter.

There is not, there cannot be one road for those that are to pursue the world and to possess it, and those that are to renounce it. I could write you a volume, to prove that a pious parent should not, and could not, stimulate and fill the young imagination with unhallowed images of forbidden things, to become the torment and the taint of a mind devoted to God, and conformed to his holy will; while not one word that I might say, should be applicable to the parent who wishes and intends that the child should succeed and shine among the gay, the loved, the happy of this world's society. For after all, the world's poetry is better than its prose—the dreams of fairy land are better than the drudgery of mammon—the wildest disciple of romance is more lovely in her generation, than the cold, calculating drawing-room coquette. That her delusion will be the shorter and her disappointment the surer, is no great evil: for the fashion of this world passeth, the game is soon played, and it matters little whether it be won or lost, when it is ended. If I look to gather winter stores into my garner, I plant my ground with one thing; if I want it to look pretty through the summer season, I plant it with another. Is not this so? But no more now, except the sincere esteem of,

Yours ever,
CAROLINE WILSON.

XLV.—TO LADY * * * * *

August 29, 1842.

My dear Lady ———

I received your note, and soon after it the promised book; on the eve of departure from Blackheath for a short season; and thank you much for affording me another opportunity and excuse to write. I thought the time had expired for your sea-side address, and that I must wait another. The book I looked hastily over before I left it behind, quite sufficiently to be satisfied of its character, and I trust it will be very useful to a not unimportant class,—that of young men entering on the profession—with a wish to reconcile its practices with the mind of God. The difficulty of this in every profession, trade, or calling, as now carried on in the world,—the more than difficulty, I should say impossibility, of following any after a godly sort, without the sacrifice of its temporal advantage to a greater or less extent, is a thing that has much fixed my attention through life, by the opportunity I have had of observing the spiritual difficulties of every class of persons. From the least to the greatest, I have seen that the utmost the god of this world proposes, must be foregone, unless some manner of service or of homage be conceded to him. "All this will I give to thee, IF"—must be heard in every believing heart; and the choice made in every faithful one, to be less rich, less honourable, less successful, in this world, than he might have been if the love of Christ constrained him not. I am so persuaded of this myself, I always purposed if I had children, to keep it before their eyes and my own, as a matter of course, that the great things of this world must be righteously renounced, and no question made, how they might be righteously attained: not in one path only, but in all, from the bar downward to the poor waterman, who could make money on a Sunday, IF. Is there any stronger evidence of human corruption, and the present reign of the evil one, than this—that the most lawful calling cannot be righteously pursued without departing from the common practices of the world, and leaving its utmost advantage to the ungodly. I was much pleased with your approbation of our dear friend C—— M——, and so was he, for I made him a party to your observations. Authors sorely need encouragement, and they will need it more and more, who in these days are to stand against the turning tide. When I leave home, I feel the truth of your observation, that I am happy to live out of the sphere of contention, and fire my poor missiles from a distance. It is difficult to go many miles from home, and take the chances of a single Sunday, without encountering the mischief in some form or other. I was sadly grieved in this way at * * * last Sunday, more perhaps than the thing was worth; for though Mr. —— had some reputation at ——, as an evangelical minister, I never heard him fully preach the truth, nor quite believed he did, though others thought so. I was quite unprepared, however, and proportionately shocked, to hear him tell a large congregation, well enough disposed I dare say to believe him, on the text: " Make your calling and election sure;" that the only calling and election here spoken of was *already their's*, by birth and baptism in the Christian church; and their only care must be to *keep it*, and make sure of its ultimate benefits, by a holy and virtuous life. And so deeply leavened is the sometimes religious world with this insidious poison; so confused and confounded are minds not really persuaded or perverted, that numbers sate contented with the hearing, and departed satisfied with what they would sometimes not have endured to listen to. This is the forecasting woe, that threatens all people, to strive against Popery and Puseyism all the week, and on the Sunday listen to their perversions without knowing it. For myself, I am a faint-hearted coward, and would gladly be out of hearing of these rumours of wars; but I am ashamed to be saying all this to *you*, who have to bear with it, and to deal with it so much more nearly. Does it not sometimes make you cry, " How long, O Lord, how long ?"

I have not your former letter by me, and am afraid there may be something in it I neglect to answer to. If you see the —— ———, you will find in the ensuing number a review of Tractarian Novelists; Paget and Gresley in particular, of which you will detect the writer perhaps. They are monstrous.

It is rather grievous to observe to what extent also the periodical press is in possession of the enemy. You see I am terribly out of heart. Nevertheless, there seems to be a sound gospel ministry here. I call to mind your question respecting the *clearness* of Mr. M———'s writing. In his preaching, being extempore, it is something *quite extraordinary.* I was pleased to have my impression of it confirmed by your notice of it, in connection with the eagerness and rapidity of his delivery; it indicates a mental power of a very peculiar character; because it is a rapidity and perspicuity of *thought,* not of mere language: it is the mind, and not the tongue, that acts with such extraordinary velocity and exactness. I am afraid you will discover by my prating, that I am under the influence of watering-place idleness. I expect to return home next week, and hope to be soon obliged with another communication from you. Meantime, my dear Lady ———, believe me,
    Sincerely and obliged yours,
      CAROLINE WILSON.

XLVI.—TO MRS. T——.

September 7, 1842.

My very dear Friend,

The newspapers have made known to me your great affliction: what can I say to you? Nothing of comfort that the Holy Ghost has not already said within you, but only a few vain and empty words of human sympathy and love,—" The Lord gave," or rather lent, and if we ask, why should he resume? we must first answer, why should he have ever given?

Yours was indeed a brief loan, poor dear! and because I know your more than common desire for children, and more than common delight in them, I estimate very deeply your present suffering. That you are upheld and supported under it, I am also sure, for your heart has been too long given to Jesus, for you to refuse him any thing beside; and He has been too long given to you, for any other loss to leave you destitute.

These are lowering and darkening times, dear; and they who see their loved ones safe on shore before them, will die happier than they who leave them on the deep: you cannot feel this now, but you will. Be comforted and wait; you know that I say to your dear husband, all I write to you, and comprehend him in all I feel for *you*. At your leisure, and entire inclination, not before, I should like to hear of both of you. We are just returned from our usual summer holiday; thank God in health. With Mr. Wilson's most kind regards, and feeling sympathies, believe me, dear,

Ever affectionately yours,

CAROLINE WILSON.

XLVII.—TO MRS. T——.

September 20, 1842.

MY DEAR FRIEND,

Your letter is just such as I expected from yourself; the voice of thanksgiving from a broken heart—praise in the depth of affliction. Such choice and lovely flowers bloom but a short season in general; there seems but little of the dross of earth about them, and why should they bide the fire.

In respect of your wish about the Epitaph, I think those you selected very appropriate; and should hardly expect to substitute a better of my own. But if it is the feeling of your love to put something of mine upon the tomb of your precious child, perhaps the inclosed will meet your wishes, which I have penned for the purpose. It is not easy to select within the given compass; I send it only on the condition that you make no ceremony of rejecting it, if you prefer another; since it is your estimation of it only, that can give it value for the purpose. I write in haste lest you should be anxious for it. Yes, dearest, I have ceased to wish for children long before my death-bed. It is the natural desire of a wife, but I very soon found I had enough to love, and enough to lose. The very feeling, at first so painful, that if I should lose my husband, I should have nothing left, was soon converted into a thought of satisfaction. I should wish to have nothing left in this world, that my whole heart's affections might be transferred at once, and the last tie be broken. This has been long *my* feeling; but you are younger, dear, and must not so desire. You have blessings left, and they must bring their duties and their cares, and you must try yet to enjoy the one, as well as fulfil the other; and you will—God will comfort you.

CAROLINE WILSON.

EPITAPH.

Brief thrall of sin
  His spirit held—in Jesus risen again,
Brief be the tomb
  That holds his body now, till Jesus come.

XLVIII.—TO LADY * * * * *.

October 25, 1842.

My dear Lady ———,

Though I have been too long in saying it, I hope you will believe that your first letter, saying most of yourself and of what is yours, was by no means the least interesting to me. Indeed, apart from the near interest I have in Desford Rectory, that is a story might deeply affect any heart, feeling and liking to feel its entire dependence, trusting and liking to trust, everything to the control and determination of the Most High. Indeed you say right, there is enough there, and enough everywhere, to shame us out of anxiety of any kind. Mistrust in a child of God, is the most irrational thing in the world; but seeing that we are such poor frightened children, striking interferences of providence like that you mention, are very graciously given from time to time, and may be most profitably repeated and contemplated, for our encouragement as well as for our reproof. You have a right to be assured, and must be assured, *that* you will not be turned aside permanently, however opposed by adverse influences for a season; and we will hope not even this. I have no doubt myself, and it is the feeling of the most decided people I meet with, that it is *war*, not *peace*, for which we must prepare ourselves: separation not union, to which we must be ready to submit, if it please God to suffer the extremity of this mischief. We do expect the Evangelical party must stand out, with such a show of resistance and determination, as will either force respect by its numbers, influence and consistency, and afford for Zion a stronghold, and a safe one within the establishment; or, as will, on the other hand, so array the hierarchy against us, that we shall be cast out, ministers and people together, from the parental roof; and if on the one hand we see many, who seemed to be of us, going out from among us, or compromising all that is most precious to us, those who abide are waxing stronger and stronger, and gathering as it were in expectation of the conflict. Such are the signs of the times, I would *you* had no more *personal* difficulties and anxieties about it than I have, for though sore distressed, and often very sad in spirit about this declension in the church, and obscuration of the light so long enjoyed, it is as the member feels for the body, rather than individually for itself. I shall stand by the established church, as long as she will let me; but I feel that I could do very well without her, if it became necessary. It would be a *great loss* for this world; but what is there of this world that we cannot do without, and count *but loss* that we may win Christ: and having won him, maintain the purity of his faith, and the glory of his name. No, my dear Lady ——, I have not discovered that remedy, nor have I, like some others, looked for it, for I never believed it was intended in the present dispensation. A great deal was thought at one time, about getting pious men into parliament. Men whose social position did not require it of them, (for I would not have them shrink from it where it does,) put themselves forward, and were supported by the religious body as such, in the expectation of dethroning Satan there; there was an honest purpose and expectation of a great deal of influence for good; and I found myself almost alone in my opinion, that they were doing wrong. In the stir about the Sabbath again, instead of catching eagerly and thankfully at such poor crumbs of relaxation, as would have been thrown to us by that hard taskmaster, God's people thought to have, and would have nothing less, than the utmost limits of his law, and purpose. Perhaps, too, the increase of religion in the high places of our church, has wakened a too lofty expectation there, which, like the others, will disappoint itself. I have had but one mind about it all, it is a very simple view; but nothing has disproved it yet. Our Lord is *gone* to receive a kingdom of his Father, he did not commit to his servants the government of the world in his absence; but left the usurper on the throne till He returns. Far other was his last behest to *them*, "Love not, touch not, taste not, handle not." He did not ask his Father then to give it them; far other was his last prayer for them. His people will reign with Him, they cannot reign without him, they may not prevail to have the domination any way until He come again, and the God of this world is cast out.

The Assistant of Education, respecting which you inquire, was a periodical publication edited by me for many years, and really written *almost wholly by myself.* The Listener was a part of it, also the Scripture Readers' Guide, now a separate work, in the 11th edition. Several of those you mention, I hope may be separate works some time, as I have them so prepared; but would not take, and could not get others to take, the risk of their publication. About the advertisement you speak of, I am surprised; as I believed the work, as a whole, to be out of print. My publisher failed and disappeared. I cannot tell who has advertised it. Still, if you get it, there is nothing of consequence in it that is not my writing; and a good deal that might be used in education, religion apart. Indeed I should consider the " —— ——," a very nice and valuable gift to make to many persons. Your secrets, be assured are quite safe with me, and I doubt not so with S——; and I shall be pleased to see your Letters in print. I can hardly make up my mind, what to be doing next: but I cannot be idle long, for my own mind's sake. Circumstances give more weight to the question of *profit*, than I could wish it had, in the choice of subject: but this too is of God, and perhaps I require the impulse to keep me going. Nevertheless I hope I wait, and am sure I ask, for his direction in it.

This is, I fear, a desultory epistle; but your kindness excuses everything, and you will

    Ever believe me yours,
      CAROLINE WILSON.

XLIX.—TO LADY * * * * *

November 22, 1842.

MY DEAR LADY ———

I have received safely your inclosure, which shall be carefully kept till I have further directions from you respecting it. Greatly indeed I am grieved to hear of your serious indisposition; I can only hope and pray it may be but a temporary alarm,—a word I do not apply to you, but to those who cannot spare you. I will not impose a long letter on you now, lest you weary yourself to answer it; instead of just telling me you are getting well. I think I do not understand your proposition respecting regeneration: that is, I understand your negative as to the baptismal service—there is, and ever must be a weak point, when we attempt to defend our church, in her formularies at least, though I believe not in her intentions. I say, "defend the church," because heartily as I would at all times defend our establishment by Holy Scripture, I refuse all defence of Holy Scripture by the opinions of our church. What I do not understand is your view of regeneration as a change of state: I think you do not seem to mean a change from a state of nature to a state of grace; from a state of condemnation to a state of justification; as the high church party do, and as we do; and yet I cannot think what other change of state can be in your mind. In the passage you allude to, the word regeneration evidently, I think, means the resurrection of the body to renewed existence; which by analogy would strengthen our view that its ordinary meaning is the resurrection of the soul to spiritual existence, when it passes from death unto life. This we believe regeneration to be, and this we wish to disconnect from the baptismal service, otherwise than as between the sign and the thing signified; which may or may not be in connection at any given time. And this we wish to make our church say, as far as we can, because if she will not, we must not defer to her opinion against what we believe to be the mind of God as manifest in Holy Writ. Mr. ——— wished to make the church in the right; but many who think him scripturally unanswerable, are not satisfied with his defence of certain phrases in the Prayer book. For my own part, as I profess not to expect perfection in anything that comes from the hands of man, I would rather stand upon the Articles, and the general purport of her services, and give up, as unfortunate and objectionable, the few expressions that have led to so much mischief and misapprehension. I would rather regret the blemish on her fair cheek, than attempt to paint it out. But I should like to know what *you* mean by a change of state as effected in baptism; only, not till you are well enough to write at ease. The Bishop of London's Charge has thrown a huge mass of ballast into our sinking boat, which threatens to swamp us utterly. But no more now; while God is on our side, we will not, and we do not fear what man can do against us. With the deepest interest in your health, and all that concerns you, believe me, my dear Lady ———

Very sincerely yours,
CAROLINE WILSON.

P. S.—I should like to know, whether in the case of your death, the secret of your authorship is to be for ever kept.

L.—TO LADY * * * * *

January 3, 1843.

MY DEAR LADY ———

Many thanks for all your kind communications: I am now so much on the debtor side, I think we shall not cross upon the road. I quite understand your term now, as synonymous with what we call High Church; but still think the latter the better, because the more familiar term. Perhaps, to avoid all the difficulties, of calling things by different names, which are only degrees of the same thing, is better. Nevertheless Tractarian, High Church, and Evangelical, would be three things in the eyes of most readers. I think your proposed addition to the book, quite unobjectionable; and as regards the *word* catholic, it may be useful. I was much pleased to get another copy of your little book, as it enabled me to send the first into the servants' room. I have received also the two volumes of Poetry: but alas! I do not pretend to be no lover of poetry. I was born a poet, and bred a poet; and am perhaps too much of a poet still, but alas! What a requisition you have made, to read two volumes of—what shall I say? However, I will try at your request to look again; at present I simply confess, I have found more Puseyism than poetry. There are many reasons for reading bad prose; but I never yet could find a reason for reading or writing bad poetry; just because there is no necessity for poetry at all. I hope you will not be angry at this affront to your friend's muse; but you confess *you* have not read them.

I have not written any more in the C——— ———, than I have named to you—except two; when I do so, I will tell you.

I note your suggestions about Union; but fear I am too hopeless, to be the instrument of promoting it. I never knew a moment at which it seemed so impossible, except by previous separation from the church; and even then, if the people of

God within the church should become, as I think they ultimately will, a severed but united body, the state of the dissenting churches is most unfavourable to anything like union with us, on that side. Already they are taking advantage of our strife, to attack both sides; and it appears to me also, that their spirituality as a body is as much on the decrease, as their ill-will toward the Establishment is on the increase. I am entirely persuaded myself, that there can be no *union;* but an agreement to *differ* in love, about all that is not necessary to salvation. Never alas! were we apparently so far from this. It may come, but I think it can be only through a time of such opposition, and persecution, from the world and *its* church, as shall force the church of Christ to stand together, in its defence. Accept the best wishes, of this beautiful and bountiful season, come in with such unusual brightness.

I am indeed rejoiced and thankful, that you are tolerably well again. My dear Lady ———
Yours in *real union*,
CAROLINE WILSON.

LI.—TO LADY * * * * *

February 6, 1843.

MY DEAR LADY ———

I am in arrears, I fear, with all your kind communications, and books too; which I am giving away discreetly, and hope they will do good. I mean ten copies of the "——— ———." All you write about disunion is most true, most sensible; but alas! it is retrospective, and what can that avail? You say "if dissenters *had* remained, instead of separating." I doubt not you are right; but that is past. I do not know to what particular period of separation your extract refers. If to that of the ultra-calvinist separation, under Messrs. B———, &c.; they long ago broke up, and God and the world took each their own amongst them. If the Irvingite party,—they are already joined in heart to the Puseyite faction; and will join hand, when they can do it without shame. Other denominations of dissenters already show themselves awakened by our strife: but are taking arms, to wound us on both sides. Even if they were better disposed to peace than I fear they are, we can no longer invite them to return into our fast-crumbling edifice, out of which we are momentarily expecting to be expelled.

A very learned and pious clergyman here the the other day, wished to change the name, Dissenters, and unite the pious of all sorts, under the name of *Consenters;* you would *consent* to this, but would you be prepared to see the whole body of God's people in the Establishment withdraw from it, to form this Consentient Church! For my own part, I *could* be content to see it, if God did it; but I could not resolve to be the doer of it: because, better as the vital part might be without its encumbrance of worldly intermixture, the dislocation would be terrible, and its effects upon the world and *its* church most lamentable. Besides, I agree with you about the *present* and *temporal* advantages, among many spiritual disadvantages, which the temple of our God derives from the surrounding mass of outer-court worshippers; or the advantages, at least, which society derives, from the temporary amalgamation. Alas! it is not on our side *now*, that the pulling-down of bulwarks is threatened: and our words will have little effect upon our opponents. It has been always foreseen by the far-seeing and deep-thinking, that the high-church and evangelical parties, being not *differing* but *opposed* in principle, could only adhere by sufferance on the part of the majority:—unity was impossible. Most of us fear that the time is come, when that sufferance will be refused; and then the minority must secede. I desire, on my own part, that it should be the act of our unnatural mother, to cast us from her bosom, rather than ours to abandon her, even in her corruption, while liberty of conscience is allowed on the disputed points. Approving therefore entirely your "Extracts," I do not see them applicable to the present crisis. I pray God to protract it,—and he may; but the feeling of most is that the crisis approaches, more or less near, some say ten years—some say ten months. Much depends upon the government. If they grant a convocation, or meddle with church matters in parliament, the *numbers* are against us; and the church *in* England, will not long be the church *of* England; for which we shall all deeply grieve, and Satan will triumph gloriously; but it will not be *we* who have removed our tents, or extinguished our lamps within her.

How artful those people are!—among the host of them, there is not a more dangerous and perverted or perverting one than ————. Your "Worldly Religion" is a true painting, and will be a true likeness of more than it is drawn for. You may be quite at ease respecting the principles, likely to be derived by your orphan niece, at Miss B———'s; their reputation for *religion* stands high; but there is said to be very great deficiency of *instruction* in every thing else, which is a great evil for one who may have to maintain herself, hereafter as you say, by the exercise of her mental acquirements. Would it be any satisfaction to you, that I should see her? Accept this return of little for your much; and the inclosed from my valued pastor, against that enormous heresy of the Tractarians; "No regeneration before the ascension." Ever most truly yours,

CAROLINE WILSON.

LII.—TO LADY * * * * *

February 12, 1843.

MY DEAR LADY ———,

You have so entirely misunderstood my last, I must undeceive you; not only for the ease of your own mind, but, lest you should impart to any one else the thought which is founded wholly on misapprehension. I almost think it would be enough to ask you to read my letter again: but I may have written obscurely, and you may have forgotten to what I was *answering*, when I put the interrogatory that you quote. *You* had exhorted to *union*. I saw but one union at this time possible, which was to be deprecated: I asked you if you would consent to *that*, not asking you *to consent*, but meaning to express my certainty that you *would not;* and when I added that *I could*, IF, &c., it was an expression of painful resignation to the Divine will in that which I *anticipate*. From what part of my letter you could draw the inference that it is *God's people* who are *banding together* to secede, when I meant to express the deep and anxious fear with which all the evangelical party see the high-church party banding together to *force them out*, I cannot at all guess; but I must have expressed myself ill indeed for you so to understand me. I do not know a single individual, lay or clerical, who wishes, purposes, or even thinks of leaving the church; but I know few thinking and feeling and informed persons, who are not *afraid* that under the growing influence of Puseyism, the Establishment will so change its ground as to *leave us* a separate body. That this does not occur to you as a possibility, without our own act, may arise from your not knowing what is doing, or is likely to be done. But suppose to yourself, the bishop of Exeter refusing ordination to every man, who will not subscribe that we are justified by baptism; and suppose him next to suspend all the curates, and withdraw all licenses within his power, on the same ground—or because they won't bow to the altar—or any other anti-scriptural thing. Such power he *already has*, and to an extent has exercised. But suppose further, that the Queen grants what they want; a convocation empowered to act in church matters, and make changes in the ritual, under the pretence of settling disputes. Immediately the majority may decide for doctrines and practices, which no righteous minister can comply with; articles which he cannot subscribe, because they are unscriptural: forms which he cannot use, because they are idolatrous. What *must* follow, as regards the ministry? What would, and ought to follow as regards their flocks? This is the view I meant to exhibit, the only one I or my friend from Oxford, to whose words I seem to have done great injustice, ever contemplated. This was meant by Dr. Arnold, whom I quoted to you; by Mr. Blunt, who on the verge of eternity expressed his belief, that less than ten years will accomplish it *certainly*—of some who think that *ten months* will see it done— of many a devout heart, I feel assured, now earnestly praying, that when the trying time shall come, he may stand fast in the Lord; though it may be at the cost of all he holds most dear. Now I must ask of your justice to read my letter again, and see if it will not fully, and in every part, bear this explanation as its obvious sense; if it will not, then it must have been a very stupidly-compounded effusion.

When this time comes, my dear Lady ———, it is not the little band who will rally round the Lord's forsaken ensign, that will have to determine who is, and who is not to be among their number: as you seem to think. True, we may hope, and trust, and pray; but we must not sleep upon our watch-tower in a time of siege. It may please God *you* will not live to see it. I sometimes hope, and if I might, could *wish* that I may not,—who am a little younger—for it will be fraught with grief to many whom I love, if not much affecting myself *personally*. We both may pray for *delay*, even if we are hopeless to see the ill finally averted; but to suppose that any godly person within the Establishment can *wish* it, *promote* it, *purpose* it; no, really I could not have written any thing that *could* bear that construction. I write under a press of occupation, and will therefore delay answering all the rest of your kind propositions. With many apologies for this haste.

Ever affectionately yours,
CAROLINE WILSON.

P. S.—My picture of the church of Christ in England now, is of a besieged city, (not a *rout*,) of which the weakening garrison, after a brave defence, will be ultimately marched out,—I *hope* with their colours flying.

LIII.—TO LADY * * * * *

March 25, 1843.

MY DEAR LADY ——

If you are ashamed of writing, I am sure I ought to be ashamed of not writing; after all your kind communications. I offer but one excuse, because I had in fact but one reason for not doing so, viz., the having another book in hand, which generally impedes my letter writing. If there is any difference in our view of the sad subject of our correspondence, it arises wholly, as I think, from the different position from which we view it. You take your view from the centre—you see the picture in detail—you individualize the effects—you have Puseyism embodied, as it were, in those about you—I may almost say, *within* you : even at your heart's core. Possibly this propinquity may vary the bias of your opinions, about as much, and no more, than the light summer breeze gives its direction to the waving corn. I draw from a distance, and see only the broad outline, the larger features. I never meet with the individuals, except an empty youth, or foolish young girl now and then, who meeting me as a stranger of well-known sentiments, will seldom venture a talk with me by broaching their opinions. Consequently, I know less than you of the interior working of the system, and am not within reach of personal influence. I do not know such persons as you speak of, as being converted to seriousness by the Oxford party; I think every such case must stand upon its individual merits. If the dissipated youth is indeed a broken-hearted penitent, learning to *hate* the sin he lately loved, and to renounce it for Jesus' sake, he will assuredly not rest always in Puseyism; it may prove to have been the schoolmaster that led him to Christ. But if the change be only from self-indulgence to self-righteousness, an alarmed conscience taking refuge in a formal devotion, the convert is no safer than he was before. I am not sure that he is not in a more dangerous position, by reason of his false security; he is like one, who in a storm of wind, should betake himself for shelter to a baseless roof. It appears to me, that these cases, be they many or few, are so very individual, and so impossible to discriminate, that they need not in the least degree affect our judgment of the Tractarian influence.

I think things wear rather a different aspect in Ireland than in England; our *pious* ministers might, *if they would,* read the cold formulary to the empty benches, while the untaught labourer perished in his prayerlessness and ignorance; but if any one set about to do what your son does, he would be impeached and perhaps suspended for altering the service. Our dear pastor has a service for *communicants* on the Friday before the sacrament; but having no place large enough to address them except the church, he dares not omit the smallest portion of the service, which is not the object at all, but a really inconvenient detention; so that we in England are not likely to misconstrue *daily service.* Such a one as yours, with a gospel address at the end of it, would be a blessing everywhere, if the people would go; but in England they would not. The Puseyites may say *vicarious* prayers for the people, if they please, but nothing will take the English poor to church *bodily,* but a good stirring gospel sermon. I say not this of the rich, they will do anything, rather than renounce the world, and its affections, and lusts; as required by the gospel. Truly you say, exterior trifles of dress &c., do not signify in themselves. Intrinsically we should not care to choose between the tri-color and the drapeau-blanc; but when they were the insignia of legitimacy and of usurpation, they *did* signify. I fear it is so now between the black gown and the white: and we must not hoist the enemy's colours in the day of battle, or follow them. This is, I think, the whole extent of the difference in our views. I would rather you were right, for then the case is not so bad as I think: and so God grant it may be. Be assured you never wrote one word that gave me anything but pleasure. I have never heard anything whatever as to Dr. T——, but I know a quarter in which I am likely to learn when occasion serves. I do not know anything of the circular you speak of respecting Puseyism * * * Mr.——, of whom I think you ask me somewhere, though I cannot find the passage, has a district church in Greenwich, and is the Editor of the 'C—— R——,' the most bitterly anti-evangelical periodical, and he is the strongest Tractarian in our neighbourhood. Personally, I do not know him, for we are understood as exclusive here; and it is one advantage of authorship, that people know both Mr. ——'s mind and mine too well to ask us to meet. If, in speaking to this, I am answering an inquiry made by somebody else, excuse it, as a confusion in my mind. I have not yet received your book. Again begging you to believe you never wrote an unsuccessful letter, and hoping you will oblige me with many more, believe me, my dear Lady ——,

With esteem and affection, yours,
CAROLINE WILSON.

LIV.—TO LADY * * * * *

April, 1843.

My Dear Lady ———,

I have become so much accustomed to the indulgence of receiving your letters, I almost take it to heart when they cease to come, though I feel the fault is with myself on most occasions. I have to thank you for your books, duly received; and really valuable in my opinion. If your gentle remonstrances will not stay the torrent, they may rescue many a pious spirit from its headlong course. I will tell you anything I hear about it; but shall be much surprised that any thing objectionable can be pointed out. Our world is sadly dividing upon books, as well as every thing else; so that Seeley says there are just *two sets* of buyers, one for his books, &c., and the other for Burns', &c. Still there is and ever must be, a middle class of readers, who have come to no decision; and dip into both urns with their eyes shut, for the chance of what they may draw up. It is this class that I hope may lay their hands on both your books, and be profited thereby. On your responsibility, in publishing, I am sure that *you* at least may be at rest; for *harm* they can never do to any one. My writing has not progressed much of late, owing to a very little indisposition, and a good deal of earthly care. Meantime, I believe we only desire to be directed rightly, in what we do; and to be relieved, if it may be, from anxiety about the future; to which end, grant us your prayers. I assure you, I more welcome than resist your "good words, and comfortable" about the church. The *May meetings*, though I go not to them, I hear have taken a very satisfactory tone this year; firm, determined, zealous and affectionate;—what passed in the House is also thought to bear a favourable aspect. It is said that the strong opposition to the Factory Education Bill, has warned the government of increasing distrust of the Establishment, on account of Tractarian influences in it. But perhaps you know more of these matters than I do. If you meet with any works you think it would do good to review for the —— ——, will you kindly point them out to me?

I do fully concur in all you say, respecting the treatment of the erring *in personal* and *individual* intercourse, whenever opportunity occurs, though I deprecate every concession made to the *party* or to their *principles*, by word or deed, in general conflict; and on the open field—in the pulpit, in writing, or however else. Even there we may earnestly contend for the truth, without assailing persons or parties directly; but we may not modify and dress it, to avoid giving them a wound, or driving them away still farther from the Gospel. So I think, but still agree with all you have said, upon our communications with the misled, and the misleading individually. Excuse all this, and grant me the pleasure of hearing from you.

Most truly yours,
CAROLINE WILSON.

LV.—TO LADY * * * * *

August 25, 1843.

MY DEAR LADY ———,

I too had thought the *hiatus* unusually long, which only shows how much you have humoured me heretofore. I was apprehensive lest it might be caused by increase of anxiety for your precious grandson; and am delighted it was only the idleness, or rather relaxation,—for I do not believe that the first word ever applies to you,—of domestic pleasures. I perceive that I agree much more with you about the Millennium than with those from whom you differ. I do not think it so near as many do; and have a perfect persuasion of its being the seventh thousand of years: but then our dates are not sufficiently certain, to rest the calculation upon. I wholly agree with you in the rejection of those limited views of the Millennial kingdom: of which indeed I was not aware. I think too, assuredly, that all present things will be at an end; churches, ministrations, &c., all that characterizes the dispensation of the Spirit, which will itself be ended; but perhaps I anticipate a *sudden* termination, at the coming of the Son of man; you a gradual overthrow preparatory thereto. It may be so. I profess to *know* nothing.

I cannot define the C———'s views of baptism, because it does not seem to me they can do it themselves, owing perhaps to more than one person having treated the subject therein; and it is indeed not many of the *via media* people who can say what they mean. Like Armitage, they often think to rid themselves of the difficulty by inventing a new definition; which turns out to be only a new term, that really defines nothing. As I hold what are called *extreme views*, they are easily enough explained; though it may be thought not so easily proved. Calvin never cleared his *language*, whatever he did his views, of scholastic obscurity. Query: When he says infants are regenerated in baptism, does he mean *water* baptism, or baptism of the Holy Ghost, which may not accompany the ceremony; but which ceremony without it is *no baptism* in his mind? Or when he says regeneration, does he mean being born again of the Spirit unto life? It is quite certain the school-men used the word in a very different sense? These questions I cannot answer, being little acquainted with his writings. My view is different any way; for I believe nobody is *entitled* to be baptized at all, except on the assumption that they *are* regenerate, of which the required faith and repentance are the evidences received on profession from the adult,—

in hope and charity from the infant. If the assumption be a false one, there is (in Scripture language) *no baptism*, but an empty sign of a nonexistent thing, the *invalid half*, if I may so speak, —a seal set upon *nothing*. If I am right in supposing *previous regeneration* to be required of them that come to be baptized, it is plainly not baptism that confers it. You will perceive I thus make water-baptism nothing in the world but a *recognition* of a *fact*, and not the doer of it. If ever the Scripture seems to speak of baptism as more, I believe it means the baptism of the Holy Ghost and fire; and it is probable many of our older writers meant so too. As to the language of our church, I give it up, and stand upon her *intentions*, to be learned by weighing together the *whole* of her testimony. If she requires faith and repentance of them that come to be baptized, she requires the fruits of regeneration; and therefore cannot intend to *confer* that of which she requires the fruits beforehand. What unregenerate heart ever repented or believed? Of the other sacrament, I take just the same view; the bread and wine are *nothing*, as the water is *nothing, but the emblems. If* the soul is *previously* united to Christ, it feeds on HIM, *not them*—if it be not, it receives *nothing*. I have thus expressed my views in brief, as I have fully in my last work, "Christ our Law." It accords with those of Dean Milner, and others of his time, who exhausted the controversy, which we are reviving so painfully. I agree with you, both in judgment and in apprehension, about that master-piece of Satan—apostolical succession; may I not rather write, that *master lie?* * * * * I am glad to hear you have kept *something* of a journal, it *must be* valuable. There is one thing excites my curiosity, but I do not ask: It is,—I cannot think *how old* you are.

My life *has* been peculiar, in nothing so much so as my *conversion;* as unsought as Saul's of Tarsus, and far more resistant. I had no religion when you saw me. Perhaps that was the reason you refused me. I can remember nothing about our interview, but my disappointment: and I was too light-hearted to care a great deal about that. I think I wanted to go to Ireland. Unhappily I never kept a diary, or a memorandum of any kind; unless others have kept letters, there can be no material for my life but in my memory; but *seventeen* year's almost daily correspondence with my precious husband, will suffice for *that* period. These are preserved, but cannot be used in his lifetime. Up to that period, I shall put down from memory; there is little to relate since, in the quiet tenour of domestic happiness. God mercifully veils the future. Don't think me conceited, but God *must have his* glory in my salvation: there will be *none* to me—if the story is told rightly—but shame from first to last. Small ground for exultation, if I have had ten talents and paid the usury for only five. *You,* I am sure, will not construe this expression into a boast, nor disbelieve that the writing of it fills my eyes with tears. I *know* my mental powers to have exceeded the results: and if I write my life, instead of affecting to underrate them, I will *say so:* for it is to this hour *my heart's grief,* and will be to the end, my *grief of griefs.* It is so much so, so abidingly so, that any allusion to my talents goes through my heart like a sharp sword: producing an almost involuntary cry for pardon. I see so much more done, even *now,* by those who have less mental power than I have, to say nothing of the past. This is a terribly long gossip: but a proposed fit of idleness at the sea-side has been delayed a few days, and so left a vacuum. I think to be at Dover, but not more than three weeks, from Saturday next. Everywhere, believe me, dear Lady ——,

Your affectionate and obliged,
CAROLINE WILSON.

LVI.—TO LADY * * * * *

November 1, 1843.

MY DEAR LADY ———,

It is a too long time again, since I have written to you; one of the evils of which is like that of putting aside a book, one forgets where one left off. But yours is before me, and I must first say, that it really comforts me to find you are *not older*. Perhaps you will not thank me, for this sort of self-congratulation. You must needs be very weary, on so rough a road, although it has been no longer a one; but the double generations over whom your life has so near an influence, and so dear an interest, will prevent your counting impatiently the *other ten;* if it so please your Father you are to reach the natural age of man. Thank you, very, *very* much for the brief recital of your spiritual life. It is deeply interesting, just one of those that for God's glory, and most sovereign love, should be remembered and recorded. Whatever may be the advantage,—and there is much of *early* religious habits and impressions, by parentage and education,—there is the advantage on the side of adult and more sudden conversions, that they give an *experimental* witness to the *doctrines* of the gospel, much more difficult to shake than opinions otherwise imbibed. The "I know that I have passed from death to life;" is seldom in these cases assailable by human doubts and difficulties; or the mode and manner of the purpose, likely to become obscured, by the confusion of human disputation. Furthermore, *such* conversions do and must enhance our knowledge, of the "preciousness of Christ,"—" love much for much forgiven."

I am pleased again to find how little we differ. I think I may say, not at all, on the two subjects alluded to; Baptism and the Second Coming. The reason, I suppose, that mine are called *extreme* views, or that I at least, took possession of the word on my own behalf, is that among the persons called evangelical, (who would be included in the Puseyite term, *low church*,) there has arisen a confused, *higgledy-piggledy* notion of they know not what efficacy in the sacrament as such. Some confine it to the children of believers, some ascribe it to the faith of the sponsors; the most part mean nothing at all by it, only they will have it so; and dispute for words, against those who give a straight-forward avowal of just their own sentiments in plain terms. B——'s book is the stronghold of these confounders; and since the advance of Puseyism, all the moderados have betaken themselves to this confusion, in order to find shelter from the thunders of the *church;* and call all *extreme* who will not be puzzled too. So being of no such mind myself, for playing hide and seek, I took up the word these trimmers throw behind them, without very much care on whom it falls, so they escape the opprobrium of "*low church*," by proving an alibi for themselves. A name is shorter than an argument, and often does as well.

Poor S—— has certainly returned, *from* Rome, but *to* what? That is hard to guess; but he has expressed his conviction, that Rome is Babylon, and her worship of the Virgin, idolatry; and on that confession has re-communicated with us. More I know not. I know no more of the Christian Union Association than I learn from the *Record;* I think its tendency surely is to what you desire: a willing movement toward that union perhaps, which God alone can accomplish, or which I, at least, can anticipate only from a forcible separation of his people from all others. I still do not know, as I did not when you named it heretofore, any such movement toward separation in the church as you have heard of, nor can tell in what papers you have seen the apparent effort making. Every *English* churchman with whom I have spoken, without one exception, regrets the separation in Scotland, and considers it a mistake. True, our hearts are with them, for they are *the* brethren in Christ, suffering for conscience' sake, as they believe; but our judgment is against them, universally, as I believe. That many *expect* a similar separation among ourselves, is another thing; expectation is not intention. Noah expected the waters, and prepared; he neither wrought for them, nor invoked them. Surely it must be from the church's enemies you hear of these intentions; I mean from Dissenters or Puseyites. The only other quarter I can think of, is that of the Plymouth Brethren; but that is too inconsiderable and unstable a party to be worth the name of secession,—true godly souls as I believe they mostly are.

I am rejoiced to hear no worse a report of your little grandson, and trust the precious loan may be prolonged.

I hope I shall soon hear from you again. I wish among other things, to know if you are safe. You will be sure I feel with you respecting your two sons' opposing notoriety in the conflict, and read with peculiar interest every mention of their names: not without apprehension that it may at this moment be adding to your many cares.

Believe me with
True affection, yours,
CAROLINE WILSON.

LVII.—TO LADY * * * * *.

January 8, 1844.

MY DEAR LADY ———,

If any thing can heighten the interest of your letters to me, it is their containing matters so deeply interesting to yourself, as the subjects of your last. Being a great newspaper reader, and having you always in mind, I remark your son's progress with painful attention, and look out for his name, as if it belonged to me. Mr. M———, in his sermon yesterday on Abraham's trial, said many things that might have comforted you; but I am bad at repeating, having no verbal memory: the main purport was, that the blessings attached to affliction are not *direct*, else they would be most blest in hell: but the use of trial is, to put the mind in a fit state to *receive* a blessing—a state of humility, submission, and confidence. This is better effected by *not seeing* the purpose of God in it, which is comparatively a small exercise of faith. Abraham could have no idea *why* he was to slay his only child, nor may another father, whose only child is slain or taken from him; thence came the simple and pure faith, which fitted Abraham to receive the greatest blessing God himself could confer, but only such faith made him *capable* of enjoying. Are you not in Abraham's case, with respect to your son, and perhaps your grandchild too?

I feel some confidence that we should agree about *particular* and *general redemption*, if we could first define our terms. I don't know Luther's letter, or forget it; there is in some Calvinistic writers a hard, cold mode of setting forth these most precious doctrines, which is anything *but* like the way in which the Scripture gives them, and God intends them. "If Christ did not in *any sense* die for all mankind, why, I ask, is there a human soul at this moment out of hell?" said our preacher the other day. If Christ, in dying, *redeemed* all mankind, why is there a human soul in hell? The two questions will fence both sides, and *swamp* human reason, if you please, between them, for there is no way out. To the believer, there is no *experimental* difficulty, but most abundant blessedness in the mystery of the divine purpose; but it is as you truly say, an *incommunicable certainty*. Old William Howells was used to say, "Never mind these doctrines now; wait till you cannot do without them. Whenever you *fully* know the iniquity of your own heart, you will find you cannot be saved without election." I confess myself very grateful, however, for having had this point settled for me experimentally at the beginning, by the manner of my conversion, and so I think had you.

I wish I had written sooner, as I am rather anxious to hear from you again about yourself. That I did not, as I wish I had done, was occasioned by mere press of writing, in getting a book to press, and reviewing for the ———. If you meet with it, my articles are on Dr. C——'s Insanity, &c., Charlotte Elizabeth's Wrongs of Women, and a book, which I believe must be written by an *Irishman*—a Roman Catholic undisguisedly—perhaps you know? " Rome, Pagan and Papal." It is laughably mischievous, or mischievously laughable. I wonder if you ever got your MS. from C—— E——, which was the happy first occasion of my hearing from you. Her odd marriage turns out very well, I believe really happily; but she is going quite *beside herself* about the Jews: her last publication is painful to think of, as coming from so useful and respected a pen.

I suppose I am safe in using your last address. How does your book succeed? Believe me, dear Lady ——,

With great esteem, yours,
CAROLINE WILSON.

LVIII.—TO LADY * * * * *.

February 14, 1844.

MY DEAR LADY ——,

My gratitude must weigh against my ill-deserving, for your long and acceptable letter. A new book in hand, and a too cold house, which dulls down my faculties most miserably, have made me to be so great a defaulter of late. The thought of your having been ill, stimulates my self-reproach, which can only be appeased by writing immediately. Upon the subject-matter on which your mind is so ill at ease, I will only now tell you what I think *myself;* perhaps of some better authorities, as I meet with them, hereafter. I have not seen the book you speak of, but it is not a new thought to my mind, nor a new subject of discussion in my circle. Mr. —— would, I think, agree with what I am about to say exactly: and so would my heretofore *pope*, William Howells, who cleared my brain on that and many other points. Now what *I* think,—for I speak of myself, and for myself alone,—is, that Christ died for the whole of humanity, to the extent of removing from every one the *guilt* and *punishment* of imputed, original, or birth-sin, as it is variously called; so that nothing but actual sin will be brought into judgment against any one. Now if this be so, no child who dies before the age of responsibility, can perish; from imputed sin it is freed by the death of Christ; of actual sin it has not been capable. Into condemnation therefore it cannot come: to hell it cannot go. Now there is only one alternative; it must go to heaven—to glory. But while the remission of the original penalty of sin is thus made sure to the entire justification of the guiltless babe, by the work of the Son, on behalf of all mankind; the *principle* of sin derived from Adam remains, unless the Spirit also does His work; the fallen nature cannot go to heaven; the babe must be sanctified as well as justified; it must be born again. We assume, therefore, that those who die in infancy, are as necessarily regenerated by the Spirit, as they are justified in Christ. If you say this is inference only, and not proved, I think the latter position can be proved from Scripture, and that the former is a certain conclusion from it. It will be at once apparent, that if this is the process of infant salvation, there can be no difference between one child and another; an unconscious babe can neither lose nor acquire capability of sin by surrounding light or darkness. When the Bible tells me that Christ's blood was shed for the sins of Christendom, I will believe the remission of Adam's sin so limited; but while it is written, "the sins of the whole world," I can draw no lines of demarcation. As to supposing that a child is saved by Christian parentage, or Christian baptism, it is to me the purest fiction that human fancy ever invented: and something worse; for it is of the very essence of antichrist, making another Saviour, an earthly depositary for the benefit of the death of Christ; another "pair of keys," to lock and unlock, to kill and to make alive, which I would as soon trust to the "holy father" of Rome, as to the "holy mother" of England, or any ordinance or parentage therein. I find no such thing in Scripture; 1 Cor. vii. 14, having, to my mind, no relation to the *salvation* of a child. As to that Protean personage called "The Church," when she can be produced, we may come to some better understanding of her mind; at present her sons are all at variance, unable to decide on what she *says:* still less what she *means;* and should these be brought to agreement from Exeter to Chester, or the Shetlands, the all-important question would remain; If she be right, or wrong? I do not think, however, that the view we speak of is impugned by the expressions you quote; we *all* suppose them to be, *by nature,* the children of wrath; the question is, whether that nature has been changed by grace. In respect of burial, I hope " our mother" knows it has as little to do with salvation as baptism has; the one is the door of admission, the other of egress, to the *professing* church; there is abundant profession without faith, there can scarcely be faith without profession; and such cannot be accepted of the church unless it be made; how then can she bury an unbaptized adult? But nothing of this applies to infants; and for once only I can agree with Henry of Exeter, that it is very odd that people, who do not care to be baptized into the church, should wish to be buried from out of it. I have not quoted from Scripture, because your own two passages, 1 Cor. xv. 22; and Rom. v. 18, are the strongest I can recal to the establishment of my view, though assuredly not alone. All this is struck off in haste, because I would not delay to acknowledge yours, and inquire, not unanxiously, about your health. And this was the first subject of your letter, though there are many more that should be answered; whereas there is no point on which my mind is more thoroughly made up and made clear, to my own apprehension.

More I cannot write now; but soon again. I feel much for your family griefs and apprehensions. May they be blessed, or averted; and why not both? It has been to invalids dangerous weather, I apprehend. May *you* at least be spared to the many who cannot spare you. Indeed I shall not fail to be delighted with the shawl you so kindly propose to send; but why so kind to the unworthy?

Farewell—God and good angels guard you, in sickness or in health. Ever believe me,

Very affectionately yours,
CAROLINE WILSON.

P. S. Your last book is going to rebuke Tractarianism in Petersburgh.

LIX.—TO LADY * * * * *

March 8, 1844.

MY DEAR LADY ———

The book is finished, and the review gone to press, and I must give myself a holiday to write to you, or I shall never tell you what you wish. Your last kind letter made me sorry, as it implied that I must have expressed myself, otherwise than

I meant; since it produced regret on your part, for what you had written. I certainly did not *think* there was the least objection to the discussing of the subject between us, or any others of like mind, sedate and reasonable; but I did think M—— rash to put the thought in *print,* for the weak-minded and apprehensive. Whatever I said, this was what I meant. The "legitimate boundary" I spoke of, was not of "inquiry" into God's ways; but that while we *may* say God *permits* evil and sin for his own good purposes, we may never say or suppose he can for any purpose, be the *occasion* of it. I fear that remark led you to suppose, that I thought the discussion of the subject unwise; which I did not. Having set this matter right, I scarcely need say next, how much I should like to see you; and yet I have felt just as you do —the disappointment that always comes of a drawing-room interview—where people have previously expected much. In my own case, it is sure to come; by my natural and total want of tact and self-possession, which makes *nothing* of me at all times, except after long intimacy. Indeed, my want of confidence in conversation, even with the simplest and the meanest, limits my usefulness almost wholly to my pen, and is at times a great grief to me; especially since reputation has given a weight to my counsels, which might make my words useful, if I could only *get them out.* The fact is, I am in every sense of the word *timid.* All this does not mean that I will not see you, if you will allow me; in any manner that may be most agreeable to you.

I want to tell you what you ask about myself; but how shall I convey a just impression of what I was when mercy found me, in few enough words for a letter? For years I had never bent my knee in prayer, or any way recognized the existence of a God. I hated, and *knew* I hated—which is not commonly the case—the very *name* of God. Mine was an *understanding* enmity. I knew not only what is in the written word, but even the shades and colourings of opinion, in the construction of it. I had heard the Gospel and read controversy, as I read every thing else; and had even made up my mind, that if there were any thing in it at all, the Calvinists were right. But I believed it was all fiction together, and beneath an *intellectual being*, to be troubled about at all. Happily, I was always modest, and therefore I never gave utterance to my opinions. I believe even my brothers and sisters had no idea of *more* than absolute *indifference* to religion. It was far more—*indifference* has no existence in my nature—it was *hatred*. My brother, though he knew nothing of *this*, said of me that I was the most hopeless of his family. "There is the pride of intellect, that will never come down," was his expression. I *delighted* to hear the name of God and the truth of God made a jest of; but as to disliking the people of God, or saying anything to pain them, I should as soon have thought of hating a man for believing or disbelieving the Copernican system. You must guess the rest, or I shall never end; at the time of conversion, I was in a clergyman's family in Lincolnshire,—of the true old-fashioned high-church, in its coldest, stupidest, most inoffensive character. Mrs. Trimmer was their whole gospel. The necessity of going to church, the necessity of *hearing* the Bible read by my pupils, was to me a painful and *degrading* task; which could not but betray itself, though words they heard not from me about the matter. I held them, I fear I treated them, who only admired and petted *me*, in sovereign contempt. Without a shade of real religion themselves, they were of course shocked at my manifest disregard, of what they called so: but they never spoke to me upon it.

At this time, I violently attached myself to a lovely young woman of my own age, daughter of a neighbouring clergyman. *After my manner*, I wrapped myself up in this one satisfaction—my idol for the time being. I invested her with all the excellences she had or had not; no matter what she really was, (about which I have no clear opinion:) quite certain it is that she had *no* knowledge of true religion *at all*, and never pretended to have, and despised the GOSPEL OF CHRIST to the full as much as I did. But she had *a* religion— a *sentimental* desire for a better world, such as comes simply of disappointment in this. My inferior mentally, she surpassed me in the very thing I prided myself upon;—philosophy—in the conduct of ordinary life, to be *above* circumstances, misfortunes, disappointments, and all manner of " this world's wrongs," which we used to set ourselves to abuse, while we read Young's Night Thoughts, to avenge ourselves. In short, she always behaved well and acted properly, and spake wisely; while I, with all my knowledge and philosophy, was "a wild ass's colt:" with a mind beyond my own control, or that of any body else, and too artless to wear the guise of any thing I was not. I saw her advantage, and spoke often to her of it, lamenting my own want of self-control and submission to circumstances. This finally occasioned her, not having courage to *speak* to me of my want of *religion*, to write me a a letter, remonstrating with me upon it, and assuring me it was *religion* alone that gave her that advantage over me, which I so much admired and coveted. Now I can fully say that in this letter was no mention of *Christ*—no reference to the *Spirit*—no one word of the gospel method of salvation, or anything that might not have been said by a Socinian or a Deist; any one who believed in an over-ruling God, or a future state of happiness or misery.

On first reading it, my indignation knew no bounds: It was an insult upon my understanding —a presumption upon my friendship; I sat down and answered in all the bitterness of wounded pride, and unrestrained contempt. It happened the letter could not go that day, it was some miles off and nobody could take it. The next day—O what a day was that—I must not make remarks, but merely state facts. I felt that I was *moved, shaken.* What shame, what degradation; I, even *I* moved by such things as these! impossible. I could have buried my head in the earth for shame and humiliation. The only comfort was, *nobody could ever know it.* But this changed my purpose; —if I was to seem unmoved, why should I be angry? I burned the letter and wrote another, very kind, very dignified, very philosophical and high-minded, but quite indifferent, of course. It happened again the letter could not go, but my conflict was now with God; I loathed, I scorned, I refused, I told the blessed Redeemer, who by his Spirit was contending for me, that I would not yield—I *would not* have him—I *would not* be his. Words are not adapted to describe things like these, that pass between spirit and spirit without voice or word; and yet are more real than words could make them. I hated my friend for telling me; I hated myself for caring about what she said: but Oh! I hated most the blessed One who was thus trying to force upon me the *degradation* of his *name.* It was soon over; on the third day I wrote another letter; I owned the precious truth of what she had reproached me with; avowed my altered purpose, and acknowledged my obligation to her. Beyond that, I said nothing to any body at the time—they would have only mocked and and wondered and taken me for mad, and my friend would have been foremost in that opinion. All that they saw was, that I had *become religious* —that is, I read the Bible.

I became ill, and was almost immediately removed. But from *that third day*, all was changed to me; I read, I praised, I prayed, I rejoiced with joy unspeakable. I had nothing to learn as to the nature and manner and meaning of the change. I knew all *that* before, as *a fiction;* it was now an experimental truth. From that time Jesus was mine, and I was his; but Oh! what a soil it was for the seed to grow in! what a time before it could be wrought upon to profit; all to do, all to undo, and everything in the natural character against the work. However, you know the issue; it was hard work He undertook at first, and has been hard to the last. I have defeated Him, dishonoured Him, denied Him, *practically*, never professedly, a thousand, thousand times; but from that hour to this, I have never *doubted* Him. How could I? Had Paul himself more evidence than I had? No, for he had never been what I was, and he made no resistance. The recital is long, my time is gone; I leave you to make the comment on the bare text; but it may interest you to know, that my *friend* subsequently married a dignitary of the church, of high birth and indifferent character; forgot in her change of fortune, her preference of another world; affected fashionable life, derided all I said to her and wrote to her about the change, of which she had been the instrument; till, as my religious profession grew, being really unacceptable to herself, and offensive to her worldly irreligious husband, our acquaintance was broken off; and I know only by common report, that she died last year suddenly while dressing for a ball. Thus God has secured the whole glory to himself, there was none to the creature on any side. But I must break off here, and if I have omitted anything in your letter, that should be noticed, it shall be so hereafter:—The subject always *overwhelms* me;—meantime, believe me,

Very sincerely and affectionately,
CAROLINE WILSON.

LX.—TO LADY * * * * *

April, 1844.

MY DEAR LADY ———,

I delayed answering your last kind note, to find if any one here knew Mr. ——— well enough to desire him to call on you, which of course he would be well-pleased to do, if he knew you wished it. I do not know him, nor have I yet found any one who does. By report, I suppose he is the most evangelical in your part; whether up to our mark of divine orthodoxy, I am not sure, I never heard him. I believe he was a convert from Rome originally, and is certainly of good repute.

As to Mr. B——, I like none of all the things you speak of. "There is a way, that seemeth good unto a man," &c. We might say, it cannot be a bad way that gets a worldling out of bed, takes him to church, brings him within hearing, &c.; but is it so? Has not this been the way of Antichrist, from the beginning? Does not Satan know, that he has a stronger hold through the security of a false religion, than in the felt risk of no *religion.* Is not experience against our conclusions in this matter. I like your "words" from Abp. W—— on the unedifying use of Scripture. However, if I *liked* to go to church at eight o'clock, which I do not, I should abstain from it *now*, as I should from wearing a certain coloured ribbon at an election-time, which might please my fancy at any other period harmlessly. B—— is very notorious, and has made efforts to go farther, but was checked, either by the bishop or the people, as is stated variously. The eleven o'clock service, is a choice good luck, to the fair fanéantes of the West End; to ease them of a morning or two per week.

I am half tempted to ask, if I may send my husband to call on you some day. You would like him better than me;—everybody does; and they are right. But do not say Yes, if you had rather not be disturbed by strangers. I shall go on hoping to see you in some way. We are going, as I expect, to Tunbridge Wells on Monday next, for ten days at the utmost.

My new book is not christened. If you ever drive to Seeley's, ask him about it; for I cannot get him on with it. It is but a trifling concern, which seems to suit the age. "Too grave," "too deep," "too good;" is the bookseller's language now. So much for Gresley, Paget and Co. The gravest pens must betake themselves to lightness. My book is *intended* for the reading of idle people, on a Sunday afternoon; but I hope there are truths in it. Dear Lady ———

Very affectionately,
CAROLINE WILSON.

LXI.—TO LADY * * * * *

May 27, 1844.

My Dear Lady ———,

I inclose you C. E.'s answer. I just tore off the part of your letter that concerned her, and transmitted it without note or comment, on the subject-matter of it. You certainly have awakened my curiosity too, about Mr. Close, and will tell me, if you satisfy your own. I will ask Seeley about your friend's book, &c.; as to reviewing, I did ask, and am always obliged for a hint to this issue. Writing is as necessary to my brain, as to my purse: and the greatest part of the difficulty is always to find the subject. I am very glad of your report of Mr. Burgess; I never knew before, on sufficient authority, on what ground his good reputation stood, although I knew he had it. Still I wish he did *not* keep saints' days. I appreciate all the *bon hommie*, as well as Christian love, of your method of conformity; letting every body do as they like in things that do not signify; and would indeed that that were so, though I apprehend it is hardly compatible with the idea of an establishment, even in externals; however that be, it does not seem to me applicable to the case in question. Things unimportant in themselves, become important when they become significant of other things. When the wars of York and Lancaster deluged our land with blood, through great part of two centuries, no man, I apprehend, supposed it was the colour of roses about which they were contending; but I am afraid the peace-maker who should have adopted your plan, by wearing the red rose one day, and the white next, to mark his indifference to the colour of a flower, would have received a Lancastrian shaft through one lobe of his brain, and some Yorkist bullets into another; and verily, if our clergy will be doing the same thing, the fault is their own if they be mistrusted on both sides; and have their best intentions misinterpreted. Blood has flowed, the blood of the holiest and the wisest, has flowed abundantly and widely, about the worship of saints and the value of ordinances. We cannot plead ignorance of Satan's design in all this movement; we might know, we *do* know, that war has been proclaimed within our Protestant Establishment, against the Protestant faith. It is not *we* who are on the aggressive: we made no attack upon the taste of others for white and black; Wednesday or Thursday; fish or flesh. We *were* at peace, and then it did *not* signify. We are now attacked—besieged in our entrenchments; whether under these circumstances we should hoist our enemies' colours, and cede all our outworks at their first summons, I must refer you to the Duke of Wellington. My own view is, that in decision, not in compromise, our path of duty and of safety lies.

With respect to our intercourse with the party in the affairs of common life, I suppose the duty must vary with the circumstances. You have experienced, more perhaps than any one, the difficulty of holding spiritual intercourse and conversation with them. Where it does not resolve itself into disputation and contention, it must be very desirable to bring the truth to bear upon the erring and deluded proselytes of either form of apostacy; but it must still be simple, straightforward, uncompromising truth: or God will not bless it to the hearer or the speaker; and in most cases, it is difficult to get through without offence. I would not, however, discourage the attempt in any one who has at once courage and self-possession enough, to bear their master's banner unscathed through the enemies' lies, without making it a call to arms; an unavailing strife of words to no good issue.

Ever affectionately yours,
CAROLINE WILSON.

LXII.—TO MRS. * * *

July, 1844.

MY DEAR FRIEND,

It is due to your love, to tell you among the first of the final arrangement of our long expected move. Within three weeks, we draw our stakes and loosen our cords, to fix our tent elsewhere. I hardly know how I feel about it: perhaps as you would if you were leaving * * *; perhaps as a donkey does when he has tossed his load on his head, and stands kicking his heels up in the air, without well knowing what is to follow. *Glad*, I am sure I am, but whether to be eased of superfluous good, or of the care that for the two last years has embittered it, I am not sure. Dishonest indeed I have been to my heavenly Father, if I have not truly told Him in every prayer, that I am willing to relinquish any temporal enjoyment for the spiritual advantages I expect. *I am* willing, I am desirous: I am very grateful to be allowed the change, if this is to be the issue, which He only knows, who hears my constant and abiding prayer, to have less of the world, and more of *Him* and *His*.

We have taken a very comfortable house at ———, very pleasantly situated, but with *no* garden. Only think how I shall enjoy myself when I come *thence* to visit you; and, dear friend, if ever you come to visit us, you will take of *our* fruits and flowers, as we of yours, for you *shall* stay one Sunday. Meantime, you must think of me as half-distracted with cornices and canopies and carpeting; and *all* longing for a house not made with hands, that will not need this trumpery. Till this is over, I may not see you, scarce think of you—but still be,

Ever affectionately yours,
CAROLINE WILSON.

LXIII.—TO MRS. * * *

July, 1844.

MY DEAR FRIEND,

I wanted you to speak to me of your position, not because I did not know it, but because until you did so, I could not properly speak of it to you, to express my sympathy and feelings for you. These are greater than my surprise, for I think you have had apprehensions of the kind for some time, and many other things gave indication of what might come to pass. But farther than this I have thought, that if God had purposes of lovingkindness towards all or any of you, some such thing *must* come to pass, to arrest a course as painful I am sure to *you*, as grievous to all your friends, and ruinous to your dear children. Now the messenger has come, and you must call the place *Bochim*.* And so you will; and you will think beside, how much severer a message of reproof it might have been. There might have been a summons without warning; there might have been the cutting off of children, in the midst of earthliness and error; or *you*, dear, might have been called upon to leave them, uncertain whether they would have followed where you go. Now all of these things are spared you, and time given for finding, or returning, to the way of life. It is a painful, very painful dispensation: do not suppose I think lightly of it, but I do hope the temporal loss, and temporary privation, may be your gain in spiritual enjoyment even now, besides the eternal issues affecting those you love. Be sure that all that concerns you remains upon our hearts with real interest. If you should remain the summer at ————, and at any time feel that our coming would not be oppressive and disagreeable to other parties, we should have great pleasure in seeing you there

* Judges ii.

once again. I always find my love grow on the declining prosperity of my friends; I rather think it is the character of *Christian* affection to do so, for I believe our gracious Master does the same; more tender towards the sick ones of the household. But worldly feelings understand not this: and you must be candid, and not ask us, if it will be unpleasant to any body. I could most wish to hear the place was gone, for I know by experience, how painful the *going* is, and how much better over. But I tell you how the delay will act to your advantage; you will look upon every thing with painful feelings, till your heart is wholly weaned from them; and then, when the leaving comes, instead of being a painful effort to resign them, it will be a grateful sense of satisfaction as for a great relief. So, dear friend, let your heavenly Father manage it in his own way. If you have retained the light of His countenance, that is enough for *you*, and for the rest, *hope all things;* striving only to be faithful to them, as you are to Him; and not to do, as He does not, lose his children by too indulgent love. I was, as usual, much pleased with ———, and much with all she seemed to feel upon this painful subject. In her, God has, I trust, given you an abiding blessing, that will, under all circumstances, administer to your comfort or consolation.

Let us try to look on the bright side still, and count your gains instead of losses. I do not wonder at your temporary depression; but that will not return; it was only to break you into more peaceful submission. This done, the opposing barrier of self-will broken away, the stream will run more smoothly: though at times it swell, it shall not overflow, to go over you. "When thou passest through the waters, I will be with thee."

Ever affectionately Yours,
CAROLINE WILSON.

LXIV.—TO LADY * * * * *

September 14, 1844.

MY DEAR LADY ———,

Much and many thanks for two prompt and welcome notes. I shall give all attention to your lists, but rather apprehend you are in the wrong class of books, for the C——— ———. Such as the ——— ———, &c., are too trifling, others too long out. Reviews of that sort take only notice of new publications; the C——— ——— only of those that, more or less, can be made to bear upon religion; and are of some weight for or against the truth. Not tales or novels, I apprehend, unless weight be given by the names of men, who write them; as was the case with Messrs. Paget and Gresley.

The thing that most astounds my incapability, is how you can read so many sermons. I cannot read any; and Seeley would tell you *nobody* reads sermons: as he says to all that propose to print them. I do not think more than the *brief notices*, at the end of the C——— ———, could be acceptable on that head, not worth the work of reading for. The only one you have so kindly troubled yourself to register, that does not appear to me too old, or too trifling for a lengthened review, may be Lady C. L———; if, as you say, it is likely to have influence:—query whether it can have any, or will be heard of, where the ——— ——— is read, which is not among *fashionables* assuredly; whereas we of the graver sort, who read and write, do not require information upon works that never appear amongst us. You may know otherwise; but I have an impression, the ——— ——— only moves among the clergy and others, of the more decided tone. I will ask S———, if Lady C. L——— is suitable; but, you ask me to tell you, what I hear about it: the probability is, I shall never meet an individual who has heard of it; so little are such books thought of in my sphere. For myself, I deprecate religious novels wholly and entirely; and never should open one, but for the specific purpose of reviewing. Re-perusing your former letters, I can heartily join in your *wish*, if not your *hope* about field-preaching. Our church is *not*, in her present form, the church of the people, but of the upper half of them; and so it will remain, while the supposed remedy for our need is church-building, instead of gospel preaching. But, alas! the tide runs all in that direction, and I see no prospect of a reflux. I rather anticipate that the dominant party will lay the cold hand of formality on all of life or utility that is within its reach, until,—I cannot, and you will not wish that time arrived—when here, as in Scotland, we shall worship in the highways, for lack of the churches, from which we shall be ejected. So speaks my prophetic muse. May she prove a lying prophet, is my wish and prayer; but, "Give peace in our time, O Lord," is the very utmost that my faith can compass, even in the prayerful utterance of my wishes.

It is needless to repeat, that I do not agree with your *Clericus,* as to where our safety and our wisdom lies; having so fully heretofore explained myself to you. I see no authority in the Bible for his views. I shall meditate the subject, on which you wish me to "write a book, for I terribly want to begin one now; and I shall be greatly obliged by any explanation of your views about it. Assuredly you know *that* world better than I do *now;* though once I did, which made the " Listener" so mischievously efficacious. I rejoice to find you well enough to dine *en masse.* I am too nervous, (vulgariter, *shy,*) for a table d'hôte, it takes my appetite right away; but I dare say you often find very pleasant acquaintance in that manner. *Out of doors* gaiety is by no means so disturbing to me; and I delight myself greatly with the drums, trumpets and guns, flying artillery, and battery practice, that goes on before my windows every day.

C. WILSON.

LXV.—TO LADY * * * * *.

Woolwich Common, Dec. 16, 1844.

MY DEAR LADY ———,

While I have not written to you, I have been doing your bidding—smashing Lady C. L——— to my heart's content—shame on her; if she is a child of God, if not, I have nothing to say about it. It is sensible and well-written, after her manner, but I wish I had power to extinguish such books for ever. You will see what I mean in the next ——— ———; I wish *she* could read it without knowing whence it came. I would not criticise minutely what I deprecate *wholly*—the *better* the *worse* is all I can say. To please S———, I touched on all the other books, which is as you suppose, a common practice, where there is something in common, and not gone by in time. The worst of reviewing such books is the necessity of reading them—the pleasure of abusing them is great.

Do tell me everything you take the trouble of thinking about my writing, past, and especially future, for I am really at a loss often what to set about. Miss F——— is a near neighbour, but I have not met her yet, nor do I know her writing. I do not think you say truly of yourself respecting the unconverted. Our feeling towards them *cannot* be too strong; is never, I believe, strong enough, at least my own is not; and yet I would do any thing to save a soul, if I thought I possibly might, in preference to every other work of love, for it is surely first. Whether I think the *preaching of the law* in the first instance is the best and likeliest method to bring the soul to Christ, is another thing; perhaps I do not, but it may be so sometimes: and I am still thinking of what you suggest, and always am delighted and obliged with your suggestions,—so pray go on. I am sure your walk in life is a very important one, and God has especially endowed you for it, to sing the Lord's song in a strange land; where I, alas, should hang my silent harp upon the willows—for very sadness. How easily would you answer your own question. " Why is this?" I wish I could transmit you *all* a sermon I just now heard upon " We have this treasure in earthen vessels;" but there is enough in the text to solve your problem. If we had it always in the fine porcelain of the earth, we should straightway fancy there was some value in the vessel itself; and if it were gilded quite over the base clay, we should straightway believe the clay itself was gold. Is not God's glory always his first object in those he loves and saves? and does He not well to manifest, how little *his Pearl* can lose or gain by the more or less beauty of the setting?

This I say with reference to your first remark, about good feeling and high principle in the people of the world. I cannot admit the fact generally, that those who live in sin *are God's people at all,* whatever they may have professed. False profession is truly very painful and disheartening, and sends us to the *Word,* to try our ground again; whether we believe an empty fable. No more now, but do write to your

Most undeserving,
CAROLINE WILSON.

LXVI.——TO LADY * * * * *

November 22, 1844.

MY DEAR LADY ————

I feel it a long time since I communicated with you. I think continually about you, nevertheless, wonder how you are going on; hope you are getting more accustomed to your strange position; more cheerful and peaceful under your reverses; more joyful in anticipation, and in memory less sad; and then I ask myself why, since I want to know all this, I do not write and ask? Thank you for all such information given in your last, and do believe that you cannot write anything, about yourself and yours, that does not wake my sympathy to pleasure or to pain. It is always a satisfaction to me, that I know your island-home; and where you walk, and what you see, and who you live amongst. I can imagine winter makes as little change in your beauties, as can be anywhere,— one great advantage of the sea, and the sea-tempered atmosphere. Glad I was to hear you had achieved anything like a *home of your own*, that is a house to yourself, instead of furnished lodgings. I could think of few things, so little likely to *be mental improvement*, as the study of German and Italian authors; wherefore it was I wished ——— occupied with something better. Meantime do not take my words for more than they mean. She is young, unformed, and inexperienced, quite capable and quite likely to grow wiser as well as older; and to be turned away from the erroneous views and dangerous fantasies that now bewilder her. But of deep importance, of tremendous importance is it, what influence she abides under now, whether of companionship or books; for that which makes one smile, as the folly of a girl, will make one sad indeed as the delusion of a woman. Truly sorry I am on her account as well as yours, that the S———s have left you; and so withdrawn the better influence of their better minds. May the Divine light and grace, dearest friend, make you all I once knew you; except in that which cannot be restored here, but will be hereafter; and make your dear child, all that you once wished her, and I once hoped to see her: then we shall be agreed again in opinion, as we are now in love for each other and interest for her. That it will be so I hope and expect, because in looking to the future, I cannot forget the past. We are all here going on prosperously, and I hope thankfully; liking Woolwich extremely; and not insensible of our great responsibility, if with so much privilege, of those that plant and water, and Him that giveth increase, we grow not up in daily increasing stature, and fulness of Christ.

Dear Milady, may we meet again; meantime, let there be openness and faithfulness and confidence, not *mystery*, between us, even while there cannot be agreement. With kindest wishes to the young Islander, believe me,

Ever yours, most affectionately,
CAROLINE WILSON.

P. S.—There is but one subject, dearest, of your letter which must be an embarrassment between us; because I cannot speak my mind upon it, without giving you pain, at a time when I feel that you have pain enough; and yet you must feel my *silence* says as much as if I spoke my mind; with more liability of misapprehension. *Prejudice* in my mind, must necessarily be all in *favour* of *your child*. But after all, there really cannot be much mystery between us, about the matter. You have known my mind so long and intimately heretofore on all matters, but especially on religion, and that mind remains so wholly and entirely unchanged, it cannot be unknown to you or any wise a secret from you, that your dear child *is not* what *I* would have her; and in other and better days, did confidently hope from her. The miserable nonsense I saw her read, the mistaken views I heard her express, and the influence under which I saw her to be thinking, feeling, and acting, gave occasion to my earnestly-expressed hope, that her new friends would be wiser than her old ones; and lead her back to the paths of truth and peace.

LXVII.—TO LADY * * * * *

January 6, 1845.

My dear Lady ——

I cannot think how it is I am so long in writing, while the non-arrival of letters from you is to myself so great a *miss*. Thought rather than time, has perhaps been pre-occupied—to say nothing of *Christmas in London*, which slays my intellectual being dead.

I have just lost another of my sometime many sisters; for I was at the *fag*-end of a family of ten. It is no cause of grief, but rather of exalted joy, that one so sweet and saint-like, at an advanced age, and with nothing to leave on earth, has put on a long-expected crown. My only thought of sadness is something about survivorship in a fast-emptying world—a sort of *lag-behind*, when so many are gone before. We must put away such feelings, and be ashamed of impatience in our day's work. If I did it better, I think I should be less impatient. Enough of self. All compliments, good wishes, and bright blessings of the season to *yourself*.

We are in some spirits about your neighbour of Exeter; we shall beat *him*, and thereby keep other meddlers quiet, I trust. It is encouraging, too, to find in the laity so much care about the matter. That *the people* would not become Tractarian, I was always sure; and one of the many evils therefrom to be anticipated, I thought was, that we should have one religion for the people, and another for the aristocracy: a calamitous point in any nation's history. I scarcely hoped for so speedy and spirited a resistance of the first inroads. *You* will not be so much pleased as I am, to see the first battle fought and victory gained, over the black and white gown. I have not read the "Cross and Crescent." It was ordered for our Reading Society, but I believe is to be suppressed as too *free:* in which case I shall not see it. I am not for reviewing *much*, having a book in hand; only in case of something *very* desirable.

We find your Dublin Magazine very *intelligent;* I have forgotten to say, "thank'ye" for it. Let me have the pleasure of hearing soon, if only that you are well; and I will try to seem more grateful in future. Reverting to your letter, I see your mention of Dr. Arnold. Why! you would *laugh* if you could hear *all* I say about it; because my admiration exceeds the limit of common parlance, and runs riot. It is long since I have or shall *so* like another book; so new, so fresh, so lofty, so pure, so independent; but if I were to characterize it all in one word, it would be SENSE. Farewell, I hope you will mention the precious child when you write.

Most affectionately yours,
CAROLINE WILSON.

LXVIII.—TO LADY * * * * *

February 22, 1845.

MY DEAR LADY ———

I must take occasion of the thanks due to you for the pretty shawl, just arrived, to perfect my answer to your letter. The shawl arrived by post two days since, and also a note from Mrs. ———, requesting me to let her know that I received it, which of course I did. The workmanship is very good, and the texture most delicate; I beg you to believe I shall have much gratification in wearing it as your gift. For the subject-matter yet unanswered of your last nice long letter——I am not surprised that *you* cannot *feel* the importance of these petty innovations, seeing that to you they are not so, being really habituated to such things in ———; but if any clergyman *in England* now persists in them, contrary to the known habits and wishes of an English congregation, it is a perversity impossible to conceive, if *he does not* attach importance to them; and *if he does*, that importance stands upon the ruinous corruption of our faith. If they *be* insignificant, why offend with them even *one* of the weakest of their flock; much more, why offend the whole weight of public opinion in our country? It is difficult to set limits to mortal absurdity; but the man who does this, *without* an ulterior meaning, passes my most generous indulgence for his folly; and, moreover, exceeds my credulity of the fact. You may know otherwise. I forgot in the haste of my last, to say that I think the extract formerly inclosed, is very suitable to the times: and in effect most true, as to where the danger *hides* itself; and therefore is most dangerous.

There is an ——— influence again, perhaps, in your opinion of Arnold's book, and also a political one, which does not weigh so heavily with me. A Tory I am, most entirely; but not having, like yourself, others to think for, such matters do not affect my estimate of a character, nor my enjoyment of a book. I do not agree with Arnold in a hundred things: but I do admire him more than I have done man of woman born for many a day; and have not hesitated to recommend the work to any one. However, you are not alone; opinions run so high for and against the book, it is dangerous to name it in company, lest you open a fire of disputation. Nothing, however, seems to abate the vivacity of *my* enthusiasm in his favour; there is no accounting sometimes for peculiar sympathies with character; but never to me can superficial spots upon the disc, be conjured into an eclipse. What do you think of the Irish Education schemes?

I suppose it is yet doubtful whether the Oxford sentence against W —— is good in law; but whether or not, it is a great triumph of the right that it has been past. Like another great agitator he can only come off on a technicality: which will not affect the view of his deserts. The decease of the Camden Society is another glorious issue of our struggle. Your ——— must be, by your last account of him, very little deserving to be ranked among the innovators. I cannot but foresee he will soon doff their colours, if he still wears them.

I did not say more about the particular story of Sir ———, because *prohibition*, not *criticism*, was my object. It matters not what is in it. I wished it, and all like it, whether better or worse, *unwritten* and *unread,* which makes of no moment the morality of the story, or the lessons it conveys. I feel much as you express yourself of the baptismal tract. The man who writes it ought not to use the baptismal service; nor he who believes it; therefore it is a pity so to enhance the difficulties of a conscientious minister of our church.

I hope to hear you are better, and your interesting invalid at least not worse. What a fearful treasure is that sweet child; but the other is the darkest cloud still.

I wish you would not get up so soon in the morning; I don't like works of supererogation, and think it cannot be good for you. Now farewell, with many thanks, for all kind words and thoughts and deeds. You are the only person who extracts a long letter from me, and they but little worth: for it is a by-gone talent with me to write a letter. Yet I am

Ever affectionately yours:
CAROLINE WILSON.

LXIX.—TO LADY * * * * *

May 26, 1845.

MY DEAR LADY ——,

I was delighted at sight of your letter, which if mine reached you at all, it crossed on the road. I am not surprised that you cannot find *my felicities* in the Isle of Wight, any more than *my horrors* in London. All these things depend, most happily, on habits, tastes and feelings, infinitely and beneficently varied according to our health, position and estate. I did not think you would find very much of higher and better things; and so it proves. The main subject between us this time, is to be *Mesmerism*, you say. Upon this my mind is very well made up, in despite of C. E. and Miss M———, only I do wish that wise women would not write nonsense. *If* Mesmerism has cured *anybody* of *anything*, as I dare say it has, it is of course available as a remedy for disease; and it appears to me perfectly absurd, to suppose it less lawful than any other means. It is simply a matter of experiment and fact; and certainly I should try it, if I believed in its efficacy; which would depend not on argument but fact, taken not upon opinion but testimony. *At present* I believe it is occasionally, not generally, efficacious. For all other purposes, I believe it a mixture of delusion and imposture. I strike off a large part of its wonders, as deliberate deception; another part as ignorant delusions; and all that remains, such as real fits of insensibility, hysterics, somnambulancy, that may be superinduced on weak, sensitive and nervous subjects, to be perfectly explicable on well-known natural principles, without supposing anything supernatural. If I believed it more, I should believe it unlawful; but even so, I should avoid it as monstrously foolish and dangerous, unless medically applied. As to what *pious clergymen* may write or say, it is a fact against which experience cannot close its eyes, that the grace of God which imparts to his servants so much of better things, does not endow them with worldly wisdom, or give them sound judgment upon matters not directly spiritual; there is no manner of vagary, by which sound and good men have not been for a time deluded; and I am fain to confess thereon, that their testimony carries with it little weight to my mind, except it be statements of plain fact, or the evidence of their own senses, without note or comment. At the same time, I own no sympathy with those who, like ———, &c., refer all such matters to Satanic influence. Satan is wiser than his instruments, he takes advantage of all human follies; if he invented them he would do it better, as I think. So wonderful and curious are the operations and influences of nature, nothing of that sort passes my belief; but I am, for that very reason, slow to accept evidence of supernatural influence.

* * * * * * * Assuredly your daughter cannot be wrong, to try *all* means with her dear boy, and hope and pray to the last. Your new charge is a heavy and affecting one. I suspect few are so well endowed as yourself, to meet it and fulfil it; and wisdom and power, not your own, will assuredly be added unto you. It is an affecting case, and yet how much mercy and amelioration in it. May God support and guide you, as he will. I don't know your house by it's name; so perhaps it is not where I guessed. My writing stands sadly still, from seeing too much company; which is not so good for me as thought and paper. In haste and bustle still

Most affectionately yours,
CAROLINE WILSON.

LXX.—TO LADY * * * * *

July 1, 1845.

MY DEAR LADY ———

Time has stolen on, and I have not thanked you for a much-desired letter, desired they always are; but most after delay. Reasons about as usual with myself, writing and a good deal of company in and out, tending to distraction of thought. I hope Southampton will agree with you better than the Island; but am accustomed to think it a relaxing air, and not healthful. I believe, however, these are mostly relative rather than abstract propositions, according to the constitution on which they act. I am quite concerned for your many and not light troubles; but do trust that they will subside, as the most troubled waters are wont to do, at the Divine word. Meantime there is no more to say, but "Fear not, for I am with thee."

We are, thank God, much as usual, spared all the heavier trials of humanity, and I trust grateful for health and peace; but most of all for grace and pardon, and a brighter world to come. Next week I expect we are going from home, to Folkestone first, for about three weeks; but if you are kind enough to write, I shall be anxious for a few words of medical report; and your letters will be forwarded wherever I may be. Let me not be long ignorant where to find you, at any time. Poor Ireland seems to fall from bad to worse, and who can even pretend to read the issue? * * * * The religious aspect of things looks all of one colour, and that a sombre one, as if men—rulers at least—were determined to level all, and cast Truth quite out of the account, till God be professedly, as well as virtually, forgotten; and all distinctions of truth and error denied. This very liberalism gives the Puseyites a check, for the present at least. God knows his own purposes in all; and will give us, I trust, submission. Oh! when will patience have its perfect work? It is far from it still in me.

I pray God to restore your family to health, and to amend your own. Ever believe me,
Very affectionately yours,
CAROLINE WILSON.

LXXI.—TO LADY * * * * *

September 8, 1845.

My dear Lady ———

I was glad indeed to receive your kind note yesterday. I had been really anxious, yet was afraid to trouble you with inquiry. Thank God for your restoration, which most heartily I do, though the least of the many who cannot spare you. We always feared the Southampton atmosphere for you: but you have had a heavy weight of cares as well; and though I believe you are not so nervous a person as myself, where is the temperament that does not more or less suffer bodily for the mind's sorrowing and carefulness? I can well believe, that the near vision of eternity at hand, has so far lightened them as to increase your perception of their nothingness, and reduce to a minimum of difference life's best and worst. But then you are feeling so much for others, who have still a life before them, desolate and bereaved of their most precious child. May you be strengthened and comforted, both with them and in them. Spare yourself, meantime, from all bodily and mental labour that can be dispensed with, however much it deprives your absent friends of your communications.

Under the circumstances, I feel ashamed almost to intrude even this letter upon you, unless I know something which it would interest you to speak of. But oh! how minor interests sink and fade before the shadows of earthly sorrow, or lights of unearthly joy; and both ways your thoughts have been withdrawn from common converse upon common topics. We are just arrived at home from our short holiday, at Folkestone first, and then at *Southborough,* my haven of delightsome refuge from the *dust* and *brownness* of this worn and weary region of the habited world; where the oak-tree and the heather cure all my maladies of mind and body. In haste and unsettledness, therefore, I write to say how anxiously and sympathizingly I am,

Ever yours,
CAROLINE WILSON.

LXXII.—TO MRS. * * *

September, 1845.

MY DEAR FRIEND,

Truly glad am I to get your note, though in one sense it is just too late. We postponed as late as we could our promised visit to ——, in hope to hear from you, but could not make up our minds to write to you. You will have no difficulty, I trust, to understand our feeling in this. We knew how many you have to please, and felt the probability, that at such a time as this, our presence might not be agreeable to every body, however much so to you. We feared, if we wrote, you would not like to refuse us, and that perhaps some one would be annoyed, or you embarrassed; so that after much talk, and much hesitation, we resolved to give it up, and we only yesterday returned from ⸺⸺. My husband says he cannot make holiday again. We have three school-girls coming to us to-morrow for Michaelmas, and a further reason for *us* is, you know, that we cannot afford as many movements as we should like; therefore I fear it must be given up for this season, though I confess myself a little vexed, that your letter failed by a *single day* to find us at ⸺⸺, whence possibly we might have stolen just till Saturday or Monday. However, we felt, whilst we should have sincerely liked to come, some little delicacy about it. I am thankful, dearest, for the tone and spirit in which you are able to *wait*. That, I apprehend, is your lesson now; and when that is learned, you will be taught and enabled to *submit*. It is so our graces are maintained, our spirits perfected in Christ: here a little and there a little, as we need it, and can bear it; but done it must be. "Patience must have her perfect work," and no one grace be wanting at the last. Happiest they that are the aptest scholars, to learn their lesson fastest, and be dismissed from tutelage to their most blessed home. Do give my love to all, for in some sort I do feel for all. I have been a little out of health this summer, but was much mended by my sojourn at Southborough; and am still further improved by the few days passed at ————. Is it not the greatest of all blessings, that you can say, you are *all* well. Let me hear of you now and then, for I get thinking of you anxiously sometimes. I don't suppose I shall be from home again till Christmas: then in town; but I fear you will not be to be seen then. Be sure I shall try to see you whenever I can, for your trials deepen my feeling of interest in you; nevertheless, you *have* cause for great praises still.

Ever affectionately yours,
CAROLINE WILSON.

LXXIII.—TO LADY * * * * *

October 20, 1845.

MY DEAR LADY ——

I do not think I can be happy any longer without writing to you; and yet not to make you write, more than six words. I know how you are occupied, with a too painful certainty, without supposing you ill.

The calamities of others dwell much upon my mind, when coming within personal cognizance; sometimes with great gratitude; sometimes with timid apprehensiveness; as if they *must* come to me next. I do not consider this last a feeling to be encouraged, because it is a prejudging of the Divine purpose, and a sort of self-influence not required of us. I apprehend, that to think with grateful satisfaction how we are spared while others suffer, is a better thing, and equally efficient to secure sympathy, and make us to go softly. That I think of your daughter, and of your suffering with her and for her, is not surprising, missing the continual pleasure of your letters, and knowing that illness or sorrowful occupation is the cause. I will hope not the former. Can I do anything for you, say anything to you, or anything about you, in all your suspended labours?

I am quite settled in again for the winter, and hope, if health and peace is granted, now to complete the book some time in hand. *We* are thinking much, perhaps as often before, with exaggeration, of the condition of the sister island. At all hands, a trying winter seems preparing for the poor. I doubt not, because I have had too long observation of the fact, that something will turn out to lessen the difficulties that overhang. In public and in private, I have always seen it so. No calamity, no grief, no difficulty, proves as great in fact, as it seems in idea; and that by reason of some uncalculated good thrown providentially into it. Have you not seen it so, not as an *accident*, but as a *rule* in the Divine economy? I think I have, and it makes me always rather impatient of *croakers* and *alarmists*, in their talk of things to come. Nevertheless, we have much to think of, and much to watch and wait for, in the aspect of things around us. The secession of Messrs. Newman & Co., seems to me unmixed good: it will undeceive the conscientious and alarm the time-serving, who were following in their steps, but never meant their conclusion; and I think it will open the eyes of the rulers in Church and State to all they care about: the political and hierarchical consequence of encouraging the movement. * * * I should like, for my own part, a more expansive besom, and a wider sweep. I suppose this *union* attempt at Liverpool is after your own heart. It would be after mine, if I had any hope of its success, but am fearful it will lack results. Nevertheless, it is worth the trial, for the sin of God's people is enormous: not by separation from the church, or adherence to it, but by separation and disavowal of each other. I know nothing, however, of this, or anything but what I see in the newspapers and magazines; so completely am I secluded here from the intercourse of men, religiously and politically informed; therefore am simply prating my own thoughts, for the mere pleasure of talking *to you*, I believe. I will trouble you with no more, lest it prove ill-timed: but must be,

Ever most affectionately yours,
CAROLINE WILSON.

LXXIV.—TO MRS. * * *

December 31, 1845.

MY DEAR FRIEND,

Very sensible of your great interest and feeling for me, expressed in your note, and well known before, I have yet purposely delayed writing, till a little further progress should be made in the treatment of my complaint, in hope to report satisfactorily. Thank God, I am fully enabled to do so. I saw A—— again on Saturday, and he seemed quite satisfied, and almost surprised, I thought, at the measure of his own success. My general health meantime, is better than it has been for a twelvemonth; my mind at rest, and my spirits restored. So I think you will say it ought to be as happy a Christmas, as gratitude can make it. I have been afraid to be too sanguine, lest another blow should come, but that is wrong. Thankfulness should not be kept in check by mistrust; seeing that if disappointment do come, I have had proof that strength and guidance will abundantly come with it. I am more persuaded daily, of what I care most about, bodily; that the disease was an accident, whilst there is every reason now to believe, it will be entirely removed. Such is the aspect now; it may be otherwise; but I am trying to do, what I am sure, it is best to do, to live *each day separately*, enjoying its own good, submitting to its own evil; but not losing the benefit and present grace of either, in looking forward to what may be hereafter. If we did always so, few days there would be, in which thankfulness for good possessed, would not preponderate; and those few would not be farther darkened, by apprehensions and regrets. It is my nature to be too timid, too apprehensive, too imaginative of unreal evils; but this is not creditable to faith and love, and I would have it otherwise." "He shall be delivered from *fear* of evil," is a great promise. Thank you, dear, for all you write, of kindly and of spiritual feeling. You are very kind to propose * * * *. We made our yearly visit at Christmas in town, and may not at present egress again. Indeed I am too marvellously well to make it at all necessary:—there have been times and may be again, when I have thought it would be a great relief to stay a few days with friends, to change the current of things; and should such return, I shall remember what you said, and ask you if it will suit you to receive us. Every kind wish and blessing of the season, to you and yours.

Very affectionately yours,
CAROLINE WILSON.

LXXV.—TO MRS. M——.

May, 1846.

My dear Mrs. M——,

Thank you, dear, for your salutations, pleasing reports, and kind inquiries. I thought on you on Sunday. I cannot say wistfully. I had made up my mind to a *dies non*, so far as human ministrations are concerned, whereas my exhilarated spirits, and the delights surrounding me, supply at once the temple and the music. I am so much better, so different to my own feelings. I had a mind to ask you, if the Mrs. W—— of Queen's Terrace is still there, so little can I believe that this is she. The weather has been so exquisite, the place is so beautiful, I cannot tell you how much we are enjoying it; perhaps it needs the long and dreary weight of dulness that has been upon me, to feel the delight of being again *alive*, in full enjoyment of God in his works, and of his works in him. In these best moments, when the soul goes free of earthly pressure, we do not feel the need of earthly help; but, alas! the pressure will return, and because "the well is deep," we then need the stronger arm to help us to draw therefrom; and very sad, and very saddening it is, that with three churches, the several ministers of which seem really intent to do their duty, and two or three curates beside; the preaching is so inefficient, one can scarcely suppose a slumbering soul wakened, or a waking one elevated by any one of them. Well, well, in that blest time you talk of, we shall have done with our rushlights; to fear their removal, or bewail their dimness, where neither sun nor moon will be any more needed, but "the Lamb is the light thereof." Aye truly, as you suggest, if this exquisite creation be the place accursed of our captivity, what will be the beauty, call it earth or heaven, of our kingly dwelling-place, when we reign with Christ. The *two last* words comprise all I know, and all I care about it. I am delighted to hear my five children are better, all kindness to them and remembrance to dear friends. Do not expect us before Monday. I am afraid to look sadly *glum* when the time comes, but ever,

Affectionately yours,
CAROLINE WILSON.

LXXVI.—TO MR. B——.

August 20, 1846.

MY DEAR SIR,

Often in the thoughts of my head upon my bed, it has occurred to me "What must Mr. B—— think? no inquiries, no renewal of invitation, or notice taken of his illness." I have been very ill too, worse than you, in some sense, since you seem to have been about your business. I have only wandered from room to room these five weeks. Illness, incident to the extraordinary season, I suppose, so dashing me, and laying me prostrate altogether, it is with difficulty I raise my head high enough to write even this. Do not come to see me now, though I want to see you, for half an hour's conversation would be a quarter too much. But write and let me know, at times, where and how you are, and as soon as I am stronger, I will answer you properly.

Our Father thus lets us approach the golden gates, and peep through the key-hole. I see only brightness, what do you see? Oh yes, the book was done before this illness came. I have scarce wit enough now, to correct the press.

We are going to the sea as soon as I am able. Mr. M—— is gone to travel for four or five weeks quite disabled. Every body is suffering except my precious husband, who is quite well; and shall add to this. I cannot, but am,

Very affectionately,
CAROLINE WILSON.

LXXVII.—TO MRS. M——.

Hastings, August 31, 1846.

My dear Mrs. M——,

Your kind inquiries deserve a more quick reply, but reports having gone to Woolwich, which would probably reach you, I thought to wait for an amended report. The time for it however is not yet, and we must wait God's further pleasure. I do not think I am better, I should say I am worse; but that one does not discern, between the sofa and the bed, how really ill one is; and so it may be only, that I have discovered in attempting to perform the function of health, that I am more ill than I thought I was; and do not, as I expected, recover all at once. Nevertheless God has favoured and prospered us in everything—all things turn out well for us. Fagged out with the journey, we were so fortunate as to get good accommodation at the best hotel, the place being crammed, where we had to stay and abide the noise, waiting for lodgings on Saturday. Beautiful indeed is the little apartment we have got, the very best we could have; and beautiful all that we see around us. Then everybody is so good to the little suffering woman—strangers send her beautiful fruit, and the very *waiters* are careful of her. And then her precious dear husband is never out of her sight, enough at all other times to cure her of anything.

This tender generous air, in contrast with our own, so ungracious and hard, it seems to me to blight what it blows upon, is so balmy and delicious, fanning you just as if it knew you were ill, and was afraid to hurt you; as if God had tempered it! and so he has to his shorn lamb and feeble sheep. Then why with all am I not better? Perhaps because he does not mean I should be: Be it so, even as he will; I feel that in being here, we are doing, as well as waiting, his pleasure; which I did not feel, so long as I refused to try the most probable means of restoration, unequal as I really did feel to the exertion.

Here I can be much in the open air, sitting on the shore, or drawn about in a chair, and even from my window *breathe in* the sea. In appetite and cheerfulness I have greatly gained, but my breathing is worse, &c., &c. My husband is getting anxious in not having medical advice. Tell Mr. B—— this if you see him, and that he is in some hurry to hear from him in answer to his letter. Thus you see, dear, whatever be the final issue of my illness, I have nothing but mercies and loving-kindness by the way; say rather *indulgences* of every kind, which thousands more suffering cannot have. I wish that you were all here, except that I believe a more bracing air might suit you better,—St. Leonard's to wit, which I hate; this I love. If you are kind enough to write again, do not omit any news you may have of Mr. M——, as well as the health of your fever-patients, and anything that may have been heard of the health of our man of God. This is a great letter for these times; pray for us, not for life or death, but for strength to wait and bear. With all love to the loved,

Ever affectionately,
CAROLINE WILSON.

LXXVIII.—TO MRS. * * *.

Hastings, September 4, 1846.

MY DEAR FRIEND,

Too long neglected. For the feelings of my kind friends, as well as my own idleness, the bulletins were safest in my dear husband's hands, so long as he could throw his *couleur de rose* upon them. But now it is time that I speak for myself. I am *not* getting better, dearest, I have never thought I was: but rapidly worse since I came here, in respect of my breathing, which must be the material thing. We have called in the soberest and most experienced man we could find, who, having plied me with the stethescope, pronounces my left lung to be consolidated; so accounting for all the distressing symptoms. If this is so, and I see no reason to doubt it, though my precious husband would fain be incredulous still, it becomes simply a question of time and amelioration. Unless I greatly improve in a few days, of which I see no promise, we shall leave this place and make progress toward London; staying perhaps at Tunbridge Wells a week, and perhaps elsewhere, to see if any change makes any difference. If not, some London physician must sign the warrant, and we must proceed to counsel what is to be done. Should *his chariot-wheels* be slow in coming, a mild, dry nook that might allow me still to take the air, and feel the sun, would greatly ease the yet remaining way; whereas at Woolwich there is no prospect for me but my bed. For my husband's sake, I would have all done to prolong, what for me cannot be too short; but the almost convulsive agonies I sometimes suffer for want of breath, makes such continuance doubtful, unless change of place relieves it. I know I am afflicting you, my dearest, by all this. You scolded me at Woolwich for the hint I dropped in the form of wishes. I had a prescience then of what was coming, without a good reason to give for it. But why did you scold me? More than one hand, and young hands too, have given mine a shake of congratulation to-day, on hearing the doctor's fiat, and wished they might go too. Why not so, dearest? Were you ever parted from your best beloved, and felt no wish to join him? That is impossible. There is but *one* counter-thought that stays the prayer: for *that one* I keep silence and say nothing. At present I suffer only in my breath, but it is great distress at times.

Thank you, these chairs are perfectly comfortable to me. With no other exercise, even the shaking is beneficial, and my moments of greatest ease are when drawn through these soft soothing breezes. Gladly would I live and die in this sweet place, endeared to me by many recollections, chiefly of those I am shortly to rejoin. But that may not be. We must be near to London, and I trouble you with all this, because I feel the friends who love us could do us no greater good at this juncture, that to suggest the place wherein to wait, least painfully, the final issue. We talk about Streatham, Brixton, Clapham, Richmond: but we know too little of the localities to judge. If you can advise us, do. I am not of those who run about the world to prolong a doomed life at any cost, but I have seen long illnesses so lightened by keeping out of doors, to even the last hour, especially in consumption, that I cannot help dreading my cold mansion at Woolwich, whence egress would be impossible. I am now not properly able to walk up stairs, and shall probably not long be able to walk at all; not for want of legs, but want of breath; however, to change seems difficult. "God will provide." If a few months be all, it very little signifies. Now write to me, and tell me that you will not fret. I know you love me, but I can render you nothing but to love again, and that I will do in heaven.

Tell dear Mr. B—— to comfort and uphold my precious husband, who will not yet give his consent to let me go. I would I could take him with me! Excuse this almost first note I have written, too full of all but what I wanted to say, dearest.

    Most affectionately yours,
        CAROLINE WILSON.

LXXIX.——TO MRS. * * *

Hastings, Sept. 5, 1840.

MY DEAREST FRIEND,

It is my fault you have not heard. I claimed to write myself, for surely best from me to your fond heart will come the news that *you* will call *sad;* and compassed, blessed, embraced as I am with kindest interest on every side, I have scarcely a right to say it is not sad that will make others so; though not myself. My illness has increased, the serious token of it with extraordinary rapidity. My breathing is terrible, and obliged us to call in advice here; and the stethescope having been applied, there seems no doubt it is a consolidation of the left lung. Dearest, God has spoken, and we have no more to do. If this be true, it is only a question of more or less time, more or less temporary alleviation. Never, never can it be sad to me to stand still and watch for the parting of the waters of Jordan to let me pass, and close on all I desire to see no more; and not from me can ever the cry be heard for a little more time to suffer and to sin, and wait and long for Him my soul desires. If it ever should be so, He will have cause to say I have held strange language with him heretofore; when for very love, as I believe, I have entreated, implored, reproached Him that He would not let me come to Him, when I could not be satisfied with any thing beside. No, no!—His Spirit will not let me be so false—to-night, to-morrow, if it be His pleasure! But there is one thought that stays the prayer—my precious husband is not yet content; it takes him by surprise, he thinks a prolonged period of expectation, even without hope, would be good for him—would reconcile him—wean him—water and mature perhaps the Divine life in his own soul. If so, be it so. At least we must do all that can be done. Neither am I indifferent, if awhile his chariot-wheels delay their coming, how that interval is passed. A milder atmosphere than Woolwich is indispensable. Our house at Woolwich might soon be got rid of, but where find another; our thoughts run many ways, mine run as they always did run, after my affections. I do not like to go where I love nothing. Then the gospel, its preached voice I shall probably hear no more; but to my husband, and in private to myself, the ministry is important. My choice is towards ——; or ——; —perhaps —— itself will be too damp and low;

but is there not higher ground within a mile or so; ——— or ———, or some common or other;—not a town, not a street, but where I may sit under a tree, or be drawn about in a garden, or at least breathe to the last the pure breath of heaven, and see nature's beauties, and hear nature's music.

This is my whole desire if I live; If I die immediately it little matters where. About those parts I have many friends, who would watch over me temporally, and sympathize with me spiritually. But you, dear, to whom, whenever I depart, I shall go more indebted for past kindness than to any other being left behind, need I say how pleasant it would be to me, to be near enough to see you more frequently; to receive the out-pourings of your own heart's sorrows; perhaps to lighten them by my own growing joys. All this must be God's arrangement if he wills it; for we are much at a loss.

I tell it you, on the chance your knowledge of the neighbourhood may do us service. We came here on Monday. My daily increasing suffering, simply from my breathing—for I suffer nothing else—a difficulty amounting, at times, to almost convulsive struggles for existence, warn us to try another change.

We mean to go to Hawkhurst for a night or two; thence, if we can get lodgings, to Tunbridge Wells. Monday or Tuesday you might write to the former, afterwards to the latter place, to the post-office. I have written more than I am well able, and should write to many others. Give prayers to us both—most for the comfort of my most dear and precious husband. This must be all now. If there be time, I shall have more, much more to say. Bless you, dearest.

Yours, most affectionately,
CAROLINE WILSON.

LXXX.—TO MRS. M———.

Hastings, Sept. 6, 1846.

DEAR MRS. M———,

The Sabbath bells have rung you to church, and hundreds of others; among the rest, my dear distressed husband, unused to break the bread of peace *alone;* may Jesus comfort him! it is my only care. I want to tell you how much brighter a Sabbath I am allowed to contemplate; not *through* the *key-hole* now, the door itself is opening. My illness has taken a more serious character, is considered now to be upon the lungs, and capable of nothing but alleviation: longer or shorter as the progress may be. Too soon for me, the bright dawn cannot come, who have grown so sadly weary of the night; nay on that very night itself a light has come, that was not there before, since

I was told the fact, cheering the dark, and making the fair more beautiful. But the blow has come suddenly on my precious husband, and he thinks if I linger awhile, even in sickness, and without hope, he shall be better reconciled and profited by the prolonged warning. If this be so, I am content to wait. At present I only suffer from distressed breathing, and utter incapability of any kind of effort. As I am getting manifestly worse every day, we are advised to leave here immediately, to try another change. We propose to-morrow to move to Hawkhurst for a night or two, and thence to Tunbridge Wells, if we can secure fit accommodation; if not, somewhere toward home. I hope no new troubles have prevented your writing to me. I feel very anxious to hear of the M———s, unheard of when Lady W——— wrote. I do not think of your hearing him to-day, but trust he may be on the return, with renewed powers, to warn the happy, and to cheer the sad, with his most blessed message.

By me, the voice of the charmer, charm he never so wisely, will probably be no more heard from the pulpit. We do not want, by day-light, the guiding stars of night: provision for the living, not the dying. Nevertheless, if I reach home with breath enough remaining, I do hope yet to speak with all my friends again of the past and coming things, in which we take mutual pleasure. The difficulty of speaking is a great distress to me now, wishing to talk more with my husband, of what can be no longer kept out of sight; nevertheless, there may be more time allowed for this. We shall probably be at home within a fortnight, even if no more pressing symptoms bring us forward. If it appears probable I shall live the winter, it must not be at Woolwich, I apprehend; if not, it little matters. God must give us guidance in this matter, for we know scarcely what to do, or where to go. Remember me most affectionately to your dear girls. Write to me, if you can, at Tunbridge Wells, unless to-morrow at Hawkhurst, and let me be,

Ever affectionately yours,
CAROLINE WILSON.

Mr. B—— writes that people live with consolidated lungs for twenty years! What a Job's comforter! to one so nearly without breath already!

LXXXI.—TO MRS. * * *

Hawkhurst, Sept. 8, 1846.

My dear Friend,

It is even so. He has heard my cries; He has seen my tears; not to add unto my life fifteen years,—I have not asked him for as many days; but to turn another way the current of a disease I so peculiarly dreaded. So at least it appears, and if it so proves, remember, for encouragement, it *is* a direct answer to prayer. When I thought I had an incurable disease I did not ask a miracle to cure it; but I did ask earnestly that something else might carry me off before the time arrived; and certainly I never, so asking, left my knees without an encouraged feeling that some how or other my prayer was heard. Apparently now the answer is made plain. My illness has assumed a decided character, my lungs are affected, and faster or slower, I seem to be sinking into consumption. At Hastings, where I went to mend myself, I grew daily worse, and the doctor then first warned me of my real state. We consequently left it yesterday, to try other air, and move ourselves gradually home. In this sweet spot we rest ourselves a night or two, and proceed to Tunbridge Wells if we get lodgings, but shall in any case make homeward next week. What next, we know not; if my life is likely to be prolonged, we must remove for the winter. A little time will develope the more or less rapidity of that which seems to admit of no doubt and no remedy. One lung is said to be consolidated: and my respiration is so dreadful! at times almost an agony. I have no other suffering at present; but that is great, making me afraid to move or speak, lest I bring on a paroxysm. To you I need not say, how all this is to me: but my darling husband earnestly pleads for time: he thinks it would soften the blow, and increase its usefulness. God only knows that, and if it would I am content to linger. My dear friend, as many will hear, and will not understand, why *I* want no time of preparation, often desired by far holier ones than I: I tell you why, and shall tell others, and so shall you. It is not because I am so holy, but because I am so sinful. The peculiar character of my religious experience has always been a deep, an agonizing sense of sin: not past, but present sin; the sin of yesterday, of to-day, confessed with anguish hard to be endured, and cries for pardon that could not be unheard; each day cleansed anew in Jesus' blood, and each day loving more for more forgiven; each day more and more hateful in my own sight, and hopeless of being better; what can I do in death, I have not done in life? What do, in this week, when I am told I cannot live, other than I did last week, when I knew it not? alas, there is but one thing left undone: to serve Him better; and the death-bed is no place for *that*. Therefore I say, if

I am not ready now, I shall not be so by delay, so far as I have to do with it. If HE has more to do in ME, that is His part. I need not ask him not to spoil his work by too much haste. I try to ask nothing, for my loved husband's sake: but I am a timid and impatient sufferer.

Now I know in all this, I am putting you to grief; but you must hear of it, if not from me; and ought not to be left to do so. This is as much as I can write now. If power remains you shall hear from me again. Pray for me, and write to Tunbridge Wells Post Office.

Very, very affectionately yours,
CAROLINE WILSON.

LXXXI.—TO LADY * * * * * *

Tunbridge Wells, September 16, 1846.

DEAR LADY ———

Hardly, and with much delay, I consented to let my husband tell you that God has spoken now, audibly, and not in broken whispers, as of late, respecting my failing health. To lose the power of speaking or of writing, just when I feel I have most to say, is very painful to me. Doubtful now, whether they may be in any measure restored, seeing them at present diminishing every day; one word I must have with you while I can. The bright, the blessed hour for which I have toiled and waited so many years; the panacea at all times of every painful, every fearful thought, has seemed in my spasmodic agonies of breathlessness, immediately at hand; of these I have been much relieved by a distinguished practitioner here. I cannot count the issue now by days, but whether weeks or months or years, it is, I believe, inavertible.

It is sudden, but you know how welcome, as surely He knows, who has heard my cries under the loathed burthen of remaining sin, with almost reproaches, that He kept not his word, to fill the hungering and thirsting after righteousness. The relief derived by Mr. H———'s treatment delays us here some days longer;—then to Woolwich. I want to say some parting words of love and gratitude and sympathy, but I find I cannot. Write to me, I can yet enjoy and profit by your words, and will repay by proxy if not otherwise. Believe, all I would but cannot say,

Most affectionately,
CAROLINE WILSON.

This was the last letter my dear wife wrote. The night which followed was passed without much uneasiness; and when she awoke in the morning after a short sleep, it pleased God that she experienced neither pain nor the slightest restlessness of body; her voice was little altered, and her mind as composed and clear as before her illness.

Finding herself much weaker, she said:—" Oh! if I die to-day, what a mercy! but the blessing would be so great I dare not calculate upon it."

Having taken her breakfast and looked out upon the beautiful sunny prospect which the open window commanded, she exclaimed:—

" I want no more of the world! how dark is all behind—how bright the prospect before! so unclouded—so safe—so secure! Jesus! so true to me! I so untrue to thee! whom have I in heaven but Thee—and there is none on earth I desire besides Thee!"

At another time:—

" This is my bridal day, 'the beginning of my life.' I wish there should be no mistake about the reason of my desire to depart and to be with Christ. I confess myself the vilest, chiefest of sinners, and I desire to go to Him, that I may be rid of the burden of sin—indwelling sin—the sin of my nature—not the past—repented of every day—but the present, hourly, momentary sin, which I do commit, or may commit—the sense of which at times drives me half mad with grief."

Some very dear friends had come from Lee to see her. To Mrs. B. who was applying Eau de Cologne to her face, she said, "Oh! if this is dying, what mercy!" To their daughter she said, "Jessie, I do not wish you to be like me, as I am the chief of sinners, but as I am in Christ." When they had gone away for a short time, I asked her if she would like to see them again. "Oh yes, let them come, what have they to hear but of the love, faithfulness, and truth of God—but at what time did they say they would come?"—"At four o'clock." "They must come soon, as I am sinking very fast." Afterwards she said;—"I have written a book to testify that God is Love! I now testify that He is Faithfulness and Truth. I never asked a petition of God, that sooner or later, I did not obtain."

About half past four, doubtless feeling that the desire of her soul to be with her Saviour was about to be granted, she said, "Oh! I am sinking *so* fast!" These were the last words she uttered, and her countenance glowing with heavenly joy, at twenty-three minutes past five, she fell asleep in Jesus without a struggle.

The following lines are taken from her "*Poetical Catechism:*"—

Our home! what spirit has not felt the charm,
  The untold meaning, hidden in that word?
Can any not recal one throb of joy
  That swell'd the bosom when that name was heard?

Far banished from the beings most beloved,
  Strangers and pilgrims on a foreign soil;
Where even that we have is scarcely ours,
  Claimants to nothing but to care and toil.

Chill'd by a rugged and ungenial clime,
  Despised as aliens, taunted and disclaimed,
What brilliant visions animate the soul,
  Whene'er our country or our home is named?

Heaven is our home—our best beloved is there,
  And there is all that we can call our own;
Treasures far other than earth's borrowed joys,
  There are our wealth, our sceptre, and our crown.

What then is death? Is it the mournful shroud,
  The soldered coffin, and the sable train?
The brief inscription, and the mouldering stone
  That tells the careless stranger, we have been?

Mistaken emblems of unreal ill!
  Phantoms that pale the conscious sinner's cheek;
Spectres! that haunt us in life's gayest hours!
  When Christians die, how false the tale you speak.

Far other visions crowd his closing eye;
  Death comes to him a messenger of love—
He hears angelic hosts their songs prepare
  To greet his coming to the realms above.

He sees the Saviour stand with hand outstretched
    To wipe the tears of sorrow from his eye;
He hears the Father from his lofty throne,
    Invite him to his mansion in the sky.

Behind him—he beholds earth's thousand ills,
    With all the folly of its mad pursuits;
And sin disrobed of passion's artful guise,
    Stands forth confessed with all its bitter fruits.

Before—what mortal accents may not tell
    Something, life's grosser vision cannot see,
The bright beginnings of eternal bliss,
    The gleam of coming immortality!

PRAYER.

O Lord, hear! O Lord, have mercy! Thou seest what I am. The fear of thy judgments has taken hold of me, I am cast out from thy presence, there is no life remaining in me by reason of this oppression. O Lord, how long? Why dost thou not come unto me, to comfort, and to bless me. Have my sins separated between me and thee? Is it to try me, and to prove me, and to show me what is in me?

O Lord! I confess my sin, and my iniquity is ever before thee. I have been wrong in every thing. Thou hast done every thing for me, and I have rendered Thee nothing. Thou dwellest with him that is of a contrite spirit; a broken and a contrite heart thou wilt not despise. Lord! thou knowest my heart is broken, it *is* contrite, and trembleth at thy word. Now then I entreat thee to fulfill thy word, and speak peace to my soul. Lord! thou canst do it; I know thou canst; I know how great, how sufficient thou art. O that I could see thee, as I have seen thee in the sanctuary. I want nothing else—thou knowest that I want nothing else. Jesus, Master, blessed, blessed Lord! O when wilt thou return and take me to thyself. Forgive me this impatience—if it be sin, O pardon it. Thou too wert tempted—thou too wert afraid, thou hast known the weight and bitterness of sin. O Jesus, pity; Saviour—help me, and let not the enemy prevail against me. Show me what it is that has offended thee. I am utterly purposed not to offend. I desire holiness more than my necessary food,— my soul is athirst after righteousness. I would be, thou knowest that I would be, conformed in all things to thy will; but I cannot, O I cannot! Thou hast tried my nature, thou knowest I have no power against my sins; I lay myself in the dust before thee. Wilt thou not, wilt thou not help me! Speak one word of peace, that I may go on my way rejoicing. Speak the word, and there will a great calm. O God! I will not let thee go, unless thou bless me. Thou *wilt* bless me, thou wilt keep me, thou wilt bring me through. Be quieted within me, O my soul, for I shall yet praise Him, who is the strength of my life and my portion for ever!

THE END.

VALUABLE AND IMPORTANT BOOKS
LATELY PUBLISHED BY
J. W. MOORE, 193 CHESNUT ST.,
OPPOSITE THE STATE HOUSE.

HAHN'S HEBREW BIBLE, reprinted from the last Leipsic Edition. Edited by ISAAC LEESER, V. D. M. and JOSEPH JAQUETT, V. D. M. 8vo., half bound in German style.

"This edition of Hahn's Bible is a fac simile of the last Leipsic edition, printed on fine paper, and bound in a superior manner, in all respects a more attractive volume than the German edition. For its accuracy, we have the pledges of two distinguished Hebrew scholars, who revised the proofs; all the vowel points and accents are in their right places—which cannot be said of all former editions, and therefore the student can never be in doubt respecting the letters to which they belong."—[*Christian Observer.*

MYSTERIES OF CITY LIFE, OR, STRAY LEAVES FROM THE WORLD'S BOOK. By JAMES REES. 12mo., paper or cloth.

"The book is original in the conception and execution: its details carry such evidence of reality with them, that the reader can scarcely take them for fiction, and we doubt much if they are; at the same time the incidents are often so startling and vividly, and painfully represented to the mind's eye, that we could wish they were not facts; or rather, we wish there were no such facts really existing in the darker vistas of human life."—[*Pennsylvanian.*

"This book is full of powerful pictures and passages, illustrative of city life."—[*Inquirer.*

"We commend this book as a good one."—[*Despatch.*

"Mr. Rees has written his sketches with much care, and his reflections are the result of a philosophic study of human nature."—[*Ledger.*

WEISS'S HAND-BOOK OF HYDROPATHY, FOR PROFESSIONAL AND DOMESTIC USE. 12mo. ed.

"Those who wish to know what Hydropathy is; how it regards diseases and applies its remedial virtues, and on what principles establishments are formed to carry out its practices, could not perhaps be referred to a better adapted guide than this production of Dr. Weiss."—[*Presbyterian.*

"The work will be found highly interesting."—[*City Item.*

"Dr. Weiss has a high reputation as a hydropathist, and we doubt not this work will be much sought for."—[*News.*

"This work must prove highly interesting and useful to those who desire to obtain a knowledge of Hydropathy."—[*Messenger.*

MEMOIR OF THE LIFE OF ELIZABETH FRY, with extracts from her Journal and Letters. Edited by two of her daughters. 2 vols. 8mo., embossed muslin, with portrait.

"It is a work which, in our estimation, outweighs in value, a whole cargo of the trashy literature which is poured out upon the country from so many of the popular publishing offices."—[*Pennsylvanian.*

"The Memoir is one which it is impossible to peruse without interest and instruction, and it ought to have a place in the library of every Christian lady; for no one can arise from its perusal without softened, yet elevated thoughts."—[*Doylestown Journal.*

STATISTICS OF COAL, THE GEOGRAPHICAL AND GEOLOGICAL DISTRIBUTION OF MINERAL COMBUSTIBLES OR FOSSIL FUEL. By R. C. TAYLOR. With numerous Maps and Plates, and upwards of 900 pages of letter press.

"There is no such work on the subject of Coal in any language; it is a mine of instruction, and a whole library of reference, which not coal and iron mines only, but statisticians and statesmen, will find worthy of their attention."—[*North American.*

IN PRESS.

BOWDLER'S FAMILY SHAKSPEARE, the first American edition, printed on fine white paper, and will be done up in embossed muslin. Thick 8vo.

LIFE OF GRAHAM. 12mo. cloth.

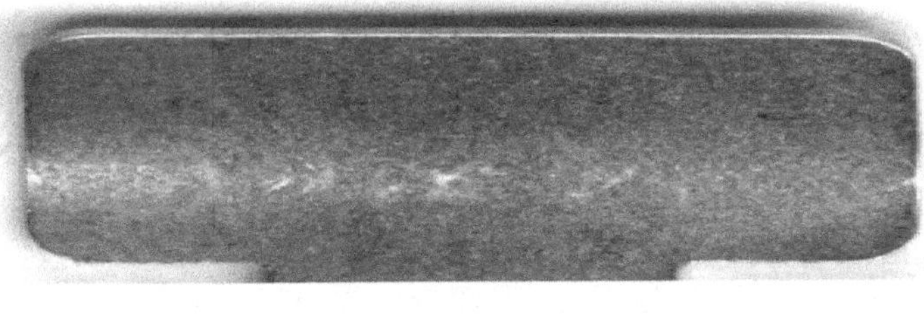

Check Out More Titles From HardPress Classics Series In this collection we are offering thousands of classic and hard to find books. This series spans a vast array of subjects – so you are bound to find something of interest to enjoy reading and learning about.

Subjects:
Architecture
Art
Biography & Autobiography
Body, Mind &Spirit
Children & Young Adult
Dramas
Education
Fiction
History
Language Arts & Disciplines
Law
Literary Collections
Music
Poetry
Psychology
Science
…and many more.

Visit us at www.hardpress.net

Im TheStory
personalised classic books

"Beautiful gift.. lovely finish. My Niece loves it, so precious!"

Helen R Brumfieldon

★★★★★

UNIQUE GIFT

FOR KIDS, PARTNERS AND FRIENDS

Timeless books such as:

Kids

Alice in Wonderland · The Jungle Book · The Wonderful Wizard of Oz · Peter and Wendy · **Robin Hood** · The Prince and The Pauper · The Railway Children · Treasure Island · A Christmas Carol

Adults

Romeo and Juliet · Dracula

- **Highly** Customizable
- **Change** Books Title
- **Replace** Characters Names with yours
- **Upload** Photo (for inside page)
- **Add** Inscriptions

Visit
Im TheStory.com
and order yours today!